PROGRAMMING LEARNING DISABILITIES

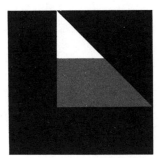

Fearon Publishers *fp*

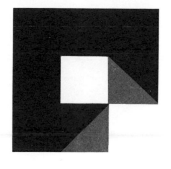

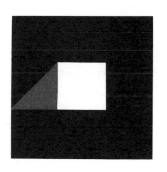

PROGRAMMING LEARNING DISABILITIES

Robert E. Valett, Ed.D.

Psychoeducational specialist and director of the Learning-Resource Center for Exceptional Children, Sacramento City United School District

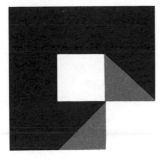

This book is dedicated to
those teachers and parents everywhere
who have had both the courage
and the stamina to pioneer in the
psychoeducational programming of
children with learning disabilities.

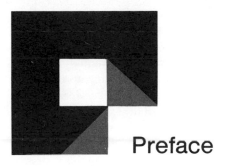

Preface

Throughout the years of my practice as an educational psychologist and special educator, the haunting question raised by parents and teachers alike concerning children with specific learning problems has been: "Yes, but *what can I do about it?*" A great deal of reliable information is now available about what to do with and for children with learning disabilities, although relatively little of this information has been fully utilized in the public school system. Times *are* a-changin', however, and we have seen the beginning of meaningful parent involvement in effecting legislative provision for learning disability programs. Parents have also made a significant impact on educators by their help in bringing many new educational programs and innovations into the local school district.

This book has resulted from the author's experience in helping in the birth process of such a program; this program is no longer in its infancy, but now appears to be rapidly entering the adolescent stage with all the accompanying growing pains and problems. As a result the need has emerged to establish a beginning rationale and some frame of reference in which learning disability programs might continue to grow and prosper.

Most programs for exceptional children appear to succeed or flounder dependent upon the presence or absence of a rationale and organizational procedure for the programming of specific learning disabilities. It is now being recognized that, in addition to a well-trained teacher with the necessary personality characteristics for working with exceptional children, the program itself must have a solid frame of reference and must not depend on the inclination of individual teachers. Ideally, all programs are based on a philosophy of education with certain theoretical constructs and resulting research data that have instructional relevance. Although a growing body of theory and research on learning disabilities is available, no attempt is made in this book to review it in any great detail—the interested reader will have to turn to the references for this information. The primary purpose of this book is to make a beginning attempt at bridging the gap between existing theory and practice by presenting a framework for the actual programming of learning disabilities.

It is assumed that there are three stages in the over-all programming of learning disabilities. The first stage consists of *planning* and includes development of an operational rationale and the consideration of its educational implications in practice. The second stage is *implementation,* with emphasis on the psychoeducational evaluation of the pupil with learning disabilities by the teacher who will be directly responsible for the education of the child. The last stage is *remediation.* This stage includes all of the problems of programming and school organization with which the professional educator is so familiar. An attempt is made in this book to cover each of these three stages, but priority has been given to remediation. The problems of providing individualized instruction, classroom organization and materials, parent involvement, and in-service training and supporting services have been discussed in depth. It is hoped that those interested will find some help and guidelines in the planning of their own unique system for the programming of learning disabilities.

Although this book has been written primarily for use by teachers, psychologists, and administrators concerned with the establishment and operation of learning disability programs, it should be of value to others as well. In particular, parents of exceptional children, pediatricians, and students of learning disabilities and related disciplines should find it of some help in clarifying their thinking concerning educational implementation. It should be realized, however, that this book emphasizes *programming,* and for total perspective the reader should use it in conjunction with the author's earlier works, *The Remediation of Learning Disabilities* (Fearon Publishers, 1967) and *The Psychoeducational Inventory of Basic Learning Abilities* (Fearon Publishers, 1968).

Some acknowledgments are in order—first, to the many children and teachers from whom I have learned so much, and second, to the many school and educational psychologists who are contributing to the development of individual evaluation and programming approaches that attempt to apply what we already know about effective learning. Specifically, appreciation is extended to the *Journal of School Psychology* for permission to reprint four articles, "A Clinical Profile for the Stanford-Binet (L-M)," "A Psychoeducational Profile of Basic Learning Abilities," "A Developmental Task Approach to Early Childhood Education," and "The Evaluation and Programming of Basic Learning Abilities." My thanks go also to *Exceptional Children* for permission to print in part, "A Social Reinforcement Technique for the Classroom Management of Behavior Disorders." In addition, I wish to express my appreciation to the following teachers who supplied the specified information: Jack Radisich (Figure 9-2), Joan Smith (Figures 9-3 and 9-7), LaVerne Graf (Figure 9-5), and Eva Fong (Figure 9-8).

Special acknowledgment is due to Consulting Psychologists Press of Palo Alto, California, for their permission to use the following copyrighted test profiles: A Clinical Profile for the Stanford Binet (L-M), A Psychoeducational Profile of Basic Learning Abilities, and The Valett Developmental Survey of Basic Learning Abilities.

My sincere appreciation is also extended to my wife for her help and understanding, and to my five children—Steve, Rick, Pam, John, and Larry—for their stimulation and tolerance in becoming the subjects of many of my informal games and experiments.

Sacramento, California
January, 1969

ROBERT E. VALETT

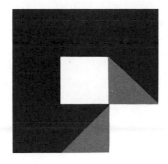

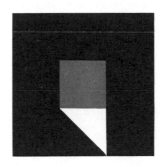

Contents

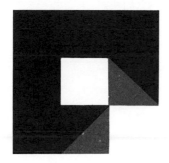

Figures

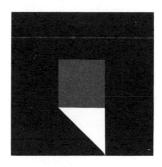

A Rationale for the Programming of Basic Learning Abilities

By education most have been misled;
So they believe, because they so were bred.
The priest continues what the nurse began
And thus the child imposes on the man.[1]

This poetic expression of the power and misuse of education remains as true today as it was when it was written three hundred years ago. In most places throughout the world, however, the influence of the priest in determining educational values, goals, and procedures has been weakened through the emergence of the new coalition of professional educators and psychologists. Unfortunately, until fairly recent times this new fraternity appeared to have offered little in educational innovation when compared with its predecessor, as evidenced by the continued imposition of age-old, quaint approaches to teaching the young with questionable success.

With the gradual accumulation of theory, and its experiential testing through trial and error and formal research, the present generation of psychoeducational

[1] John Dryden, "The Hind and the Panther."

1

coalitionists has within its grasp the knowledge of truly effective teaching and learning. There are even indications that an educational revolution may be in process if we examine the degree of change in the attempt to actually apply the principles of behavior to teaching and learning situations. Such a renowned revolutionist as Mao Tse-tung has said that "If we have a correct theory, but merely prate about it, pigeonhole it, and do not put it into practice, then that theory, however good, is of no significance."[2] Although few would advocate that we look to Mao Tse-tung as the new priestly guide for educational reform, there is no doubt that this is an apt statement of the early history of learning theory when there was little formal application to the broad stream of public education.

Within the past ten years or so this trend has been reversed by the introduction of systems analysis, behavior modification techniques, programmed materials, computer applications, refined approaches to evaluating and remediating learning disabilities, and numerous other developments. With the training and establishment in the public school system of school psychologists, consultants, and administrators versed in the application of the principles of behavior and learning it may well be that we are witnessing the beginning of a truly significant period in education that could dramatically transform our entire society for the better.

Within this rapidly changing context the role of the school psychologist is beginning to emerge. It is now felt that his primary role is as a professional consultant to teachers and administrators in the application of learning theory to teaching and to pupil learning situations. The old role of the psychologist as a tester and classifier of children with learning problems is passé, and the profession is moving rapidly from the current diagnostic-remediation practice to what Barbara Bateman has recently called the task-analysis approach.[3]

The general approach to the evaluation of learning disorders advocated here is not primarily focused on normative references, but rather on the task analysis and programming of what are termed the *basic learning abilities* that extend from infancy through adulthood. The dangers of fixating on normative data and the mere reporting of test results cannot be stressed too strongly; indeed, the early caution of Maria Montessori that "When we shall have instructed (clinical teachers) in anthropometry and psychometry in the most minute manner possible, we shall have only created machines whose usefulness will be most doubtful"[4] is equally appropriate to the school psychologist. Montessori's insistence on the development of the spirit and intent of teaching rather than the mechanical analysis or skill alone is what might today be called emphasis on the artistic application of the principles of learning by the psychoeducational specialist—either teacher or school psychologist.

My approach to the psychoeducational evaluation and programming of basic learning abilities is based on the operational analysis of behavioral tasks and their implications for subsequent learning experiences. It assumes an orderly sequential acquisition and development of skills and abilities through the integration of behavioral standards that, in part, become what Hunt has called "... the coded residues of encounters which are stored within the nervous system."[5] The demand on the professional worker concerned with learning disabilities is thus to give primary

[2]Mao Tse-tung, *Quotations from Chairman Mao Tse-tung* (New York: Bantam Books, Inc., 1967), p. 176.
[3]Barbara Bateman, "Three Approaches to Diagnosis and Educational Planning for Children with Learning Disabilities," *Academic Therapy Quarterly*, Vol. XI (1967), pp. 215-222.
[4]Maria Montessori, *The Montessori Method* (New York: Schocken Books Inc., 1964), p. 7.
[5]J. M. Hunt, "Introduction to the Montessori Method," *Ibid.*, p. xxvii.

attention to the nature of the learning experience or the "environmental encounter" that may eventuate in the development of the desired behavior.

To this end, the specification of 53 *basic learning abilities* that have been developmentally grouped and operationally defined in the six major learning areas—gross motor development, sensory-motor integration, perceptual-motor skills, language development, conceptual skills, and social skills—will enable the psychoeducational specialist to identify and program the specific behavior of concern regardless of chronological age or grade level.

A Functional Definition

In order to avoid semantic confusion, it is important at this point to examine briefly the concept and nature of learning disabilities prior to discussing the over-all schema of basic learning abilities and their implications for educational programming.

A *learning disability* is here defined as any specific difficulty in acquiring and using information or skills that are essential to problem solving. A significant learning disability exists when the individual's actual performance or achievement in any given ability is found to be far below his capacity or potential. A discrepancy between classroom achievement and mental age of one or more years is usually cause for concern, while a discrepancy of two or more years calls for immediate educational intervention.

"Specific difficulty" implies some disability in one or more of the six major learning areas. For example, a nine-year-old boy of normal intelligence who has no apparent physical limitations is having difficulty differentiating right from left with constant reversal tendencies in his writing. This boy could be classified educationally as having directionality and laterality disabilities. Other examples might include children with special difficulties in learning body localization, fine muscle coordination, vocabulary, classification systems, or socially anticipated responses.

Learning disabilities may result from prenatal factors, birth trauma, developmental anomalies, environmental deprivation, psychological frustration and failure experiences, and inadequate instruction—to name just a few causes. Although it is important to be aware of the etiological aspects involved because of their implications for both medical and psychoeducational treatment, no attempt is made here to consider these factors in any detail. The primary focus of the educator must be on the immediate situation and the need to take the child forward through careful programming of learning tasks appropriate to the child's needs. To this end, restricting physiological and mental conditions, home and family factors, and prior educational approaches and successes that can be used in programming the present learning disabilities being experienced by the child should be considered.

Whenever possible, children should be given special education relative to their learning strengths and disabilities instead of educational placement by any gross classification system based primarily on etiological categories. For instance, some children, whether they are mentally retarded, cerebral palsied, aurally handicapped, or exceptional in other ways, can best be educated by remaining in a regular class while receiving supplementary special education for specific learning disabilities as may be needed. These children should remain with their peer group but receive the special help they need as early and as long as may be necessary. For other children, however, it will always be necessary to provide a more effective educational environment through the use of special equipment, significantly reduced class size, teacher's aides, a specialized teacher, and other provisions.

It should be remembered that even in a special self-contained class for exceptional children, the emphasis must be on individual differences and the programming of specific learning disabilities. Although group approaches and class lessons can and should be used for pupils with mental retardation, minimal cerebral dysfunction, aural handicaps, etc., it must be kept in mind that such children do not display homogeneous characteristics suitable for educational planning. Therefore, this definition of learning disabilities is as applicable to exceptional children as to so-called normal children.

Characteristics and Needs of Children with Learning Disabilities

As with all children, pupils with learning disabilities can best be understood through individual evaluation and consideration of their distinctive personal characteristics and needs. Many children with learning disabilities do, however, share a few characteristics that provide the basis for understanding their educational needs. These common characteristics are:

1. *Repeated failure experiences:* Although everyone fails at times, pupils with learning disabilities have had repeated failure experiences in their educational pursuits that negatively affect future learning. Many of these children have failed so often that they are convinced they cannot learn regardless of how hard they might try.
2. *Physical and environmental limitations:* Many children have learning disabilities caused in part by physical anomalies or limitations. Thus the essentially bright child with a peripheral hearing loss may have an expressive language and conceptual disability requiring special education. Similarly, the child reared in an impoverished environment may have limited information and conceptual disabilities. Another common illustration is the child with minimal cerebral dysfunction who has an organic predisposition causing perceptual distortion and a variety of specific learning disabilities.
3. *Motivational problems:* Largely because of repeated failure experiences, the child with learning disabilities tends to lack interest, drive, and enthusiasm for educational situations. In many cases, an outright rejection of teachers and academic school tasks has occurred. This lack of motivation to try and learn must be recognized as a primary problem in working with these pupils.
4. *Anxiety:* A vague anxiety, usually stemming from a sense of impending failure, is also characteristic of many of these children. Because of personal difficulties in learning and a feeling of rejection by teachers and parents, children with learning disabilities tend to develop poor self-concepts. These feelings are quickly generalized to a sense of personal inadequacy that may be marked by inattentiveness, daydreaming, and nervous mannerisms.
5. *Erratic behavior:* Children with learning disabilities tend to demonstrate erratic behavior in most learning situations. On test profiles they are marked by extreme variations in strengths and weaknesses, with normal or superior performance in many areas and significantly low task performance in others. General behavior also tends to be erratic as the child searches for areas of success and interest while avoiding or rejecting those situations that he perceives as threatening.
6. *Incomplete evaluation:* Most pupils with learning disabilities have been educationally hindered because of incomplete evaluation or improper diagnoses. Too often we find children who have been labeled as "retarded," "slow," or

"emotionally disturbed" when actually little or n⟨
evaluate and understand their specific learning pr⟨

7. *Inadequate education:* The overwhelming majority
   disabilities have not been properly educated. They l
   inadequate facilities, untrained teachers, and public ii
   characteristic of this group is the lack of any attempt at

The general needs of children with learning disorders ca⟨
many ways and are not distinctly different from those of all ch⟨
major difference is one of degree or emphasis since the regular ⟨
notably unsuccessful in meeting their needs. Within the framework
four major areas of needs for children with learning disabilities can ⟨

1. *Personal acceptance and understanding:* Many of these childre
   misunderstood, having been rejected as retardates, nonreaders, p⟨
   dren, etc. If it is recognized that many of the behavioral manife⟨ ⟩ns of
   pupils with learning disabilities can be modified, then increased understanding by those concerned should result in greater awareness and acceptance of
   the child. This acceptance of the pupil as an individual with potential to be
   developed is the primary need in effecting motivational change both within
   the child and within the educational system.
2. *Specific psychoeducational evaluation and diagnosis:* In order to help children with learning disabilities adequately, teachers and psychodiagnosticians
   must combine their talents and efforts to arrive at a truly meaningful evaluation of the child that will aid in educational programming.
3. *Specific instruction:* Learning disabilities can be modified only through
   highly specific instruction and educational procedures. It is essential that the
   disability be clearly identified and that a sequentially organized program be
   developed to fit individual pupil strengths and weaknesses.
4. *Success in learning:* Instead of failure, children with learning disabilities
   need to be carefully programmed to insure success experiences. The development and use of individualized lessons with accompanying reinforcement
   and reward systems is basic to insuring success in learning.

There are many approaches to meeting the educational needs of children. The
four major needs of children with learning disabilities as indicated here can best
be met through a consideration of more precise educational objectives and the
rationale for their attainment.

The Basic Learning Abilities

The primary objectives in educating children with learning disorders are the
identification and the remediation of specific disabilities. To achieve these two
objectives all disabilities need to be operationally defined in educational and behavioral terms. While medical and psychological terminology is of supplemental
value in clarifying etiology and in specifying diagnosis and relevant treatment goals
and plans, the primary model must still be educational.

In working with learning disabilities the only classification system that should be
used is one that has meaningful educational relevance. That is, the categories
should be such that concrete objectives for training purposes can be recognized
and arranged therein. For example, a child might be described in part as being
emotionally disturbed or autistic, but it is much more objective and meaningful
educationally to indicate his body schema problems, spatial organizational dis-

bal fluency and encoding difficulties, etc. With such an approach a
t will facilitate communication and further evaluation can be evolved.

accord with these objectives, the author has recently compiled and operationally defined 53 *basic learning abilities* in six major areas of psychoeducational growth
and development.[6] Each ability has been behaviorally illustrated and given an
educational rationale for training and instructional purposes. In his handbook, *The
Remediation of Learning Disabilities*, the author has provided a model for teacher
evaluation of the basic learning abilities, with supplemental resource programs
listing concrete activities and exercises that may be used by the teacher in developing whatever special program is required by the individual pupil. Each resource
program also contains a number of related program references, suggested instructional materials, relevant evaluation and diagnostic aids, and various readings.
Both the evaluation device and the resource programs can best be used and implemented through the conjoint planning of teacher, administrator, and psychological
consultant.

Gross motor development, which is defined as the development and awareness
of large muscle activity, is the first of the six major areas under which the basic
learning abilities have been grouped. The abilities included in this area are rolling,
sitting, crawling, walking, running, throwing, jumping, skipping, dancing, self-
identification, body localization, body abstraction, muscular strength, and general
physical health.

The second area is *sensory-motor integration,* which is defined as the psychophysical integration of fine and gross motor activities. Abilities grouped here include balance and rhythm, body-spatial organization, reaction speed-dexterity,
tactile discrimination, directionality, laterality, and time orientation.

Perceptual-motor skills comprise the third area of basic learning abilities. This
area has been defined as the functional utilization of primary auditory, visual, and
visual-motor skills. The skills include auditory acuity, auditory decoding, auditory-
vocal association, auditory memory, auditory sequencing, visual acuity, visual
coordination and pursuit, visual-form discrimination, visual figure-ground differentiation, visual memory, visual-motor memory, visual-motor fine muscle coordination, visual-motor spatial-form manipulation, visual-motor speed of learning, and
visual-motor integration.

In all motor and perceptual areas attempts are made to emphasize the actual
behavior desired in the remedial program because, as Hunt has pointed out, "Motor
control may be less a matter of educating the child's muscles than it is of his having
clear images of what he is trying to make with his hands"[7]—or body.

Next, we move into higher order abilities, beginning with the fourth area—
language development. This area is defined as the current functional stage of total
psycholinguistic development. An illustration of a selected language ability, fluency
and encoding, will emphasize the complexity of this area. Fluency and encoding is
operationally defined as the ability to express oneself verbally. The behavioral
description states that the pupil can communicate verbally, has average fluency of
speech without undue hesitation or stuttering, and uses coherent sentence structure. One of the remedial program ideas is the use of nonsense verse, mental
games, rhymes, and poems as suggested by the outstanding work of Chukovsky.[8] It

[6]Robert E. Valett, *The Remediation of Learning Disabilities* (Palo Alto, Calif.: Fearon Publishers, 1967).
[7]*Ibid.,* p. xxxi.
[8]Kornei Chukovsky, *From Two to Five* (Berkeley, Calif.: University of California Press, 1963),
pp. 89-113.

is immediately apparent that fluency and encoding is developmentally dependent on many sensory-motor and perceptual-motor-auditory skills and that any training program must integrate numerous psycholinguistic and conceptual functions. The illustration demonstrates that, in reality, much overlap exists among the basic learning abilities and that in no sense do they represent independent or factor-pure entities. They are, however, fairly distinct classifications for basic educational programming and remediation. Other abilities under language development are vocabulary, articulation, word attack skills, reading comprehension, writing, and spelling.

The fifth grouping of basic learning abilities is in the area of *conceptual skills*. This area is concerned with the functional level of concept attainment and general reasoning ability. The abilities included here are number concepts, arithmetic processes, arithmetic reasoning, general information, classification, and comprehension. The selection and programming of these abilities was highly influenced by the work of Piaget and some of the applied innovations with first-grade children developed by Educational Testing Services of Princeton, New Jersey.

Social skills, defined as the skills involved in social problem solving, make up the last area. Since there are many social abilities, this has been a difficult area to consider. There is no question that many individuals have never learned to adapt successfully to the minimal social demands of their environment and that this has been their primary disability. One of the early, classical experiments in social learning was conducted by that outstanding social psychologist, Mark Twain.

In truth, man is incurably foolish. Simple things which the other animals easily learn, he is incapable of learning. Among my experiments was this. In an hour I taught a cat and a dog to be friends. I put them in a cage. In another hour I taught them to be friends with a rabbit. In the course of two days I was able to add a fox, a goose, a squirrel and some doves. Finally a monkey. They lived together in peace; even affectionately.

Next, in another cage I confined an Irish Catholic from Tipperary, and as soon as he seemed tame I added a Scotch Presbyterian from Aberdeen. Next a Turk from Constantinople; a Greek Christian from Crete; an Armenian; a Methodist from the wilds of Arkansas; a Buddhist from China; a Brahman from Benares. Finally a Salvation Army Colonel from Wapping. Then I stayed away two whole days. When I came back to note results, the cage of Higher Animals was all right, but in the other there was but a chaos of gory odds and ends of turbans and fezzes and plaids and bones and flesh—not a specimen left alive. These Reasoning Animals had disagreed on a theological detail and carried the matter to a Higher Court.[9]

Considering the abundant need for programming successful social learning, four major abilities were grouped in this area. They include social acceptance, anticipatory response, value judgments, and social maturity. The social skills area has proven to be quite subject to remediation, and, as a result of progress through the use of many new behavior modification procedures, the author can only agree with Mark Twain that man is indeed foolish—but not incurably so!

A Theoretical Rationale

Although the basic learning abilities have been behaviorally defined for educational purposes, there is a theoretical basis underlying their general scope and sequential arrangement. The major areas of theoretical relevance are those of educational objectives, intellectual evolution and structure, and teaching strategy. Four widely recognized contributions have been selected and integrated into the schematic presentation in Figure 1-1, which attempts to illustrate the sequential-developmental aspects of the basic learning abilities and their theoretical foundation. The educational goals, stated in operational terms for each basic learning

[9]Mark Twain, *Letters from the Earth* (Greenwich, Conn.: Crest, 1962), pp. 180-181.

THEORETICAL RATIONALE OF THE BASIC LEARNING ABILITIES

SOCIAL SKILLS
- Social Maturity
- Value Judgments
- Anticipatory Response
- Social Acceptance

CONCEPTUAL SKILLS
- Comprehension
- Classification
- General Information
- Arithmetic Reasoning
- Arithmetic Processes
- Number Concepts

LANGUAGE DEVELOPMENT
- Spelling
- Writing
- Reading Comprehension
- Word Attack Skills
- Articulation
- Fluency and Encoding
- Vocabulary

PERCEPTUAL-MOTOR SKILLS
- Visual-Motor Integration
- Visual-Motor Speed of Learning
- Visual-Motor Spatial-Form Manipulation
- Visual-Motor Fine Muscle Coordination
- Visual-Motor Memory
- Visual Memory
- Visual Figure-Ground Differentiation
- Visual-Form Discrimination
- Visual Coordination and Pursuit
- Visual Acuity
- Auditory Sequencing
- Auditory Memory
- Auditory-vocal Association
- Auditory Decoding
- Auditory Acuity

SENSORY-MOTOR INTEGRATION
- Time Orientation
- Laterality
- Directionality
- Tactile Discrimination
- Reaction Speed-Dexterity
- Body-spatial Organization
- Balance and Rhythm

GROSS MOTOR DEVELOPMENT
- General Physical Health
- Muscular Strength
- Body Abstraction
- Body Localization
- Self-identification
- Dancing
- Skipping
- Jumping
- Throwing
- Running
- Walking
- Crawling
- Sitting
- Rolling

Valett's Basic Learning Abilities

PSYCHOMOTOR DOMAIN

COGNITIVE DOMAIN

Evaluation (internal and external judgments)

Synthesis (unique communication, plan of operation, abstract relations)

Analysis (elements, relationships, principles)

Application (use of abstractions)

Comprehension (translation, interpretation, extrapolation)

Knowledge (specific and universal)

Bloom's Taxonomy of Educational Objectives

Figure 1-1

AFFECTIVE DOMAIN

Value Complex
(set and characterization)

Organization
(value conceptualization
and organization)

Valuing
(acceptance, preference)

Responding
(acquiescence, will,
satisfaction)

*Receiving-
Attending*
(awareness, motivation)

SENSORIMOTOR INTELLIGENCE

*Egocentric
Organization*

*Perceptive
Movement*

INTUITIVE PREOPERATIONAL THOUGHT

*Beginning
Abstractions*

CONCRETE OPERATIONS

Permanence

Classification

Relationships

FORMAL OPERATIONAL THOUGHT

*Propositional
Thinking*

*Symbolic
Operations*

**Piaget's
Intellectual
Evolution**

THEORETICAL RATIONALE OF THE BASIC LEARNING ABILITIES

SOCIAL SKILLS

Social Maturity
Value Judgments
Anticipatory Response
Social Acceptance

CONCEPTUAL SKILLS

Comprehension
Classification
General Information
Arithmetic Reasoning
Arithmetic Processes
Number Concepts

LANGUAGE DEVELOPMENT

Spelling
Writing
Reading Comprehension
Word Attack Skills
Articulation
Fluency and Encoding
Vocabulary

PERCEPTUAL-MOTOR SKILLS

Visual-Motor Integration
Visual-Motor Speed of Learning
Visual-Motor Spatial-Form Manipulation
Visual-Motor Fine Muscle Coordination
Visual-Motor Memory
Visual Memory
Visual Figure-Ground Differentiation
Visual-Form Discrimination
Visual Coordination and Pursuit
Visual Acuity
Auditory Sequencing
Auditory Memory
Auditory-vocal Association
Auditory Decoding
Auditory Acuity

SENSORY-MOTOR INTEGRATION

Time Orientation
Laterality
Directionality
Tactile Discrimination
Reaction Speed-Dexterity
Body-spatial Organization
Balance and Rhythm

GROSS MOTOR DEVELOPMENT

General Physical Health
Muscular Strength
Body Abstraction
Body Localization
Self-identification
Dancing
Skipping
Jumping
Throwing
Running
Walking
Crawling
Sitting
Rolling

Valett's Basic Learning Abilities

Intellectual Operations: BEHAVIORAL   SYMBOLIC   SEMANTIC   FIGURAL

Content: DIVERGENT THINKING   CONVERGENT THINKING   COGNITION   MEMORY

Guilford's Structure of Intellect

Figure 1-1
Continued

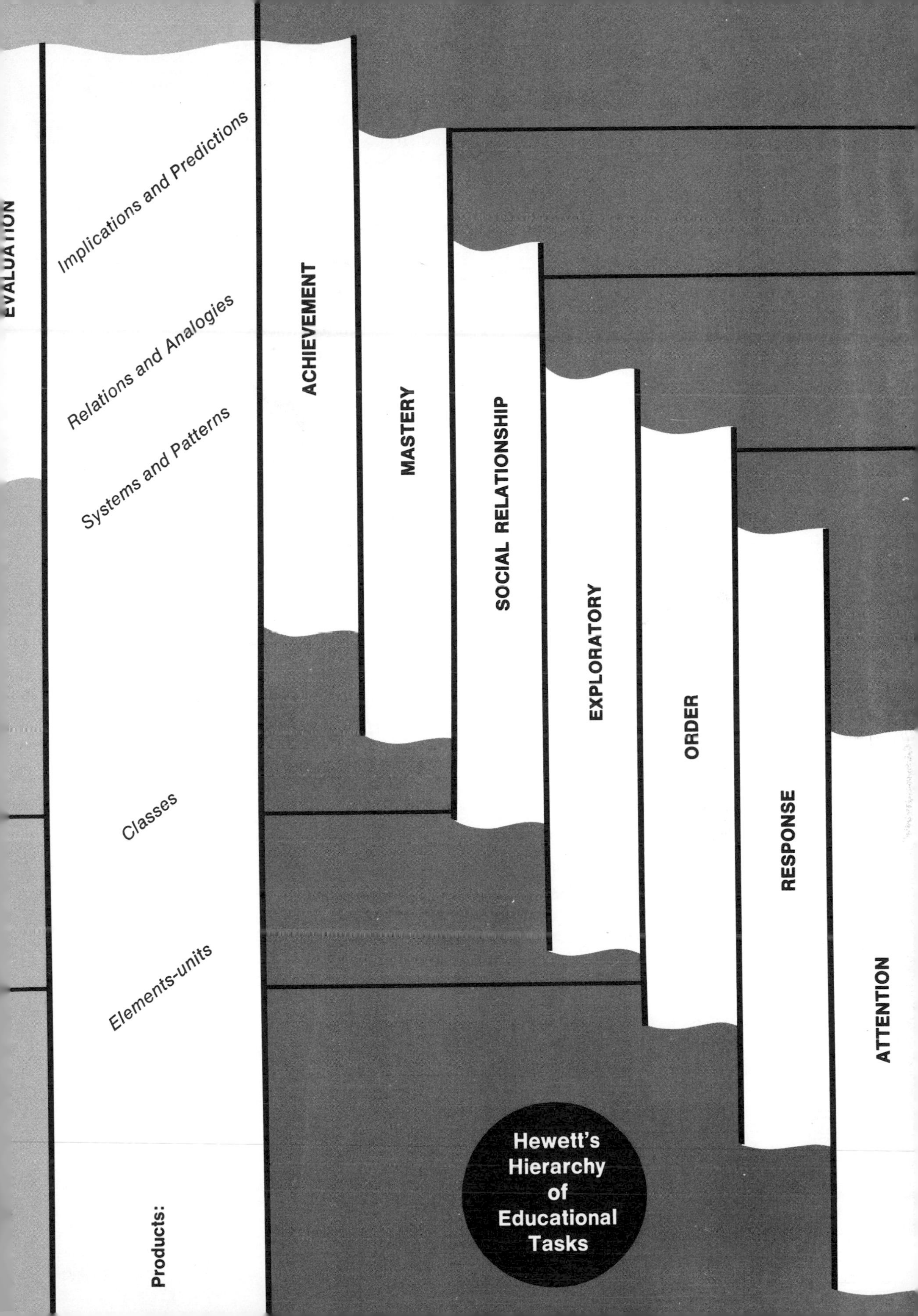

EVALUATION

Implications and Predictions

Relations and Analogies

Systems and Patterns

Classes

Elements-units

Products:

ACHIEVEMENT

MASTERY

SOCIAL RELATIONSHIP

EXPLORATORY

ORDER

RESPONSE

ATTENTION

Hewett's
Hierarchy
of
Educational
Tasks

ability, are reflected in Bloom's *Taxonomy of Educational Objectives*.[10,11] The theories of intellectual evolution and structure that have the most meaning for the educational specification of the basic learning abilities appear to be those of Piaget[12] and Guilford.[13] The teaching strategy through which the basic learning abilities can be taught is best seen in the behavior modification approach as typified for programming purposes in Hewett's "Hierarchy of Educational Tasks."[14]

EDUCATIONAL OBJECTIVES

The goals inherent in the *Taxonomy of Educational Objectives* are classified into a psychomotor domain, a cognitive domain, and an affective domain. At this time Bloom has not yet specified the objectives that might be included in the *psychomotor domain,* although it logically seems that they would be task- and skill-orientated such as those specified by the basic learning abilities in the areas of gross motor development, sensory-motor integration, and perceptual-motor skills. The *cognitive domain* focuses on the acquisition and utilization of skills and abilities. For example, the specific learning abilities—visual coordination and pursuit, writing, classification, etc.—all involve cognitive processes such as comprehension, application, synthesis, and evaluation. The educational implication is that lesson plans having to do with the development of writing abilities, for instance, should proceed with these specific educational objectives in mind. Hence, concrete knowledge pertaining to the nature of the writing skills required in the lesson should be provided with exercises that proceed until the pupil has learned how to evaluate his own writing skills. The *affective domain* transcends most content areas of learning and stresses the importance of recognizing the given level of emotional commitment to the learning task.

To continue our illustration of writing skills, the teacher must not only identify what cognitive level of writing is to be the immediate learning objective but also must determine whether the affective objective should be merely one of obtaining some response such as marking or scribbling, or whether a higher level value complex is to be recognized as the objective that might result in various forms of spontaneous written expression.

INTELLECTUAL STRUCTURE

Educational objectives must be considered relative to the developmental level of the learner and the intellectual requirements for success. Too often have teachers selected learning goals that were either developmentally or intellectually inappropriate for the child and, therefore, predestined to failure of accomplishment.

The basic learning abilities encompass the range of developmental and intellectual skills from gross motor tasks through high level social skills. It is important

[10]B. S. Bloom (ed.), *Taxonomy of Educational Objectives, the Classification of Educational Goals, Handbook I: Cognitive Domain* (New York: David McKay, Inc., 1956).

[11]B. S. Bloom, D. R. Krathwohl, and B. B. Masia, *Taxonomy of Educational Objectives, the Classification of Educational Goals, Handbook II: Affective Domain* (New York: David McKay, Inc., 1964).

[12]L. J. Flavell, *The Developmental Psychology of Jean Piaget* (Princeton, N.J.: D. Van Nostrand Co., Inc., 1963).

[13]L. P. Guilford, "Three Faces of Intellect," *American Psychologist,* Vol. XIV, No. 8 (1959), pp. 469-479.

[14]F. M. Hewett, "Educational Engineering and Emotionally Disturbed Children," *Exceptional Children,* Vol. XXXIII (1967), pp. 459-468.

here to recognize that gross motor, sensory-motor, and perceptual-motor skill development is prerequisite to success in the higher-level language and conceptual skills that comprise the bulk of school curricular offerings. Piaget has provided ample documentation of elementary intellectual components in these more basic learning tasks and has aptly labeled them "sensorimotor intelligence" and "preoperational" intellectual stages of development. Intelligence, then, evolves to the stages of concrete and formal operations necessary for the accomplishment of complex intellectual tasks.

The structure of intellect presented by Guilford also takes into account the many components of successful problem solving. Guilford's intellectual system includes figural and behavioral operations not traditionally recognized or provided for in educational programs. His specification of intellectual content and products should prove helpful to educators in relating goals to intellectual components that, when recognized at certain evolutionary-developmental stages, may have obvious curricular implications.

TEACHING STRATEGY

As soon as the educational objectives have been selected and the program content of the basic learning abilities has been structured, a teaching strategy must be developed. The "Hierarchy of Educational Tasks" emphasizes the importance of specifying what level of commitment the learner is on so that subsequent educational programming can be more effective. To return to our writing skills example, the child with learning disabilities may reject all direct writing approaches and hence refuse to respond, or he may have passed this level and be struggling for mastery or achievement. Whatever the level may be, different approaches by the teacher will be required for effective education. The basic learning abilities specify content areas for the levels of educational tasks presented by the Hierarchy. This, in turn, gives the teacher direction as to how to begin to approach the learner with specific learning disabilities.

A Schematic Analogy

In order to integrate the various aspects of the theoretical rationale presented here, it may be helpful to consider a schematic analogy (*Fig. 1-2*). A tree is a living and growing entity. Education is certainly an ongoing and dynamic "state of becoming" in which meaningful psychoeducational programming must be conceived of as an evolving growth process. The tree, then, represents the learner whose roots are found and understood in developmental psychology. The developmental psychology of Piaget with its evolutionary stages of intellectual growth is primary to the learning process. Of similar importance is an awareness and utilization of Guilford's structure of intellect, which provides the psychologist and educator with a knowledge of some components of the cognitive growth process that contribute to many programming possibilities. From this rich, nutrient source springs the learner as a dynamic being with great potential for growth.

Within the formal educational institution of the school, the 53 basic learning abilities presented here become the operational content or "curricular basis" for specific educational programming. The trunk of the tree represents these basic learning abilities with all their possibilities for future development in behavioral accomplishment through cultivated growth. The tree limbs branch off the trunk to permit fruition as an eventual possibility. Realization of the desired fruit of knowledge is dependent on the specific objectives that have been clarified by Bloom's *Taxonomy* and that are achieved only through careful selection and a cultivated programming of the entire educational process relevant to the needs of the individual learner.

This schema presents the teacher with a purposive-growth model for the education of children with learning disabilities. Certainly, the teacher who has an understanding of the objectives, structure, and stage of intellectual development of the pupil, and the educational task level involved, should have a more meaningful basis for her work. By relating the basic learning abilities to these other contributions, the teacher should be able to develop a rationale and purpose for her own unique plan and approach to the child.

A SCHEMATIC ANALOGY

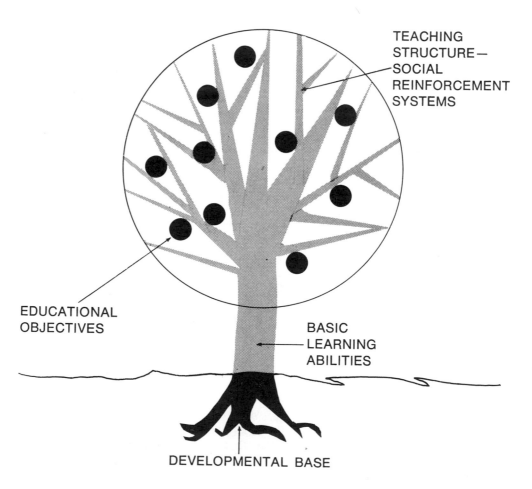

TEACHING
STRUCTURE—
SOCIAL
REINFORCEMENT
SYSTEMS

EDUCATIONAL
OBJECTIVES

BASIC
LEARNING
ABILITIES

DEVELOPMENTAL BASE

Piaget's
Intellectual Evolution

Guilford's
Structure of Intellect

Figure 1-2

2

The Basic Learning Abilities

In the programming of learning disabilities the basic learning abilities become the primary content areas of concern around which the entire instructional program is to be organized. Accordingly, these abilities and their related skills should become the focus of initial evalution by psychologists and diagnostic teachers. A definition for each ability is presented here, followed by an illustration and the educational rationale. Since effective programming and remediation is dependent on differential psychoeducational evaluation of these abilities, both the operational definition and the educational rationale must be clearly understood.

GROSS MOTOR DEVELOPMENT: The development and awareness of large muscle activity. (Basic learning abilities 1-14)

1. Rolling

Definition: The ability to roll one's body in a controlled manner.
Illustration: From a supine position, with arms over head, pupil can roll from back to stomach. Pupil can do sequential rolling to right and left, can roll down hill or incline.

15

Educational Rationale: Rolling—either parts of one's body, or the entire body itself in accord with specific instructions—furthers neurophysiological control and development. Physically immature and poorly coordinated children should be given increasingly difficult rolling tasks and taught fundamental body control skills.

2. Sitting

Definition: The ability to sit erect in a normal position without support or constant reminding.

Illustration: Pupil can demonstrate proper poise in sitting at desk with feet on floor, back straight, and head and arms in proper position for work at hand.

Educational Rationale: To work and learn effectively, children must be taught how to relax and to maintain proper sitting posture for reading, writing, and participation in varied activities. The relationship of poise and body control to fatigue and poor performance should be demonstrated and corrected where required.

3. Crawling

Definition: The ability to crawl on hands and knees in a smooth and coordinated way.

Illustration: With eyes fixated on target, pupil first crawls in a homolateral fashion. Pupil progresses to cross-lateral crawling program.

Educational Rationale: Crawling is a developmental skill, beginning with creeping and extending to complex target-oriented programs furthering neurophysiological integration. Children should be provided with ample opportunity to crawl and should be taught specific body coordination skills through varied crawling activities.

4. Walking

Definition: The ability to walk erect in a coordinated fashion without support.

Illustration: With head up and shoulders back, pupil walks a specified path and walking line. Pupil can walk backward and sideways without difficulty.

Educational Rationale: Walking is a neuromuscular act requiring balance and coordination. Children should be presented with opportunities to develop increasing skill in more difficult tasks.

5. Running

Definition: The ability to run a track or obstacle course without a change of pace.

Illustration: Pupil runs a straight track of easy distance without difficulty, can change direction through a simple obstacle course without stopping or significantly changing pace.

Educational Rationale: The ability to run requires muscular strength, coordination, and endurance, and contributes to total psychomotor learning. Running skills and related activities should be taught as an integral part of the physical education program.

6. Throwing

Definition: The ability to throw a ball with a reasonable degree of accuracy.

Illustration: Pupil throws a ball to another person so that it may be caught, can throw ball accurately into box or basket.

Educational Rationale: Children should be taught to throw various types of balls with a fair degree of accuracy. Boys should be provided with specific remedial instructions if their throwing skills are notably impaired.

7. Jumping

Definition: The ability to jump simple obstacles without falling.
Illustration: Pupil can jump from chair to floor without difficulty, can jump from jumping board without falling, can jump over knee-high obstacles.
Educational Rationale: Children should be taught to coordinate themselves as required in simple jumping tasks. Physical education programs should include personalized instruction in jumping skills and activities.

8. Skipping

Definition: The ability to skip in normal play.
Illustration: Pupil can skip, alternating feet, around circle of players, can skip rope forward both by hopping and alternate-foot skipping.
Educational Rationale: For many children, skipping is a difficult task of coordination and timing that also requires strength and endurance. Children should be taught to skip by direct imitation and guidance and through involvement in games and activities.

9. Dancing

Definition: The ability to move one's body in coordinated response to music.
Illustration: In young children, abilities are shown by free movement and eurhythmic expression. There is a progression to more formal dance steps with older pupils.
Educational Rationale: Children need to be taught the enjoyment of free movement and emotional response to music and rhythm. Dancing and related skills should be a fundamental part of all physical education and remedial eurhythmic programs.

10. Self-identification

Definition: The ability to identify one's self.
Illustration: Pupil can identify self by name, respond to name when called, and identify self in pictures and mirrors.
Educational Rationale: Primary to all conceptual learning is the awareness of self as a separate identity. The young preschool child must be taught to differentiate himself from other objects in the environment and to respond to his name.

11. Body Localization

Definition: The ability to locate parts of one's body.
Illustration: Pupil can locate eyes, hands, mouth, hair, nose, feet, eyebrows, fingernails, shoulders, elbows, knees, back, neck, chin, forehead, wrists, arms, legs, toes, etc.
Educational Rationale: Before a child can develop an adequate self-concept he needs to be able to locate himself in space. Children should be taught to find and point out body parts physically and to describe each body part by name and function.

12. Body Abstraction

Definition: The ability to transfer and generalize self-concepts and body localizations.

Illustration: Pupil can identify others by names and pictures, can locate body parts on others, generalize to pictures, complete body picture puzzles.

Educational Rationale: Children should be provided with varied experiences whereby they may gain psychophysical awareness and control of themselves. Educational programs should allow for the child to consider himself relative to given situations and should contribute to the development of a sound self-concept.

13. Muscular Strength

Definition: The ability to use one's muscles to perform physical tasks.

Illustration: Pupil can touch floor from standing position. From supine position he can sit up and touch toes, can raise legs off floor from supine position for a few seconds. Pupil can do one push-up and chin self from bar.

Educational Rationale: Muscular strength is best developed through a systematic physical fitness program adapted to individual growth patterns. Exercises and games involving all major body muscles should be included in the program.

14. General Physical Health

Definition: The ability to understand and apply principles of health and hygiene while demonstrating good general health.

Illustration: Pupil has good personal health and hygiene habits—no chronic absences for health reasons, no unusual accidents or health history, and no significant physical disabilities interfering with learning.

Educational Rationale: The child must be taught proper health habits that may affect his entire efficiency in learning. Educational consideration must be given to significant health, nutrition, and physical limitations.

SENSORY-MOTOR INTEGRATION: The psychophysical integration of fine and gross motor activities. (Basic learning abilities 15-21)

15. Balance and Rhythm

Definition: The ability to maintain gross and fine motor balance and to move rhythmically.

Illustration: Pupil is able to balance on balance board or rail, can move rhythmically in playing jacks and in bouncing on trampoline or spring.

Educational Rationale: The maintenance of body balance and the perception and expression of rhythmic patterns are fundamental to readiness for more advanced perceptual-motor experiences. An integrated balance and rhythm program should be an essential part of physical education and formal readiness training.

16. Body-spatial Organization

Definition: The ability to move one's body in an integrated way around and through objects in the spatial environment.

Illustration: Pupil can run maze on playground or in classroom without bumping, can move easily through tunnels and use playground monkey bars, can imitate body positions in space.

Educational Rationale: Body awareness and control of movement in space should be taught through imitative and exploratory exercises. Provision should be made for special playground activities together with programs designed for use within the regular classroom.

17. Reaction Speed-Dexterity

Definition: The ability to respond efficiently to general directions or assignments.
Illustration: Pupil can attend to the teacher sufficiently to comprehend total directions. He can organize self and respond adequately to complete the given assignment within a normal time expectancy. Pupil has good attention and concentration span.
Educational Rationale: Remedial activities should be planned so that they may be clearly understood and successfully accomplished within a given period of time. Children should be guided through problem-solving procedures, including listening and analytical skills, and good study habits.

18. Tactile Discrimination

Definition: The ability to identify and match objects by touching and feeling.
Illustration: With hidden toys and materials, pupil can match objects with both left and right hands, name or classify materials or substances, differentiate weights, and discriminate temperatures.
Educational Rationale: Since tactile discrimination and sensory integration are primary to higher level perceptual and cognitive learning, all preschool, primary, and remedial education programs should provide systematic training in those areas.

19. Directionality

Definition: The ability to know right from left, up from down, forward from backward, and directional orientation.
Illustration: Pupil can write and follow picture story or reading material from left to right, discriminate right and left body parts and those of other people, locate directions in room and school.
Educational Rationale: Since many learning and problem-solving situations require directional orientation, it is important that these skills be specifically taught if necessary. Such instruction should begin with body orientation and proceed to object relationships and concrete applications.

20. Laterality

Definition: The ability to integrate one's sensory-motor contact with the environment through establishment of homolateral hand, eye, and foot dominance.
Illustration: Pupil has consistent right- or left-sided approach in use of eyes, hands, and feet in tasks such as kicking ball, cutting paper, sighting with telescope, writing, etc.
Educational Rationale: Lateral consistency in body orientation to problem-solving situations reduces psychomotor conflict and furthers sensory-motor integration and learning. Where gross inconsistency and neurological immaturity exist, training programs should reinforce laterality and help to establish habitual modes of response.

21. Time Orientation

Definition: The ability to judge lapses in time and to be aware of time concepts.
Illustration: Pupil is prompt in attending class, completing timed assignments, and following directions. Child is aware of day, month, year, time of day, and seasons.
Educational Rationale: Body organization in time reflects sensory-motor integration in space and is prerequisite for advanced perceptual and conceptual skills. Children should be provided with opportunities to explore and judge space-time relationships in order to develop synchrony of movement.

PERCEPTUAL-MOTOR SKILLS: The functional utilization of primary auditory, visual, and visual-motor skills. (Basic learning abilities 22-36)

22. Auditory Acuity

Definition: The ability to receive and differentiate auditory stimuli.
Illustration: Pupil responds functionally to watch tick, hidden sound toys, and general normal conversational directions. Pupil has no significant decibel loss.
Educational Rationale: The ability to receive and to respond to auditory stimuli is a result of the integration of experience and neurological organization. The training of children in listening skills with emphasis on the development of good habit patterns of auditory attention and motivation should be stressed.

23. Auditory Decoding

Definition: The ability to understand sounds or spoken words.
Illustration: Pupil can follow simple verbal instructions, can indicate by gesture or words the meaning or purpose of auditory stimuli such as animal sounds, nouns, or verbs.
Educational Rationale: Children need to be taught to listen carefully and to understand and respond to oral stimulation and instructions. Activities should stress behavioral responses and simple "yes-no" answers rather than long verbal replies.

24. Auditory-vocal Association

Definition: The ability to respond verbally in a meaningful way to auditory stimuli.
Illustration: Pupil can associate with verbal opposites, sentence completions, or analogous verbal responses.
Educational Rationale: Children must be taught to listen and to respond verbally in meaningful ways through the use of association, logical inference, and judgment. Expressive fluency should be recognized as a secondary goal.

25. Auditory Memory

Definition: The ability to retain and recall general auditory information.
Illustration: Pupil can act out (charades) Santa Claus, simple plots of common nursery rhymes ("Jack and Jill"), can verbally relate yesterday's experiences, meals, television and story plots.
Educational Rationale: Children must be taught that what they are hearing is important and that they will be expected to recall and use auditory information following training activities. Pupils should be rewarded for increasing their auditory memory span as evidenced through individual improvement records.

26. Auditory Sequencing

Definition: The ability to recall in correct sequence and detail prior auditory information.

Illustration: Pupil can imitate specific sound patterns, follow exactly a complex series of directions, repeat digit and letter series.

Educational Rationale: Pupils need to be provided with instruction in attending to specific directions and in the identification and location of sound patterns and sequences. Drill and meaningful practice should be an integral part of the total remedial program.

27. Visual Acuity

Definition: The ability to see objects in one's visual field and to differentiate them meaningfully and accurately.

Illustration: Pupil sees without notable fatigue, holds material at appropriate working distance, has no significant loss of acuity on Snellen or Illiterate E chart.

Educational Rationale: What an individual sees is the result of a psychophysical process that integrates gravitational forces, conceptual ideation, spatial-perceptual orientation, and language functions. Children should be provided with varied visual experiences and practice in their interpretation and utilization.

28. Visual Coordination and Pursuit

Definition: The ability to follow and track objects and symbols with coordinated eye movements.

Illustration: With head steady, pupil can move eyes to fixate on stable objects in varied places, pursues moving objects such as finger positions, follows pictures and word stories left to right without jerky movements.

Educational Rationale: Coordinated eye movements are essential in order to attend successfully to sequentially-arranged symbolic learning material such as reading matter. Child should be provided with systematic instruction in visual coordination and occular control activities.

29. Visual-Form Discrimination

Definition: The ability to differentiate visually the forms and symbols in one's environment.

Illustration: Pupil can match identical pictures and symbols such as abstract designs, letters, numbers, and words.

Educational Rationale: The ability to see likenesses and differences in one's environment is prerequisite to symbolic differentiation and interpretation as required in reading. Basic educational programs should include opportunities to point out, indicate, and comment on the details and differences perceived in one's visual field.

30. Visual Figure-Ground Differentiation

Definition: The ability to perceive objects in foreground and background and to separate them meaningfully.

Illustration: Pupil can differentiate picture of self and friends from group picture, differentiate objects in "front" and "back" part of pictures and mock-ups, differentiate his name from among others on paper or chalkboard, perceive simple forms and words imbedded in others.

Educational Rationale: The differentiation of meaningful objects in the environment requires visual concentration, attention, and stability. Children should be trained in the skills of visual scanning, peripheral discrimination of boundaries, and detecting significant details; pointing, matching, describing, and kinesthetic-motor modalities should all be used in the remedial education program.

31. Visual Memory

Definition: The ability to recall accurately prior visual experiences.

Illustration: Pupil can recall from visual cues where he stopped in book, can match or verbally recall objects removed or changed in the environment, can match briefly exposed symbols.

Educational Rationale: Visual recall and retention must be sufficiently developed to insure success in reading and related abstract learning tasks. Training should be provided in the recall of material through pointing, matching, and verbal description from memory.

32. Visual-Motor Memory

Definition: The ability to reproduce motor-wise prior visual experiences.

Illustration: Pupil can draw designs and symbols following brief exposure, can reproduce letters, numbers, simple words on demand, can portray prior objects or events through gestures or drawings, can reproduce varied patterns and identify hidden materials.

Educational Rationale: The ability to recall what one has learned or experienced and to act on this information is essential to all sequential tasks in education. Without an adequate visual-motor memory span, tasks must constantly be learned anew with great loss of time and efficiency. Retention of sequential visual-motor patterns is an essential element of this learning ability.

33. Visual-Motor Fine Muscle Coordination

Definition: The ability to coordinate fine muscles such as those required in eye-hand tasks.

Illustration: Pupil can write legibly, trace, and imitate precise body movements without difficulty, can cut, can manipulate, and can judge fine physical responses without gross errors.

Educational Rationale: The coordination of visual perception of stimuli with fine motor responses required in many educational tasks is prerequisite to academic success.

34. Visual-Motor Spatial-Form Manipulation

Definition: The ability to move in space and to manipulate three-dimensional materials.

Illustration: Pupil can build block houses and designs, draw three-dimensional pictures, complete shop and craft projects, integrate form and space puzzles.

Educational Rationale: The perception of forms in space and the ability to judge motor skills required to manipulate objects relative to one another is basic to the solution of nonverbal performance problems encountered in everyday life.

35. Visual-Motor Speed of Learning

Definition: The ability to learn visual-motor skills from repetitive experience.

Illustration: Pupil can respond with increasing speed to rote learning tasks such as copying digit or letter sequences, spelling, specific arithmetic processes, and gross motor skills such as jumping over a rope.

Educational Rationale: Most visual-motor skills can be improved through refined practice and drill. The specific skill to be learned must be broken down into its component movements or processes and a systematic approach developed to accomplish the task to the point of overlearning. Both meaningful practice and drill must be utilized in order for the skill to be developed for functional use.

36. Visual-Motor Integration

Definition: The ability to integrate total visual-motor skills in complex problem solving.

Illustration: Pupil can play complex team sports, swim, draw accurate pictures including people, may play musical instrument, write extended letters, move freely about neighborhood and community.

Educational Rationale: The degree of integration of visual-motor skills is evidenced in complex tasks requiring coordination of eyes, hands, and large muscles. Varied educational experiences need to be planned in these areas to provide opportunity for integration to develop.

LANGUAGE DEVELOPMENT: The current and functional stage of total psycholinguistic development. (Basic learning abilities 37-43)

37. Vocabulary

Definition: The ability to understand words.

Illustration: Pupil has a basic receptive vocabulary in accord with chronological age and educational opportunity.

Educational Rationale: Vocabulary develops as a result of experience and neurological integration. Children must be provided with varied educational opportunities as a basis for language development. Directive teaching of basic nouns through concrete aids, imitation, and reinforcement techniques should be followed with sequential instruction in verbs, adverbs, and adjectives.

38. Fluency and Encoding

Definition: The ability to express oneself verbally.

Illustration: Pupil can communicate verbally, has average fluency of speech without undue hesitation or stuttering, uses coherent sentence structure.

Educational Rationale: Fluent verbal expression and communication develop gradually as a result of experience and verbal stimulation. When the child has the need to express himself and feels free to do so, he should be rewarded and encouraged to engage in extended forms of verbal communication.

39. Articulation

Definition: The ability to articulate words clearly without notable pronunciation or articulatory problems.

Illustration: Pupil uses words with correct pronunciation of initial, medial, and final sounds.

Educational Rationale: During preschool and kindergarten years most children evidence articulatory difficulties that gradually disappear as a result of maturation and experience. By the middle primary grades, however, the child with notable articulation problems may require special education and speech correction. Many articulation problems can be avoided through a consciously developed program of classroom speech improvement.

40. Word Attack Skills

Definition: The ability to analyze words phonetically.

Illustration: Pupil can make proper phonetic associations, break down words phonetically, recognize component words.

Educational Rationale: In order to read effectively, the child must be able to associate sounds with their written symbols and to analyze new words accordingly. Context cues must also be recognized and utilized by the pupil with increasing speed and facility. Pupils should have a basic sight vocabulary prior to introducing phonics.

41. Reading Comprehension

Definition: The ability to understand what one has read.

Illustration: Pupil can recall story and paraphrase plot, can explain or relate meaningfulness of what has been read.

Educational Rationale: Comprehension of reading material requires an accurate vocabulary knowledge and the ability to relate words meaningfully in sentence, paragraph, and story form. Comprehension develops through the feedback and consideration of what one has read.

42. Writing

Definition: The ability to express oneself through written language.

Illustration: Pupil can write simple sentences and communicate ideas through paragraph, letter, story, or essay.

Educational Rationale: Writing is a basic form of language communication requiring integration of visual-motor skills and practice. Development of basic writing ability begins with training of finger and hand muscles through scribbling exercises, tracing, copying, and the increasing refinement of free writing exercises.

43. Spelling

Definition: The ability to spell in both oral and written form.

Illustration: Pupil spells within general age expectancy.

Educational Rationale: Spelling is a higher-order skill requiring visual-motor integration together with basic vocabulary knowledge and phonic awareness. Correct spelling develops through good habits and practice, proceeding from simple to complex words that are meaningful to the pupil.

CONCEPTUAL SKILLS: The functional level of concept attainment and general reasoning ability. (Basic learning abilities 44-49)

44. Number Concepts

Definition: The ability to count and use simple numbers to represent quantity.

Illustration: Pupil can count forward and backward to 100, count by twos, group simple quantities upon request.

Educational Rationale: Arithmetic understanding and usage begins with basic number concepts—being aware of simple numbers from one to ten and corresponding sets representing such numbers. Facility in dealing with numbers in combinations to 100 and in manipulating numbers, such as counting by groups of twos, fives, and tens, is preliminary to mastery of more advanced basic processes.

45. Arithmetic Processes

Definition: The ability to add, subtract, multiply, and divide.

Illustration: Pupil can demonstrate knowledge of basic processes within expectation of his chronological age.

Educational Rationale: Pupils must be taught to apply basic number concepts in addition, subtraction, multiplication, division, and other arithmetic processes. Overlearning through the use of meaningful drill and practice is required for automatic recall and use in more advanced problem solving.

46. Arithmetic Reasoning

Definition: The ability to apply basic arithmetic processes in personal and social usage of problem solving.

Illustration: Pupil can purchase goods and account for funds, knows coinage and exchange, can calculate time differentials, understands weights and measures.

Educational Rationale: The purpose of learning arithmetic processes is to be able to apply this understanding in the solution of everyday problems. Educational programs should provide ample opportunity for the pupil to test his knowledge in practical situations.

47. General Information

Definition: The ability to acquire and utilize general information from education and experience.

Illustration: Pupil is aware of major local and national current events, knows local geography, has concept of city, state, and nation.

Educational Rationale: A child's fund of information is acquired through a variety of experiences and formal education. Early preschool and childhood opportunities for exploring the immediate environment may aid in the development of interest and motivation essential to the acquisition and retention of general information.

48. Classification

Definition: The ability to recognize class identities and to use them in establishing logical relationships.

Illustration: Pupil can sort objects by classification, recognize subclasses, verbalize common elements in class identity.

Educational Rationale: A child's mental development is gradual, progressing from sensory-motor and concrete stages to recognizing relationships inherent in groupings and classification systems. Experience in dealing with likenesses and differences in many varied sequential learning situations provides the foundation for later development of formal logical thought.

49. Comprehension

Definition: The ability to use judgment and reasoning in common sense situations.
Illustration: Pupil responds to factual reasoning when situation is explained to him. He can recognize alternatives in situations and can judge actions accordingly. Pupil can identify logical reason for given action.
Educational Rationale: Comprehension develops through experience resulting in increasing attention and in the understanding of varied situations and their implications for problem solving. General exploration, directive instruction, and practice in making inferences and behavioral responses are essential to any relevant educational program.

SOCIAL SKILLS: The skills involved in social problem solving. (Basic learning abilities 50-53)

50. Social Acceptance

Definition: The ability to get along with one's peers.
Illustration: Pupil can relate meaningfully to others and is accepted in both one-to-one and group situations.
Educational Rationale: To become socially acceptable, children must be taught self-control, cooperation, and good manners. The school must cooperate with the home in both direct and indirect teaching of these important personal habits and the related skills of social behavior.

51. Anticipatory Response

Definition: The ability to anticipate the probable outcome of a social situation by logical inference.
Illustration: Pupil can predict the consequences of his own behavior and that of others in given situations.
Educational Rationale: Children must be taught to consider alternate behavioral responses in specific learning situations and to judge the consequences and desirability of possible choices. The development of foresight is essential in social learning and should be emphasized throughout the curriculum.

52. Value Judgments

Definition: The ability to recognize and respond to moral and ethical issues.
Illustration: Pupil has a sense of right and wrong, controls own actions, demonstrates proper behavior.
Educational Rationale: Children need to be taught consistent standards of right and wrong in keeping with their culture so that they may develop respect for the common humanity and dignity of all mankind. Pupils should also be instructed in the respect for individuality and the values of democracy. Character education should enable the child to develop from egocentric to rational-altruistic behavior.

53. Social Maturity

Definition: The ability to assume personal and social responsibility.

Illustration: Pupil is socially mature and independent, demonstrates appropriate citizenship, and assumes social responsibilities.

Educational Rationale: In order to foster social maturity, the school must provide opportunities for pupils to learn social expectations appropriate to their developmental level. Instruction and practice in the acceptance of responsibility and the obligations of good citizenship should be planned to guarantee increasing personal success.

3

A Model District Policy Statement

Each school district should develop a carefully worded policy statement by which a program for the remediation of learning disabilities can be put into effect. Unless there is a clearly defined operational statement for use by professionals and all others concerned, gross confusion may result to the extent that pupils may be detrimentally placed and educationally mismanaged. Under such circumstances it would be preferable for children to continue in the regular program until a carefully thought-out policy statement can be developed.

Experience in school organization and administration has demonstrated that the professional staff who are expected to carry out a district policy must also be involved in its development and subsequent revision. Hence, a system for the cooperative involvement of this staff—special teachers, psychologists, and administrators —must be designed from the beginning of any complicated program attempting to provide for the remediation of educationally handicapped children with learning disabilities.

The following model policy statement was developed by the author over a period of several years' work with educationally handicapped children in the state of

28

California. It is admittedly incomplete in that any good policy statement must be constantly evolving and changing as a result of empirical experience derived from the program itself. However, this policy statement has been tried and has proven to be of considerable value in implementing the rationale presented in Chapter 1.

This model policy statement is presented here only as a *guide* to those concerned; it has been developed in accordance with California law and a specific local school district's organizational pattern. Accordingly, it should be changed and adapted to the needs of other districts and states as necessary. (The later chapters in this book will expand in detail on various aspects of this policy statement in an attempt to illustrate an organizational approach to the programming of learning disabilities.)

District Policy Pertaining to Programs for Educationally Handicapped Minors

It is the intent of this district[1] to develop and provide the necessary classes and programs as rapidly as possible in order to meet the needs of educationally handicapped minors. A comprehensive plan including systematic pupil screening, referral, evaluation, admission, and placement, together with organized teacher recruitment, in-service training, and adequate classroom construction, will make it possible to provide for all educationally handicapped minors within the near future.

Referrals will now be received from all schools on an open, continuous basis in accordance with the policies and procedures prescribed herein.

I. Definition of educationally handicapped minors

A. Chapter 7.1, Section 6750 of the *Education Code* defines educationally handicapped minors as, "... minors, other than physically handicapped minors ... or mentally retarded minors ... who, by reason of marked learning or behavioral problems or a combination thereof, cannot receive the reasonable benefit of ordinary education facilities."

B. Chapter 1, Article 27, Section 221 of *Title* 5 of the *California Administrative Code* states that "An educationally handicapped minor eligible for admission to a program is a minor described in *Education Code*, Section 6750, whose learning problems are associated with a behavioral disorder or a neurological handicap or a combination thereof, and who exhibits a significant discrepancy between ability and achievement."

C. This district has stipulated that the "marked learning or behavioral problems" of primary concern here will be most frequently manifested as follows:

1. *Distractibility:* Excessive motor activity, short attention span, lack of concentration or persistence, inability to delay or to control impulses or desires.

2. *Perceptual disorders:* Deficiencies or difficulties in recognizing (perceiving) by seeing, hearing, touching, or moving. These deficiencies cause pupils difficulty in accurately duplicating drawings, letters, written words, speech sounds, or body movements used in certain skills or games. Inability to attend because of slight lapse of consciousness.

3. *Conceptual disorders:* Deficiencies in storing and retaining previous experiences. In school these deficiencies cause difficulties in remembering

[1]This model policy statement has been modified from an actual statement of the Sacramento City Unified School District, Sacramento, California.

ideas and concepts, written words, arithmetic processes, and school rules. Difficulty in generalizing, abstracting, and reasoning.

4. *Emotional instability:* Excessive anger, aggressiveness, destructiveness, excessive anxiety, shyness, fear, conformity, or depression, bizarre, highly unrealistic, or delusional behavior.

II. Definition of the programs

A. A "program" is one or all of the special education programs for educationally handicapped minors described in *Education Code*, Section 6751. They are:

1. *Special classes* (elementary and secondary): Under this program educationally handicapped pupils unable to function in a regular class are assigned to a special class.

   a. This district will maintain preschool-kindergarten (ages 4-6), primary (7-9), intermediate elementary (9-11), upper elementary (11-13), junior high (13-15), and senior high school (15-18 plus) classes. All classes have a maximum of 11 pupils assigned to a special teacher. Classes may be specialized according to pupil needs and may be designated as primarily behavioral, neurological, or perceptual-motor programs.

   b. Classes may be self-contained or resource-centered. In the *self-contained class* pupils are assigned to the class for the entire school day; on occasion, when their educational handicap will permit, pupils may be assigned for specific periods or subjects to other classrooms. In the *resource-centered class*, pupils are assigned to a special class teacher who will be responsible for the educational program for each pupil throughout each day; however, the pupils will be programmed into other classrooms during the day on a much more extensive basis than for the self-contained special class.

2. *Learning disability groups* (elementary and secondary): In this program the pupil remains in his regular class but is scheduled for individual or small-group remedial instruction given by a special teacher.

   a. This district assigns the learning disability group teacher(s) to a maximum of four schools. A maximum of 11 pupils is assigned to the traveling special teacher who calls at each school on a regular schedule. The special teacher provides individual and small-group tutoring to the selected EH pupils, in most cases for 30- to 40-minute periods daily.

3. *Specialized consultation to teachers, counselors, and supervisors* (elementary and secondary): Under this program specialized consultation relative to the learning disabilities of individual pupils and special education services required by such pupils is provided for teachers, counselors, and supervisors.

   a. This district has contracted with a private diagnostic and treatment center to provide medical consultation to the members of the admissions committee.

4. *Home and hospital instruction* (elementary and secondary): Under this program a pupil who is unable to function in a school setting and who does not attend school receives instruction at the appropriate grade level at home, in a hospital, or in a regularly established nonprofit, licensed children's institution.

      a. This district assigns pupils not able to be continued in special or regular programs to a home teacher for educationally handicapped pupils. This teacher calls on each pupil on a prearranged schedule.

B. For those educationally handicapped pupils not able to profit from any of the above programs, the district may arrange to place the pupil in a private children's treatment center through special contract with the county superintendent of schools.

III. Objectives and Priorities

A. The primary objectives of this district's program for educationally handicapped minors are early identification of disabilities and provision of special education for EH pupils. The goal is to remediate specific learning disabilities insofar as this is possible in order to enable the pupil to learn more effectively and, hopefully, to return to the regular program.

B. Pupils with mild to moderate learning disabilities will be considered for the learning disability group and/or the special resource-centered class program. Pupils with severe learning disabilities will be considered for placement in self-contained classes and/or home teaching. In all programs pupils will be integrated with regular pupils as soon as possible. A pupil will be reassigned to a regular class as soon as he is functioning on an educational level sufficient to warrant it.

C. Priority for screening, identification, admission, and placement in the educationally handicapped program will be as follows:

1. Pupils with specific learning disabilities, such as perceptual-motor dysfunctions, possibly due to a neurological handicap.
2. Pupils having severe personality and emotional disturbances (autistic, schizophrenic, pre-psychotic, and severe neurotics) and significant learning problems.
3. Pupils with normal or above-normal functioning general intelligence (a *minimum* general intelligence quotient of 90).
4. Kindergarten- and primary-age children meeting criteria listed above.
5. Elementary-age pupils meeting criteria listed above.
6. Secondary-age pupils meeting criteria listed above.
7. Until the district can establish sufficient programs to meet the need, preference will be given to pupils in schools where EH programs are located in order to minimize family and transportation problems.

D. Pupils who are primarily discipline problems, slow learners who have functional intelligence in the 75-90 range with comparable school performance, and other minors who are not neurologically impaired or handicapped with a basic emotional disturbance will not be accepted in the educationally handicapped program.

IV. Legal standards for identification of educationally handicapped minors

A. Section 223 of *Title 5* states that "... individual identification of a minor as an educationally handicapped minor shall be established by a written report, including an assessment and evaluation of the minor's educational handicaps, from each of the following:

1. "A certificated employee of the school district or county superintendent of schools."

    a. In this district the referring classroom teacher and school principal will file the written report, using Special Education Form 1.[2]

2. "A credentialed school psychologist, or a certified psychologist with clinical training and with experience in working with children. Tests administered or techniques employed by psychologists in making such identification shall be those generally recognized within the profession. Other tests and techniques may be used by psychologists only with the prior approval of the state board of education."

    a. In this district the assigned school psychologist will file the written report. Other psychological reports from school and/or certified psychologists will be accepted at the discretion of the director of special education.

3. "One or more licensed physicians with experience in working with children and representing such fields as, but not limited to, pediatrics, neurology, and psychiatry, as the problems of the minor may make necessary."

    a. In this district the required medical assessment and evaluation will be obtained by the minor's parents from a private medical doctor of their choosing.

V. Referral procedures

A. The teacher requests a conference with the principal and school nurse to review the pupil's learning problem and to coordinate procedures. During this meeting, discussion should focus on the degree of severity of the behavioral characteristics outlined in Special Education Form 1 (*Fig. 3-1*) and whether or not the pupil meets the priority criteria outlined in section III of this outline. (At this point, the teacher has not filled out SE-1.)

B. For help in the initial screening of pupils, the teacher should have the child complete Special Education Form 2, "Basic Learning Abilities Pupil Work Sample" (*Fig. 3-2*), which should then be reviewed with the school psychologist for further consideration of the referral. As an additional aid in screening, the principal may administer the Slosson Intelligence Test. He should hesitate in referring pupils with a functional IQ below 85 with comparable school performance.

C. The principal arranges a meeting with the parents, teacher, and nurse, and explains the learning problem to the parents. He requests their cooperation in possibly referring the child for the educationally handicapped program.

1. The principal obtains the parents' signatures on Special Services Form 1, "Parent Authorization for Psychological Services" (*Fig. 3-3*).

2. The principal explains to the parents that the law requires a medical assessment and evaluation of the minor's educational handicaps. For this purpose the principal and nurse give the parents a copy of Special Education Form 3, "Medical Report on Pupil Referred for Educationally Handicapped Program" (*Fig 3-4*), together with a cover letter from the superintendent (*Fig. 3-5*).

    a. The principal should stress the importance of the parents' making an immediate appointment with a physician because this step in the referral process must be completed before anything else can be done. The physician is requested to send the completed medical report di-

---

[2]Samples of all forms mentioned are included at the end of the chapter.

rectly to the referring school nurse in care of the school address that is written on the front of the medical form.

3. Upon receipt of the completed medical form (SE-3) the school nurse should note its receipt on the student's health record and then forward it to the school principal. The school principal must then decide if he wishes to make a formal referral for the educationally handicapped program.

4. If the principal decides to initiate the referral, he requests the pupil's teacher to complete the "Teacher Referral Form for Educationally Handicapped Pupil" (SE-1).

5. The principal sends the completed Special Services Form 1, and Special Education Forms 1, 2, and 3 directly to the *supervisor of psychological services*. Copies of these records should be retained in the pupil's school file. This now constitutes the formal referral for the EH program.

6. The supervisor of psychological services will assign the referral to the appropriate school psychologist for the required psychological assessment and evaluation. The referral will be given priority over non-EH cases from the referring school.

   a. The psychologist will proceed to examine the child and will write a report covering: general intellectual ability, including functioning IQ with subtest scores and indicated strengths and weaknesses; an evaluation or appraisal of achievement in the basic learning ability areas of gross motor development, sensory-motor integration, perceptual-motor skills, language development, conceptual skills, and social skills; comments regarding the observed discrepancy between ability and achievement (if any); recommendations, including statements about eligibility for the EH program, priority status in the district, type of program(s) implied, specific learning needs to be considered by the committee and teachers involved, and other comments, such as special treatment, follow-up, limitations of attendance, etc.

   b. A copy of the psychologist's report will be sent to the referring school principal as soon as possible. If the pupil has been found eligible for the EH program, two copies of all records and reports, together with the complete psychological file, will be sent to the *coordinator of educationally handicapped programs*.

7. Upon receipt of the psychological report notifying him of pupil eligibility, the referring school principal should telephone the coordinator of educationally handicapped programs and request that the pupil be placed on the agenda for formal consideration by the *admissions committee*. The coordinator of educationally handicapped programs will immediately assign a date and time when the pupil will be considered by the admissions committee.

VI. The admissions committee

A. *Membership:* In accordance with the *Education Code,* Section 6755(b), the admissions committee for this district will consist of the referring school principal, the referring teacher or teachers involved, the referring school nurse, the examining school psychologist, the consulting physician, and the coordinator of educationally handicapped programs who shall serve as chairman. The director of special education and other professionals concerned may attend as *ex officio* members of the committee.

B. *Procedures*

1. All members of the committee will be informed in writing by the coordinator of educationally handicapped programs regarding the date, time, and place of the meeting (*Fig. 3-6*).

2. The coordinator will also send a form letter to the parents of the child concerned requesting their presence at the admissions committee meeting at a specified time (*Fig. 3-7*).

3. The coordinator will send an agenda of pupils to be considered, plus copies of all available reports on the referred pupils, to the consulting physician at least five days in advance of the admissions committee meeting. Following use by the physician, these records will be returned to the coordinator at the time of the meeting and will be forwarded to the receiving special education teacher upon placement.

4. The coordinator will open the meeting with introductions and will briefly review the comments on the original "Teacher Referral Form" (SE-1) as the basis for the EH referral. Then the coordinator will request the teacher to comment on the pupil's present performance. The principal will be requested to comment regarding the present status of the referral. The school nurse will summarize family and health history and present health status. The consulting physician will review the available medical reports and recommendations. The examining psychologist will make a report. The coordinator will summarize the discussion and review the recommendations arrived at by the committee. Approximately 40 minutes will be devoted to this review and summary. The parents will then be invited to meet with all members of the committee at which time the coordinator will present the committee recommendations and lead the discussion. In some cases it may be necessary for parents to have follow-up meetings with the psychologist, principal, nurse, teacher, or coordinator in order to discuss the recommendations and their implications in detail.

C. *Committee reports:* The coordinator will write and distribute a report of the admissions committee's decisions and recommendations. To comply with the requirements listed in Section 225 of *Title 5*, the committee report will be summarized on Special Education Form 4, "Admissions Committee Report on Educationally Handicapped Pupils (*Fig. 3-8*). As required by Section 225 of *Title 5*, the report will specify:

1. The committee's findings regarding the type and extent of educational learning needs and the ability of the child to profit from participation in one of the programs described in the *Education Code*, Section 6751.

2. The committee's decision regarding eligibility and a positive or negative recommendation with respect to admission of the minor to the most appropriate program.

3. The names of the members present at the meeting of the committee at which a recommendation was made.

VII. Placement in the program

A. Following official admission to the program by the admissions committee, the coordinator will place the newly admitted pupil on the waiting list. Waiting lists will be subdivided into preschool-kindergarten (ages 4-6), primary (7-9), intermediate elementary (9-11), upper elementary (11-13), junior high school (13-15), and senior high school (15-18 plus). The waiting list will also indicate the date of the admissions committee meeting for each pupil and the referring school. The pupil will be placed on one of the following waiting lists as recommended by the admissions committee:

1. Special class—self-contained
2. Special class—resource-centered
3. Learning disability group
4. Home and hospital teaching

B. Upon opening a new class for the educationally handicapped, the coordinator will assign pupils in accordance with the recommendations of the admissions committee. Initial placement will go to pupils on the waiting list from the school in which the program is to be housed. Other pupils will then be assigned according to the priorities specified earlier.

C. When placement of newly admitted pupils becomes possible, the coordinator will notify the referring principal by using Special Education Form 5, "Notification of Assignment of Educationally Handicapped Pupil" (*Fig. 3-9*).

D. The referring principal shall then notify the parents of the impending placement and obtain parental authorization for placement. Two copies of Special Education Form 6, "Record of Parent Conference Prior to Pupil Placement in Educational Programs for Exceptional Children" (*Fig. 3-10*) are to be signed by the parents. One copy shall be included in the pupil's cumulative record folder, and the second copy should be forwarded to the office of the director of special education. Parents will then be requested by the referring principal to telephone the receiving principal immediately for an appointment for enrollment.

E. During the enrollment conference the receiving principal will introduce the parents and pupil to the receiving teacher and make arrangements for the child's first day of attendance. The objectives of the EH program will be discussed again with the parents, as will the parent education program, pupil marking policies, teacher conferencing, the instructional program and behavior modification system, and transportation arrangements (if any).

F. Following the parent conference, the receiving principal will telephone the supervisor of transportation services to arrange the transportation schedule and the beginning date. The supervisor of transportation services will confirm the transportation schedule through direct contact with the parents concerned.

G. When an opening occurs in a special class for the educationally handicapped, the principal of the school housing the program will request an informal meeting to review pupils on the waiting list for placement. This meeting will take place at the school concerned and will include the principal, coordinator, and the appropriate teacher. During this meeting, the pupils most likely to benefit from that particular program will be reviewed and one or more selected from the waiting list to fill the available places.

H. Pupils admitted to home and hospital teaching may be so placed upon request by the principal concerned through arrangements with the coordinator of educationally handicapped programs.

I. Transferring pupils legally admitted to programs for the educationally handicapped in other districts will be automatically placed on the appropriate waiting list upon receipt of all required records from the previous district of attendance. These pupils will then be subject to the same priorities and procedures as all other pupils in this district.

J. On the day the child is actually enrolled in his new special education class, the receiving principal will complete Special Education Form 7, "Special Class Placement Report" (*Fig. 3-11*) and send it to the office of the director of special education.

VIII. Reevaluation and reassignment

A. In conformance with Section 226 of *Title 5*, "... an annual examination shall be made of the school adjustment and academic progress of each minor enrolled in a program, and a summary report shall be made to the admissions committee."

Within this district two such examinations are made each year by the teacher concerned using Special Education Form 8, "Pupil Progress Report by Teacher" (*Fig. 3-12*) and Special Education Form 9, "A Psychoeducational Evaluation of Basic Learning Abilities" (*Fig. 3-13*). The first examination is completed in January, and the second examination is completed in June. Two copies of the reports are prepared, one for the pupil's cumulative record folder and one for the office of the director of special education. All such reports are available to members of the admissions committee and others concerned.

B. During the spring of each year the coordinator of educationally handicapped programs will arrange for review meetings at each school housing an educationally handicapped program. At this meeting the school principal, special teacher, psychologist, nurse, and coordinator will review all Pupil Progress Reports and recommend pupil placement and assignment for the coming school year. A summary of these recommendations will be prepared by the coordinator and sent to all concerned. The coordinator will then arrange for pupil placement or reassignment according to the recommendations of the review.

C. If transfer to another program for educationally handicapped minors or return to a regular school program is recommended, a copy of the recommendation with accompanying data will be forwarded to the principal of the school that the child is to attend. Upon receipt of this information, the receiving principal will hold a conference with the parents and arrange for a smooth and orderly transfer to the new school.

IX. Marking and conference policy

A. All teachers of educationally handicapped pupils will write a personal letter to parents of their pupils twice each year summarizing the pupil's progress. The first letter will be sent home in January each year and the second letter in June. Each letter will specify pupil strengths, weaknesses, and progress as noted in the "Pupil Progress Report by Teacher" and will be written so as to be easily understood by the parents.

B. Educationally handicapped pupils in self-contained special classes or on home teaching will *not* receive regular report cards, and the letter from the teacher will constitute the only written report to the parents.

C. Educationally handicapped pupils in resource-centered special classes or in learning disability groups *will* receive regular report cards in addition to the letter from the teacher concerned. In all cases report card marks will be awarded by the special teacher in cooperation with the regular class teacher and will be based on the individual pupil's achievement and effort expended in relation to his handicap rather than in relation to an arbitrary "class" or "grade" standard.

D. An integral part of the marking policy for educationally handicapped pupils is the conference between parents and teacher. All parents will be requested to confer with the EH teacher during the regular conference periods established by the district in the fall and spring of each year. In addition, parents are encouraged to confer with teachers at other times by appointment. Teachers are also expected to make at least one home call each year to confer with parents in their own home environment.

X. Teacher orientation and in-service training

A. Following the decision to open a program for educationally handicapped minors in a new school, a faculty meeting will be arranged through the principal concerned and the director of special education. At this meeting the EH program will be presented in detail using special films and slides when possible. The purpose and philosophy of the program, including integration policies and the role of the special education teacher, will be emphasized.

B. When the new class has opened, a faculty meeting will be held in the special education room so that the special education teacher can explain and demonstrate her program. The functioning role of the psychologist, school nurse, and the coordinator of educationally handicapped programs will also be explained and discussed.

C. Wherever possible, special education teachers for EH programs will be selected from the regular staff of the school in which the new program is to be placed. During the spring of each year, a special in-service training course that will emphasize introductions and visitations to EH programs will be offered to all interested teachers.

D. Special summer workshops will be planned on a regular basis. These will provide opportunities for teachers to be involved in the ongoing development of the program, special study projects, etc.

E. New teachers in the EH program will be given priority for enrollment in joint district state college courses on the education of educationally handicapped pupils.

F. Throughout the regular school year teachers of the educationally handicapped will receive in-service training through special program meetings on an every-other-week basis. These meetings will be directed by the coordinator of educationally handicapped programs and will emphasize the development of programmed materials, behavior modification programs, teaching strategy, instructional organization, and related concerns.

XI. The instructional program

A. The instructional program for educationally handicapped minors will be based on the individual needs of the pupils enrolled. Accordingly, a prescriptive approach to learning will be used, and daily lesson plans will be developed for each pupil. Therefore, the program will be an individualized one, and "class" or "small group" lessons will be infrequently utilized.

B. The curriculum will include the fundamental school subjects; but the instructional materials and methods will be adapted to the learning characteristics of individual pupils. Special emphasis will be placed on the remediation of specific learning disabilities through the development of gross motor, sensory-motor, perceptual-motor, language, conceptual, and social skills. The daily lesson plan will provide remediation in each area.

C. Since the instructional program is based on individual pupil needs, the first month of the school year will be devoted to intensive psychoeducational diagnosis of all pupils by their teachers. During this period an inventory of special skills will be made and the teacher may administer a series of special tests including the Psychoeducational Inventory, the Developmental Survey of Basic Learning Abilities (for kindergarten pupils), the Wide Range Achievement Tests, Metropolitan Readiness Tests, Gilmore Oral Reading Test, The Frostig Test of Visual Perception, and other related tests. Following this diagnostic period, an individual profile of each pupil's strengths and weaknesses will be made. Then this will become the basis for individual prescriptive teaching.

D. Each pupil will attend class for the regular minimum day unless he has been placed on a modified school day by the admissions committee. Classes may also be organized by early and late periods with pupils divided accordingly. For self-contained classes a special teacher's aide will be provided for the entire time that the class is in session.

E. All educationally handicapped programs will utilize social reinforcement and behavior modification principles and techniques. These techniques and the reinforcement system to be used will follow district guidelines as presented by the director of special education, the coordinator of educationally handicapped programs, and the consulting psychologists involved. However, each teacher will modify and operate the reinforcement system according to distinctive classroom and pupil needs.

XII. Parent involvement

A. It is essential that parent cooperation and involvement begin with the initial referral and extend through the entire remediation program. Parents will have conferences with the admissions committee, with the teacher regularly at school, and with the teacher during informal home visitations.

B. During the school year parents of children in each EH class will meet as a group with the teacher and psychologist concerned in the school classroom to discuss the program and the pupils' needs and characteristics in detail. Normally, three such meetings will be held during the year in October, February, and May.

C. Parents new to the EH program will be requested to enroll in the adult education class for parents of EH children. This class is instructed by the coordinator of educationally handicapped programs and is usually offered during February and March of each year.

D. Parents of children who are eligible for the EH kindergarten program will be enrolled in an adult education class as a condition for placement of their child in the EH program. This class will be conducted similar to parent education preschool classes with the kindergarten teacher as the adult education instructor. Parents will be involved directly in structured observations and limited participation as decided by the teacher.

TEACHER REFERRAL FORM
FOR EDUCATIONALLY HANDICAPPED PUPIL

To the Psychologist: This pupil is being referred for psychological evaluation as a possible candidate for special education classes for educationally handicapped pupils. Such pupils have learning problems associated with a behavioral disorder, a neurological handicap, or a combination thereof, and exhibit a significant discrepancy between ability and achievement.

(To be filled in by teacher)

Pupil's name_____ Birth date_____

Referring teacher_____

School_____

BEHAVIORAL CHARACTERISTICS

The "marked learning or behavioral problems" with which special education classes will be concerned are manifested most frequently in the terms given under general headings below. Underline the specific characteristics that apply to this pupil. Evaluate the pupil further by marking an X under the appropriate number to the right of the characteristics listing. Then give an illustration from classroom experience.

Number Code

1. Behavior not exhibited at all.
2. Behavior exhibited to a slight degree.
3. Behavior exhibited to a considerable degree.
4. Behavior exhibited to an uncomfortable degree.
5. Behavior exhibited to a very large degree.

Distractability	1	2	3	4	5
Excessive motor activity, short attention span, lack of concentration or persistence, inability to delay or control impulses or desires.					

Classroom illustration:

Figure 3-1 (SE-1)

Perceptual Disorders	1	2	3	4	5
Deficiencies or difficulties in recognizing (perceiving) by seeing, hearing, touching, or moving. Cause difficulty in accurately duplicating drawings, letters, written words, speech sounds, or body movements used in certain skills or games. Inability to attend because of slight lapses of consciousness.					

Classroom illustration:

Conceptual Disorders	1	2	3	4	5
Deficiencies in storing and retaining previous experiences. Cause difficulties in remembering ideas and concepts, written words, arithmetic processes, and school rules. Difficulty in generalizing, abstracting, and reasoning.					

Classroom illustration:

Emotional Instability	1	2	3	4	5
Excessive anger, aggressiveness, destructiveness; excessive anxiety, shyness, fear, conformity, or depression; bizarre, highly unrealistic, or delusional behavior.					

Classroom illustration:

Figure 3-1 (SE-1)—*Continued*

ACADEMIC PERFORMANCE

Estimated reading grade placement_____ Comments _____

_____

_____

Estimated airthmetic grade placement_____ Comments _____

_____

_____

Describe writing ability_____ _____

_____

Describe language ability_____

_____

Why do you believe a significant discrepancy exists between this pupil's ability and his achievement? _____ _____

_____

_____

OTHER COMMENTS

_____   Date _____
(teacher's signature)

_____   Date _____
(principal's signature)

Figure 3-1 (SE-1)—*Continued*

BASIC LEARNING ABILITIES PUPIL WORK SAMPLE

Write your name._____ Birth date_____

Address_____ City_____ State_____

Telephone_____ School_____ Class_____ Date_____

Father's name_____ Mother's name_____

Print the alphabet.
Write numbers from 1 through 31.

Copy each design in the space provided.

Mark the big box.	■ ▪ ■ ■ ○ ■ ○
Mark the little circle.	○ ■ ○ ▪ ○ ○

Mark the one that is different.	b b b b d b b
△ △ △ ⊿ △	+ ✗ + + + +

Figure 3-2 (SE-2)

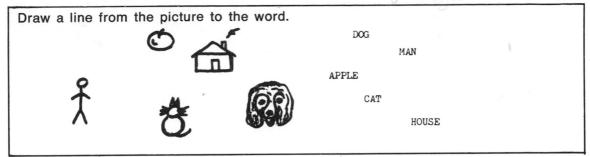

Draw a line from the picture to the word.

DOG

MAN

APPLE

CAT

HOUSE

Copy the sentences.

The big dog chased the boy.

GEORGE ATE THE WHOLE PIE.

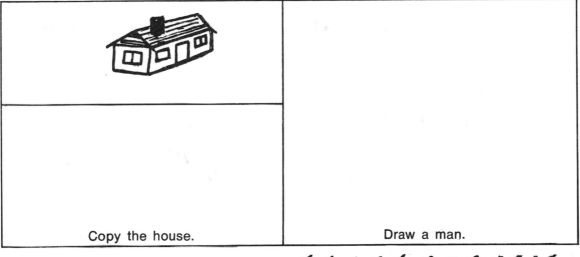

Copy the house.

Draw a man.

How many apples are there here?_____

```
  3     11     9     26      5      9     16     213
 +2    +4    -3    -17     x3     x7     x4     x 4
```

```
4⟌8          3⟌12           7⟌231          4⟌52.04
```

Figure 3-2 (SE-2)—*Continued*

PARENT AUTHORIZATION FOR PSYCHOLOGICAL SERVICES

Following a discussion with school personnel acquainted with my child, I authorize the use of school psychological services to aid in educational planning and assist in the guidance of my child.

I understand that these services may include the administration of individual intelligence, achievement, aptitude, and/or projective tests or scales given by fully qualified personnel, and that upon my request a conference will be arranged to discuss the conclusions and recommendations resulting from the service

Name of pupil_____

Birth date_____

School_____

_____   _____

(signature of parent or guardian)   (date)

Received by_____

Title_____

Figure 3-3 (SS-1)

MEDICAL REPORT ON PUPIL REFERRED
FOR EDUCATIONALLY HANDICAPPED PROGRAM

To Examining Physician: Please complete this form and return it directly to the School Nurse.

Name _____ (School Nurse)

School _____

Address _____

(To be filled in by school nurse)

Pupil's name _____ Birth date _____ Age _____

Address _____ Telephone _____

Ordinal position _____ Ages of brothers _____ Ages of sisters _____

Present concerns of the school _____

_____

_____

_____

School health history _____

_____

_____

_____

FAMILY DATA

	Father	Mother
Name		
Age		
Education		
Occupation		
Personality		
Current health		

Figure 3-4 (SE-3)

(To be filled in by examining physician)

Date of examination_____Date of last examination_____

Period of time physician has known child_____

Concerns of the family_____

_____

PREGNANCY AND BIRTH HISTORY

Place of delivery (name of hospital)_____

Delivered by (name)_____

Previous pregnancies (number)_____Miscarriages_____Stillbirths_____

Mother's health during this pregnancy: Excellent_____Other_____(describe)_____

_____

Baby's birth weight_____ Baby arrived: On time_____. Early by_____ weeks.

Late by_____weeks. Illness or complication in newborn period: No_____Yes_____

(describe) _____

MEDICAL HISTORY

	Yes	No	Date	Describe Details
Measles				
Mumps				
Chicken pox				
Rubella (3-day, or German measles)				
Whooping cough				
Seizures, fits, or spells				
Tonsillectomy				
Tuberculosis or exposure to person tubercular or with chronic cough				
Frequent bedwetting now				
Hospitalization				
Other known chronic diseases, serious illnesses, or handicapping conditions				

Figure 3-4 (SE-3)—*Continued*

DEVELOPMENTAL HISTORY

	Compared with Siblings/Peers			Comments
	Fast	Average	Slow	
Walking, running, climbing				
Talking				
Playing with toys, coloring, drawing				
Understanding what is said to him				
Getting along with peers				

	Mother, Others Say		Comments
	Yes	No	
Is particularly "difficult" or "different"			
Is particularly hyperactive			
Is particularly clumsy			

PHYSICAL EXAMINATION

Height_____ Weight_____ Age_____ Blood pressure_____

	Normal	Abnormal	Not Examined	Describe Details
General appearance, posture, gait				
Speech				
Behavior during examination				
Skin				
Eyes: Externals				
Optic fundi				
Ears: External and canals				
Tympanic membranes				
Nose, mouth, pharynx				
Teeth				

Figure 3-4 (SE-3)—Continued

Heart				
Lungs				
Abdomen (including hernias)				
Genitalia				
Bones, joints, muscles				

Neurological:
    Cranial nerves—
        nystagmus, strabismus				

Reflexes—symmetry				

Dual simultaneous
        sensory test (Bender
        face-hand)				

With eyes closed,
        simultaneously touch:
        Both cheeks				

Both hands				
Cheek and homolateral hand				
Cheek and contralateral hand				
Right and left orientation for own hand and leg				

Stereognosis—ability to
        judge shape and form
        of objects in hand with
        eyes closed (coin,
        paper, key, marble)				

From a medical point of view, does this child appear to have a neurological, emotional, or behavioral disorder sufficient to affect his learning abilities? Describe.

What medicinal or other medical treatment or supervision is recommended to improve learning and provide for the educational management of this pupil?

General comments and recommendations (including appropriate laboratory studies, e.g., EEG, skull X-rays, etc.):

Physician's name_____

Physician's signature_____

Address_____

Figure 3-4 (SE-3)—_Continued_

Dear Doctor:

The parents of this child have requested evaluation for possible placement in a special program for the educationally handicapped. Essentially, this is a small class program with a special teacher for pupils who have either neurological and/or behavioral disorders and who are achieving below their grade and ability level.

The law requires that a medical evaluation be obtained as part of the referral procedure. Enclosed is a "Medical Report on Pupil Referred for Educationally Handicapped Program" that you are requested to use as a guide in your examination of this child. Your examination and comments will be used as an aid in determining proper educational placement and programming.

Please complete the form and return it to the referring school nurse whose address has been provided on the first page of the report.

Your cooperation in the medical evaluation of this child is appreciated.

Sincerely,

District Superintendent

Figure 3-5

MEMORANDUM

To: Referring Principal   Date _____

From: Coordinator of Educationally Handicapped Programs

      Pupil _____ Birth date _____

Subject: Admissions committee meeting for educationally handicapped programs

      Place _____

      _____

On _____ your referral of this pupil for the educationally handicapped program was received. This pupil has now been scheduled for the admissions committee meeting as indicated above. In accordance with Section 6755(b) of the *Education Code* and district policy, the admissions committee consists of the referring school principal, teacher, nurse, school psychologist, consulting physician, and the coordinator of educationally handicapped programs.

Enclosed is a copy of the confirming letter sent to the parents concerned, requesting them to attend this meeting to discuss the committee's recommendations. Please arrange to personally attend this meeting with your school nurse and the present teacher of this pupil. It is also suggested that you personally follow up with the parents to assure that they understand the importance of their attendance at this meeting.

The admissions meeting will begin with a brief history of the referral to be presented by the principal. This will be followed by the teacher's oral report of the pupil's present classroom functioning. The school nurse will then summarize family and health history and present the child's health status. The consulting physician will briefly review the available medical reports. The examining psychologist will present his findings. Then the coordinator of educationally handicapped programs will summarize the discussion and review the recommendations arrived at by the committee. Approximately 40 minutes will be devoted to this review and summary. The parents will then be invited to meet with all members of the committee, during which time the coordinator will present the committee recommendations and lead the discussion. In some cases it may be necessary for parents to have follow-up meetings with the psychologist, principal, nurse, teacher, or coordinator in order to discuss the recommendations and their implications in detail.

Because of the number of referrals and limited space and time, it may not be possible to meet again about this pupil until the next school year. It is therefore important that all persons be present and recommendations be arrived at if the pupil is to be considered for placement in an EH program during this year.

If for any reason you wish to cancel this referral or not hold an admissions committee meeting at this time, please notify the coordinator, in writing, as soon as possible.

Figure 3-6

Re: Jones, Billy
Birth date: 1-13-58

Dear Mr. and Mrs. Jones:

Following a discussion with your child's teacher and principal, you signed a request on _____ that this school district make further evaluations to determine your child's educational needs and how he/she may best be helped in school.

Your child's school educational report, the medical report from your physician, and a psychological study have now been completed and received. A meeting of the admissions committee for educationally handicapped programs has been arranged for Wednesday, _____, at the School Administration Building, in the Special Education Conference Clinic Room, Special Services Office, from _____ _____ to _____ to review all of the reports and to arrive at a recommendation concerning your child's future school placement needs. This committee consists of your child's principal, teacher, school nurse, school psychologist, a consulting physician, and the coordinator of educationally handicapped programs. It is very important that you be present to meet briefly with us in order to receive our recommendations and to discuss our findings.

Because of the great number of referrals for this program and the limited time available to the admissions committee, this may be your only opportunity to meet with us this year; so we hope you will arrange to be present at the time and date indicated above. If you have further questions, please telephone your school principal who will be happy to help you in any way he can.

Sincerely yours,

Coordinator of Educationally
Handicapped Programs

Figure 3-7

ADMISSIONS COMMITTEE REPORT ON EDUCATIONALLY HANDICAPPED PUPIL

Pupil's name _____ Birth date _____

Parents' names _____

Address _____ Telephone _____

Referring school _____

Date of committee meeting _____ Place _____

Present _____, Referring principal

       _____, Referring teacher

       _____, Coordinator of EH

       _____, Physician

       _____, School nurse

       _____, School psychologist

Committee Findings

Type and extent of educational learning needs_____

Ability of pupil to profit from participation in one of the EH programs.

    _____Cannot profit. EH programs inappropriate for learning needs.

    _____Very little. Ability is limited and little profit is anticipated.

    _____Much profit anticipated. Should be given priority placement.

    _____Very much profit anticipated because of exceptional ability. Should be given high priority for placement.

Committee Recommendations

    _____Not found eligible for placement in any EH program.

    _____Not found eligible for placement at this time. Should be continued in his regular school and class, with or without educational modifications, supplementary assistance, or treatment as commented on below.

    _____Eligible for admission to a special class placement:

        _____self-contained, _____resource-centered. Level_____

    _____Eligible for admission to the EH program in a learning disability group.

    _____Eligible for admission to the EH program through home or hospital instruction.

    _____Exemption from school attendance.

    _____Later review by committee, pending receipt of further information as follows

    _____Other_____

Comments

                                      _____

                                      Coordinator of Educationally
                                      Handicapped Programs

Figure 3-8 (SE-4)

NOTIFICATION OF ASSIGNMENT OF EDUCATIONALLY HANDICAPPED PUPIL

Pupil's name _____ Birth date _____

To: _____ (Principal)

_____ (School)

From: Director of Special Education

    This pupil from your school was referred for the educationally handicapped program and was found eligible and recommended for placement by the admissions committee on _____. It will now be possible to place this pupil in a _____ at _____ school, beginning _____.

    Please notify the parents of this impending placement and obtain their signature on the enclosed two copies of Special Education Form 6, "Record of Parent Conference Prior to Pupil Placement in Educational Program for Exceptional Children." One copy of this form should be placed in the pupil's cumulative record folder and sent on to the receiving school. The second copy should be sent to the office of the director of special education.

    In addition, please ask the parents to telephone the principal of the receiving school for an enrollment appointment as soon as possible. During the enrollment conference, the receiving principal will introduce the special teacher, explain the program to parents and pupil, and make arrangements for a starting date and transportation, if necessary.

Figure 3-9 (SE-5)

RECORD OF PARENT CONFERENCE PRIOR TO PUPIL PLACEMENT
IN EDUCATIONAL PROGRAM FOR EXCEPTIONAL CHILDREN

Pupil's name_____ Birth date._____

School_____

To whom it may concern:

After our discussion concerning my child's general learning ability, school progress, and social adjustment, I hereby agree to his/her placement in the indicated educational program as soon as the necessary arrangements can be made.

I understand that the progress and development of my child will be carefully observed and that I will be informed orally or in writing at various times, or upon my special request, about the nature of such progress.

_____   _____
          (signature of parent)   (date)

_____   _____
          (signature of parent)   (date)

_____   _____
        (administrator's signature)   (date)

Indicated Program

Physically handicapped   _____
Mentally gifted   _____
Educationally handicapped   _____
Educable mentally retarded   _____
Trainable mentally retarded   _____

Figure 3-10 (SE-6)

SPECIAL CLASS PLACEMENT REPORT

To the Receiving Principal: This form is to be completed and sent to the director of special education on the day a pupil enters a special day class for the first time *or* as a transfer from another school.

Upon the basis of necessary individual examination, recommendations, and approval,

_____ was enrolled in the_____
                      (name)

_____ special education class, _____, on _____
                                              (grade)   (date)

Pupil's birth date _____

Parents' names _____

Address _____ Telephone _____

District of residence _____

School_____

Principal's name _____ _____
                                                                           (signature)

Date _____

Figure 3-11 (SE-7)

> *Note to teacher:* First, on the form entitled, "A Psychoeducational Evaluation of Basic Learning Abilities," evaluate *present* functioning in the basic learning abilities by marking the performance level. Then, in January and June at the end of each school semester, complete the "Pupil Progress Report," indicating the present educational program and progress to date. Make two copies of that report. Place the original in the special cumulative record folder. Send the carbon to the office of the director of special education for inclusion in the pupil's central file.

PUPIL PROGRESS REPORT BY TEACHER

Pupil's Name _____ Birthdate _____ Grade _____

Address _____ Telephone _____

GROSS MOTOR DEVELOPMENT   (Programs and progress in motor activities, physical education, general health, etc.)

SENSORY-MOTOR INTEGRATION   (Programs and progress in motor integration, art, music, etc.)

PERCEPTUAL-MOTOR SKILLS   (Programs and progress in perceptual skills, including listening, attention and memory, fine muscle coordination.)

(Copyright 1967, by Fearon Publishers.)

Figure 3-12 (SE-8)

LANGUAGE DEVELOPMENT (Programs and progress in language usage, including functional level of reading, writing, and spelling.)

CONCEPTUAL SKILLS (Programs and progress in arithmetic understanding, social studies, fund of information, concept development.)

SOCIAL SKILLS (Programs and progress in social and personal development, including self control, responsibility, and general behavior.)

GENERAL COMMENTS

What recommendations do you have regarding educational placement and programs for this pupil for the forthcoming semester or year?

Signed:_____ _____
　　　　　　　　　Teacher　　　　　　　　　　　　　Type of Special Class

_____ _____ _____
　　　　Principal　　　　　　　　　　School　　　　　　　Date

Figure 3-12 (SE-8)—*Continued*

A PSYCHOEDUCATIONAL EVALUATION OF BASIC LEARNING ABILITIES

	Performance Level	Learning Disabilities			Learning Strengths	
Name_____ Date_____ Age_____ Evaluator_____		Very Weak	Weak	Average	Strong	Very Strong
		0 5	25		75	95 100
GROSS MOTOR DEVELOPMENT **ROLLING** *(controlled)*						
SITTING *(erect)*						
CRAWLING *(smoothly)*						
WALKING *(coordinated)*						
RUNNING *(course)*						
THROWING *(accurately)*						
JUMPING *(obstacles)*						
SKIPPING *(alternately)*						
DANCING *(eurythmy)*						
SELF-IDENTIFICATION *(name/awareness)*						
BODY LOCALIZATION *(part location)*						
BODY ABSTRACTION *(transfer/generalization)*						
MUSCULAR STRENGTH *(sit-, leg-ups/bends)*						
GENERAL PHYSICAL HEALTH *(significant history)*						
SENSORY-MOTOR INTEGRATION **BALANCE AND RHYTHM** *(games/dance)*						
BODY-SPATIAL ORGANIZATION *(mazes)*						
REACTION-SPEED DEXTERITY *(motor-accuracy)*						
TACTILE DISCRIMINATION *(object identification)*						
DIRECTIONALITY *(right-left/etc.)*						
LATERALITY *(hand-eye-foot)*						
TIME ORIENTATION *(lapse and concept)*						
PERCEPTUAL-MOTOR SKILLS **AUDITORY: ACUITY** *(functional hearing)*						
A—DECODING *(following directions)*						
A—VOCAL ASSOCIATION *(imitative response)*						
A—MEMORY *(retention)*						
A—SEQUENCING *(patterning)*						
VISUAL: ACUITY *("Snellen")*						
V—COORDINATION AND PURSUIT *(tracking)*						
V—FORM DISCRIMINATION *(association)*						

Figure 3-13 (SE-9) (Copyright 1967, by Fearon Publishers.)

	Performance Level	Learning Disabilities			Learning Strengths	
		Very Weak	Weak	Average	Strong	Very Strong
		0 5	25		75	95 100
V—FIGURE/GROUND (differentiation)						
V—MEMORY (visual recall)						
VISUAL-MOTOR: MEMORY (designs)						
VM—FINE MUSCLE COORDINATION (designs)						
VM—SPATIAL-FORM MANIPULATION (blocks)						
VM—SPEED OF LEARNING (coding)						
VM—INTEGRATION (draw-a-man)						
LANGUAGE DEVELOPMENT **VOCABULARY** (word knowledge)						
FLUENCY AND ENCODING (use and structure)						
ARTICULATION (initial/medial/final)						
WORD ATTACK SKILLS (phonic association)						
READING COMPREHENSION (understanding)						
WRITING (expression)						
SPELLING (oral/written)						
CONCEPTUAL SKILLS **NUMBER CONCEPTS** (counting)						
ARITHMETIC PROCESSES ($+ - \times \div$)						
ARITHMETIC REASONING (problem solving)						
GENERAL INFORMATION (fund of knowledge)						
CLASSIFICATION (relationships)						
COMPREHENSION (common sense reasoning)						
SOCIAL SKILLS **SOCIAL ACCEPTANCE** (friendship)						
ANTICIPATORY RESPONSE (foresight)						
VALUE JUDGMENTS (ethical-moral sense)						
SOCIAL MATURITY (gross problem solving)						

Figure 3-13 (SE-9)—*Continued*

4

Preliminary Screening and Identification

Once the decision has been made to start a learning disabilities program, it becomes necessary to select an appropriate school for housing. Although every school should have such a program eventually, it may be best to begin with a pilot program in one or two schools. District philosophy and policy should be discussed in detail with the building principal in order to obtain his wholehearted cooperation. Plans should then be made for a special faculty orientation meeting.

Faculty Orientation

Whatever the over-all district plan of program implementation may be, the first and most important step is to introduce the selected faculty to the philosophy and procedures involved. The entire success of the learning disabilities program is dependent upon early faculty orientation and cooperative involvement.

Because the prescriptive approach to the remediation and programming of children with learning disabilities is relatively new in education, the purpose of the first faculty meeting should be to introduce teachers to the essential aspects of the program and to provide them with some means of empathizing with the children. To accomplish this purpose, the director of special education or the coordinator of educationally handicapped programs should chair the meeting and should begin with a brief statement that clearly defines the characteristics of the pupils to be involved and the nature of the educational program to be operated in the school. If colored slides or films of pupils already enrolled in similar programs in the district or other areas can then be shown, it will be much easier for the faculty to reach an affective level of understanding of what is involved and, consequently, to raise pertinent questions for discussion. Finally, the first orientation meeting should specify the beginning screening and referral procedures in which the teachers will be involved.

The next step is to determine dates when the screening procedure will be implemented in each classroom. Many screening procedures can be developed, but the one advocated here is the direct assessment of all kindergarten- and primary-age pupils with some "work sample" procedure that, when combined with school records and teacher judgment, provides extremely valuable data. In most cases this is best accomplished by having the coordinator or psychologist come to the classroom at a scheduled time and actually assist the teacher in carrying out the specified procedure. (This procedure will be considered in some detail later in this chapter.)

Following the collection of work samples or other data, the coordinator should arrange to meet individually with each teacher to review the data and to rank the most likely candidates for possible referral. The coordinator and school principal must then review all rankings and make the decision as to what pupils will actually be referred. At this point the parents must be involved through a personal conference with the principal. First, the entire program should be discussed with them, and then their child's specific situation should be explained. Finally, their cooperation should be requested in the ensuing referral and evaluation procedure.

In-service Training

Faculty orientation is only a beginning step. An ongoing, in-service training program must be planned once the learning disabilities program has actually started in the school. This in-service training should include follow-up faculty meeting presentations by the special teacher, discussions, and case conferences with the teacher, psychologist, and others involved with pupils who may be spending some time in regular classes. A very effective in-service training procedure is to hold follow-up faculty meetings in the special classroom so that special programming materials and lessons can be presented. Another equally effective procedure is to have the regular teachers visit the special class and actually see the program in operation.

Work Samples

Work samples from younger children are valuable because they help the regular teacher to understand more clearly the type of child the program is being designed for. Unless some concrete guidelines for screening are provided, it is common for most teachers to confuse pupils with behavior and discipline problems with children having learning disabilities. As a result, the special program may actually have the wrong pupils referred to it.

The "Basic Learning Abilities Pupil Work Sample" (SE-2) is one example of a screening device that has proven valuable. The recommended procedure is for the teacher to introduce the psychologist to her pupils with the remark that he is going to show them some "learning games." The work sample covers many basic perceptual-motor, language, and conceptual activities that are of primary concern in learning disability programs. The actual developmental range of the tasks extends from the three-year-old level of copying a circle to the upper-elementary level of copying advanced designs, completing written directions without having them read or explained, and working more complex arithmetic problems.

The psychologist begins work with the class by informing them they are going to be given some learning games to do, and, although there is no time requirement, they should follow the instructions and complete as many of the games as rapidly as they can without any help. For young kindergarten and immature children it is usually necessary for the teacher to write the name of the child on the top of the work sheet, together with the correct birth date. No other required information should be provided by the teacher. In kindergarten classes the psychologist or teacher may read the information at the top and then ask the children to complete as much as they can. The teacher can then proctor the class as the children proceed through the work sample. Most children will finish the project within a half hour. When each child completes the assignment, he should be provided with other work that is not distracting to those still involved.

The same work sample can be used at all grade levels, but it is best used when supplemented with samples of actual classroom assignments. Obviously, most very young children will not be able to read the directions or complete the tasks in the space provided. With increased age and training, however, the child will achieve greater motor control and skill attainment, which will result in a more sophisticated performance on the work sample. It is not too difficult for the experienced psychologist to spot even the very young child who requires further evaluation for suspected learning disabilities.

The work sample (*Fig. 4-1*) illustrates the performance obtained from a child having suspected learning disabilities possibly requiring remediation. Walter (age 7½) is in the mid-second grade but is doing beginning first-grade work. He completed his name, but he was unable to write in the other information requested. His printing of the alphabet and numbers shows correct sequencing but poor organization, control difficulties, and reversals of the letter *J* and number 9. Reproduction of the designs reflects age-level ability but shows repetition, dissociation, and problems in perceptual integration. He failed to differentiate the correct *d* from *b* and did not complete all of the tasks. He notably avoided copying the sentence in cursive writing although he attempted the printing. His copying of the house reflects poor motor control and integration. The boy does, however, have an accurate basic sight vocabulary. Further evaluation showed that Walter had normal intellectual ability but was hindered by specific perceptual-motor disabilities, which were partially indicated on the work sample.

The Referral Form

Following review of the work sample and discussion with the psychologist or coordinator, the teacher may decide to make a formal referral. Since the work sample only surveys basic skills, it is important that the referral form help the

BASIC LEARNING ABILITIES PUPIL WORK SAMPLE

Write your name. _Walter_   Birth date _BD 7-16-60_ _CA 7-6_

Address _____ City _____ State _____

Telephone _____ School _____ Class ____ Date _____

Father's name _____ Mother's name _____

Print the alphabet.

A B C D E F G H I L K I M N O P Q R S T

U V W X Y Z

Write numbers from 1 through 31.

1 2 3 4 5 6 7 8 9 10 11 12 13 14 15 16 17 18 19 20 21 22 23

Copy each design in the space provided.

Mark the big box.

Mark the little circle.

Mark the one that is different.

b b b b d b **b**

+ x + + + +

Figure 4-1 (SE-2)

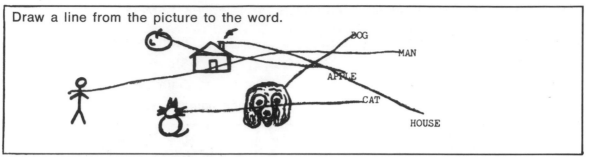

Copy the sentences.

The big dog chased the boy.

GEORGE ATE THE WHOLE PIE.

GEORGEATETHEWHOL EP

Copy the house.   Draw a man.

How many apples are there here? 12   🍎🍎🍎🍎🍎 🍎🍎🍎 🍎🍎🍎🍎

$$\begin{array}{cccccccc} 3 & 11 & 9 & 26 & 5 & 9 & 16 & 213 \\ +2 & +4 & -3 & -17 & \times 3 & \times 7 & \times 4 & \times 4 \end{array}$$

$$4\overline{)8} \qquad 3\overline{)12} \qquad 7\overline{)231} \qquad 4\overline{)\$2.04}$$

Figure 4-1 (SE-2)—*Continued*

teacher to make judgments concerning the total behavioral characteristics of the pupil. The "Teacher Referral Form for Educationally Handicapped Pupil" (Fig. 4-2) has been designed to meet this need.

The referral form begins with a concise definition of the kind of pupil desired for the program. Next, the rating scale values are introduced, with 1 signifying little or no evidence of the behavior and 5 indicating much evidence. Teachers are to give ratings in four areas—distractibility, perceptual disorders, conceptual disorders, and emotional instability—by first underlining the specific behavioral characteristics that apply to the pupil and then by marking the appropriate number from 1 to 5 on the scale. Teachers are also asked to write out a brief illustration of how this behavior has been evidenced in the classroom. The remainder of the form asks for professional judgment of academic performance and pertinent comments. The completed form on pages 66-68 illustrates a typical referral of a pupil with significant learning disabilities.

At the time of referral, Brenda was almost eight years old and was in the second grade. Individual intelligence testing had found her to be distinctly normal in ability. She had been described in school as demanding much attention, being very aggressive, and having a tendency to disturb others. Available records also reported a short attention span, poor memory, and the comment, ". . . tunes you out, doesn't understand certain concepts in stories, asks strange questions, things that most children understand."

On the referral form for Brenda the most concern is indicated in the area of distractibility and conceptual disorders—both of them being noticed to a very large degree (rated 5). Brenda's short attention span and her "difficulty in accurately duplicating drawings, letters, written words," together with the classroom illustration given, point out important perceptual problems. Conceptual difficulty and emotional instability are also clearly indicated by the illustrations given. Professional judgment of academic performance indicates reading, arithmetic, and writing problems, and varied language ability. The final comment by the teacher is quite revealing in that Brenda's ability is recognized, while at the same time she is a rather puzzling child. (The reader will be interested to know that this pupil was later identified as having perceptual-motor disabilities due to a minimal cerebral dysfunction and that she responded well to medication and educational therapy.)

TEACHER REFERRAL FORM
FOR EDUCATIONALLY HANDICAPPED PUPIL

To the Psychologist: This pupil is being referred for psychological evaluation as a possible candidate for special education classes for educationally handicapped pupils. Such pupils have learning problems associated with a behavioral disorder, a neurological handicap, or a combination thereof, and exhibit a significant discrepancy between ability and achievement.

(To be filled in by teacher)

Pupil's name __Brenda__ . Birth date __5/18/58; Age 7-11__

Referring teacher __Janet Watson__

School __Southwest Elementary__

BEHAVIORAL CHARACTERISTICS

The "marked learning or behavioral problems" with which special education classes will be concerned are manifested most frequently in the terms given under general headings below. Underline the specific characteristics that apply to this pupil. Evaluate the pupil further by marking an X under the appropriate number to the right of the characteristics listing. Then give an illustration from classroom experience.

Number Code

1. Behavior not exhibited at all.
2. Behavior exhibited to a slight degree.
3. Behavior exhibited to a considerable degree.
4. Behavior exhibited to an uncomfortable degree.
5. Behavior exhibited to a very large degree.

Distractability	1	2	3	4	5
Excessive motor activity, short attention span, <u>lack of concentration</u> or persistence, inability to delay or control impulses or desires.					X

Classroom illustration: Every unusual turn of events or change of schedule requires a full explanation to quiet Brenda. She will snatch things from children just to see them. Has attention span of 5 minutes.

Figure 4-2 (SE-1)

Perceptual Disorders	1	2	3	4	5
Deficiencies or difficulties in recognizing (perceiving) by seeing, hearing, touching, or moving. Cause <u>difficulty in accurately duplicating drawings, letters, written words,</u> speech sounds, or body movements used in certain skills or games. Inability to attend because of slight lapses of consciousness.				X	

Classroom illustration: Brenda still has not learned all of her letters. Spelling ability is very limited. She cannot count to 25 without omitting numerals. On some days she remembers more than others. I cannot decide whether she hasn't learned numbers and letters or whether she doesn't see or perceive them.

Conceptual Disorders	1	2	3	4	5
Deficiencies in storing and retaining previous experiences. Cause <u>difficulties in remembering</u> ideas and concepts, written words, arithmetic processes, and school rules. Difficulty in generalizing, abstracting, and reasoning.					X

Classroom illustration: Words or concepts mastered by the other children one day will often be completely strange to Brenda the next day.

Emotional Instability	1	2	3	4	5
<u>Excessive anger</u>, aggressiveness, destructiveness; excessive anxiety, shyness, fear, conformity, or depression; bizarre, highly unrealistic, or delusional behavior.				X	

Classroom illustration: If she is reminded that she cannot be first in line (or must put away art paper, etc.), she will stamp her feet and say, "Why can't I be first? I want to be first!"

Figure 4-2 (SE-1)—*Continued*

ACADEMIC PERFORMANCE

Estimated reading grade placement __First__ Comments __She is reading__
poorly at a primer level because we did not have a suitable group for
her.

Estimated airthmetic grade placement __First__ Comments __She is in Level__
II, Science Research Associates Workbook. However, this is not an appropriate place for her.

Describe writing ability __Very poor. In copying, leaves out words or letters.__

Describe language ability __At times it is excellent. At other times, rather__
limited.

Why do you believe a significant discrepancy exists between this pupil's ability and his
achievement? __When Brenda is quiet, she does much better work. While__
working with her individually, I find that she is quite capable and has
normal ability, but because of perceptual or emotional difficulties (I
really do not know which), she is not able to produce.

OTHER COMMENTS

Janet Watson
(teacher's signature)

Date _May 3, 1966_

E. R. Brown
(principal's signature)

Date _May 3, 1966_

Figure 4-2 (SE-1)—*Continued*

5

Psychological Evaluation

Many persons are involved in the evaluation of children with suspected learning disabilities, including parents, teachers, school nurses, physicians, and school psychologists. Although it is essential to obtain a meaningful physical examination as part of the total evaluation process, the emphasis in this chapter will be on *psychological* examination and evaluation. It is important, however, that careful consideration be given to the physical evaluation as summarized on the "Medical Report on Pupil Referred for Educationally Handicapped Program," which was presented in Chapter 3.

The psychological evaluation begins with receipt of the teacher referral form and the supplementary work sample and medical examination report. With this background information the psychologist has a frame of reference with which to begin his work. In most cases it is the psychologist's responsibility to identify special pupil learning needs and to recommend proper school placement and remedial approaches.

The initial psychological evaluation of a referred pupil with suspected learning disabilities is delimited by time and program considerations. Perhaps the first necessity is to determine what kind of pupil is to be selected for the program and to establish firm criteria by which selection can be made. It is obvious that the traditional psychological evaluation resulting in an "IQ" score and recommendation for "special education" is of little or no value in programming learning disabilities. What is needed is some differential diagnosis relative to the established special program criteria. This can then become a basis for meaningful psychoeducational consultation and planning after the actual placement of the pupil.

Within the framework and rationale of the basic learning abilities approach, three different models for psychological evaluation are presented in this chapter. The first model is concerned with a more functional use of standard instruments, such as the Stanford-Binet (L-M), for use in educational programming. The second approach suggests possible ways to integrate varied test results into a psychoeducational profile of basic learning abilities for use in teacher consultation. The last model presents an outline for the initial psychological report and emphasizes the psychoeducational prescription.

A Clinical Profile for the Stanford-Binet (L-M)

One of the major tools of the practicing school psychologist is the Stanford-Binet (L-M). Although the Binet has long been regarded as one of the more valid indicators of general intelligence, the absence of subtest categories has made the interpretation of test performance a difficult clinical task.

In the school situation some indication of individual strengths and weaknesses, together with their possible educational implications, is an important part of the psychological report. There is a need for some system of item classification on the basis of logical constructs that is meaningful for a more detailed representation of measured intellectual functioning. The Wechsler-Intelligence Scale for Children serves as one model that permits such differential diagnosis even though pattern analysis must be utilized with caution because of its questionable validity.[1]

When item success and failure on the Binet are evaluated and considered relative to other information available on the subject, such as school achievement and performance records, the test results become more meaningful. An attempt has been made here to construct an individual profile form that will aid clinical interpretation of Binet test results.[2]

CONSTRUCTION PROCEDURE

Following a consideration of the various factors of intellect as proposed by Binet,[3] Thurstone,[4] and Guilford,[5] among others, the following item classifications were established: sensory and perceptual discrimination, comprehension, motor coordination, judgment, comparisons, imagery, vocabulary, memory, arithmetic reasoning, and speed of response. Six credentialed and experienced psychological

[1]W. M. Littell, "The Wechsler Intelligence Scale for Children: Review of a Decade of Research," *Psychological Bulletin,* Vol. LVII (1960), pp. 132-156.

[2]Adapted with minor editorial changes from R. E. Valett, "A Clinical Profile for the Stanford-Binet," *Journal of School Psychology,* Vol. II, No. 1 (Winter, 1963-64), pp. 49-54; and R. E. Valett, "A Profile for the Stanford-Binet Intelligence Scale (L-M)" (Palo Alto, Calif.: Consulting Psychologists Press, Inc., 1965).

[3]A. Binet and T. Simon, *The Development of Intelligence in Children* (Vineland, N.J.: The Training School at Vineland, 1916).

[4]L. L. Thurstone, *Primary Mental Abilities* (Chicago: University of Chicago Press, 1938).

[5]J. P. Guilford, "Three Faces of Intellect," *American Psychologist,* Vol. XIV, No. 8 (1959), pp. 469-479.

examiners then proceeded to classify each item, and the degree of agreement and disagreement was discussed. The following categories were then finally agreed to as consisting of basic logical test constructs that allowed some meaningful differentiation of Binet items.

1. *General comprehension:* The ability to conceptualize and integrate components into a meaningful total relationship.
2. *Visual-motor ability:* The ability to manipulate materials in problem-solving situations that usually require integration of visual and motor skills.
3. *Arithmetic reasoning:* The ability to make appropriate numerical associations and to deal with mental abstractions in problem-solving situations.
4. *Memory and concentration:* The ability to attend and retain. Requires motivation and attention and usually measures degree of retention of test items.
5. *Vocabulary and verbal fluency:* The ability to correctly use words in association with concrete or abstract material; the understanding of words and verbal concepts; the quality and quantity of verbal expression.
6. *Judgment and reasoning:* The ability to comprehend and respond appropriately in specific situations requiring discrimination, comparison, and judgment in adaptation.

A further classification of items was then done by ten graduate students in a class on individual intelligence testing. The final classification of items was made by the author after consideration and comparison of prior sortings.

USE OF THE PROFILE

The individual profile makes possible a schematic presentation of test results and their further consideration. It is suggested that a vertical red line be drawn through the year level for the obtained basal age and that all test items successfully passed beyond this be encircled in red. This allows for a comparison of successes and failures relative to chronological age, together with a consideration of what possible individual strengths and weaknesses might be reflected in these items.

It will be noted that some items have been judged to reflect more than one test construct. This is particularly true with many of the items placed on both the general comprehension and the judgment and reasoning scales. Of course, this overlap of items exists in reality to a considerable extent, and the actual significance of an item must still be clinically deduced upon consideration of marginal successes and failures, the nature of the item relative to maturational differences, cultural expectations and total test performance, and the usual qualitative-associational aspects of test interpretation.

The profile for the Stanford-Binet (L-M) is useful in three major ways:

1. In stimulating the clinician to give further thought to individual differences and intratest performance prior to reporting results.
2. In presenting a graphic picture of test results to parents and others interested without concern as to IQ.
3. As an aid to students or beginning psychometrists in studying the psychological constructs underlying the Binet test items.

ILLUSTRATION

The profile of W. Kelly (*Fig. 5-1*) illustrates the possible use of this procedure in educational programming. Kelly passed all tests at the year 4-6 level as indicated

A PROFILE FOR THE STANFORD BINET (L-M)

Item Classifications by Robert E. Valett

INSTRUCTIONS: Draw a vertical line through the year for the obtained basal age. Circle all test items passed beyond this level.

SUBJECT'S NAME: _Kelly, W._ CA: _5-3_ MA: _6-2_ IQ Range: _114-124_ Grade: _____ Date of Test: _10-21-65_

TEST CONSTRUCTS	Year: 2	2-6	3	3-6	4	4-6	5	6	7	8.	9	10	11	12	13	14	AA	SA I	SA II	SA III
GENERAL COMPREHENSION	3 A	1 2 6		6	4 6	4 6 A		(6)	(2) 4 5	4 5 A			6	3 6	4	5	5 6 7	6	3	2 4
VISUAL-MOTOR ABILITY	1 4	A	1 3 5 6	2 5	1	A	2 2 4 6 A	(6)	3		1 3	2	1	A	A	A	A			
ARITHMETIC REASONING						5		(4)			5					4 A	2 4	2	4	6
MEMORY & CONCENTRATION	2	5	4 A		2 A			(1)	(6) A	2 6	3 6	6	1 4	4 A	3 6			4	6	6
VOCABULARY & VERBAL FLUENCY	5 6 A	3 4	2	4	1		(3)	(1) A		(1)	4 A	1 3 5	3	1 5 6	2 5	1	1 3 8	1 3 5	1	1 3 A
JUDGMENT & REASONING	1			1 2 3 A	3 4 5	1 2 3 A	(5) (6)	2 (3) (5) A	1 (2) 4 5	3 4	1 2 4	2 4 A	2 5 6 A	2	1 4 5 A	2 3 4 5 6 A	2 3 6 7 A	2 3 4 5 6 A	2 3 4 5 6 A	2 3 4 5 6 A

Figure 5-1 (Copyright 1965, by R. E. Valett. Reprinted by permission of Consulting Psychologists Press.)

STANFORD-BINET L-M ITEM CLASSIFICATIONS (Valett)

GENERAL COMPREHENSION: The ability to conceptualize and integrate components into a meaningful total relationship.

II, 3. Parts of body	VIII, 4 Similarities and differences
II, A. Identifying objects by name	VIII, 5. Comprehension IV
II-6, 1. Identifying objects by use	XI, 6. Similarities 3
II-6, 2. Parts of body	XII, 3. Picture absurdities II
II-6, 6. Simple commands	XII, 6. Minkus completion I
III-6, 6. Comprehension I	XIII, 4. Problems of fact
IV, 4. Picture identification	XIV, 5. Direction I
IV, 6. Comprehension II	AA, 5 Proverbs I
IV, 6, 4. Materials	AA, 6 Direction II
IV, 6, 6. Comprehension III	AA, 7. Essential differences
IV-6, A. Picture identification	SA-I, 6. Essential similarities
VII, 2. Similarities 2	SA-II, 3. Proverbs II
VII, 4. Comprehension IV	SA-III, 2. Proverbs III
VII, 5. Opposite analogies III	SA-III, 4. Directions III

VISUAL MOTOR ABILITY: The ability to manipulate materials in problem solving situations usually requiring integration of visual and motor skills.

II, 1. Form board	V, 4. Copying square
II, 4. Block tower	V, 6. Patience: rectangles
II, 6, A. Form board	V, A Knot
III, 1. Stringing beads	VI, 6. Maze
III, 3. Block bridge	VII, 3. Copying diamond
III, 5. Copying circle	VIII, 5. Paper cutting
III, 6. Vertical line	IX, 5. Designs I
III-6, 2. Patience: pictures	X, 2 Block counting
III-6, 5. Sorting buttons	XI, 1. Designs
V, 1. Picture completion: man	XII, A. Designs II
V, 2. Folding triangle	XIII, A. Paper cutting
	AA, A. Binet paper cutting

ARITHMETIC REASONING: The ability to make appropriate numerical associations and deal with mental abstractions in problem solving situations.

VI, 4. Number concepts	AA, 2. Ingenuity I
IX, 5. Change	AA 4. Arithmetic reasoning
XIV, 4. Ingenuity I	SA-I, 2. Enclosed boxes
XIV, A. Ingenuity II	SA-II, 4. Ingenuity I

MEMORY & CONCENTRATION: The ability to attend and retain. Requires motivation and attention and usually measures degree of retention of various test items.

II, 2. Delayed response	VII, 2. Wet Fall
II-6, 5. 2 digits	VII, 6. Days of week
III, A. Picture memories	IX 3. Designs I
III, A. 3 digits	IX, 6. 4 digits reversed
IV, 2. Objects from memory	X, 6. 6 digits
IV, A. Memory for sentences I	XI, 1. Designs I
IV-6, 5. 3 commissions	XI, 4. Memory for sentences II
VI, 6. 5 digits	XI, 4. 5 digits reversed
VI, A. 3 digits reversed	XI, A. Designs II

XIII, 3. Memory for sentences III	SA-I, 4. 6 digits reversed
XIII, 6. Copying a bead chain from memory	SA-II, 6. Passage I: Value of Life
	SA-III, 6. Repeating thought of passage: tests

VOCABULARY & VERBAL FLUENCY: The ability to use words correctly in association with concrete or abstract material; the understanding of words and verbal concepts; the quality and quantity of verbal expression.

II, 5. Picture vocabulary	XI, 3. Abstract words
II, 6. Word combinations	XII, 1. Vocabulary
II, A. Identifying objects by name	XII, 5. Abstract words
II-6, 3. Naming of vocabulary	XII, 6. Minkus completion I
II-6, 4. Picture vocabulary	XIII, 2. Abstract words II
III-2. Picture vocabulary	XIII, 5. Dissected sentences
III-6, 4. Response to pictures	XIII-6, 4. Vocabulary
IV, 1. Vocabulary	AA, 1. Vocabulary
V, 3. Definitions	AA, 3. Difference between abstract words
VI, 1. Vocabulary	AA, 8. Abstract words III
VI, A. Response to pictures	SA-I, 1. Vocabulary
VIII, 1. Vocabulary	SA-I, 3. Minkus Completion II
IX, A. Rhymes; new form	SA-I, 5. Sentence building
X, 1. Rhymes; old form	SA-II, 1. Vocabulary
X, 3. Vocabulary	SA-III, 1. Vocabulary
X, 5. Word naming	SA-III, 3. Opposite analogies IV
	SA-III, A. Opposite analogies V

JUDGEMENT & REASONING: The ability to comprehend and respond appropriately in specific situations requiring discrimination, comparison, and judgement in adaptation.

II-6, 3. Identifying objects by use	VIII, 3. Verb. absurdities	XIV, A. Ingenuity II
III-6, 1. Comparison of balls	VIII, 4. Similarities & diff.	AA, 2. Ingenuity I
III-6, 2. Patience: pictures	IX. 1. Paper cutting	AA, 3. Dif. abs. words
III-6, 3. Discrim. of animal pictures	IX, 4. Rhymes: new form	AA, 6. Direction II
III-6, A. Comparison of sticks	X. 2. Block counting	AA, 7. Essential diff.
IV-3. Opposite analogies I	X. 4. Finding reasons	AA, A. Binet paper cut.
IV-4. Pictorial identification	X. A. Verbal absurdities III	SA-I, 2. Enclosed boxes
IV-5. Discrimination of forms	XI, 2. Verbal absurdities IV	SA-I, 6. Essential simil.
IV-6, 1. Aesthetic comparison	XI, 5. Prob. situation II	SA-I, A. Recon. of opp.
IV-6, 2. Opposite analogies I	XI, 6. Similarities	SA-II, 2. Proverbs II
IV-6, 3. Pictorial sim. & dif. I	XI, A. Finding reasons II	SA-II, 3. Finding reasons
IV-6, A. Pictorial identification	XII, 2. Verb. absurdities II	SA-II, 4. Proverbs II
V, 5. Pictorial sim. & dif. II	XIII, 1. Plan of search	SA-II, 5. Ingenuity I
V, 6. Pictorial identification	XIII, 4. Problems of fact	SA-II, 6. Essential diff.
VI, 1. Differences	XIII, 5. Dissected sentences	SA-II, A. Pass. I: V of L
VI, 3. Mutilated pictures	XIII, A. Opposite analogies II	SA-II, A. Codes
VI, 5. Opposite analogies II	VI, A. Response to pictures	SA-III, 2. Proverbs III
VI, A. Response to pictures	VI, 3. Induction	SA-IV, 4. Direction III
VII, 1. Pictorial absurdities I	XIV, 2. Reasoning	SA-III, 5. Reasoning II
VII, 2. Similarities II	XIV, 4. Ingenuity I	SA-III, 6. Repeating thought of passage: tests
VII, 4. Comprehension IV	XIV, 5. Direction I	SA-III, A. Op. anal. V
VII, 5. Opposite analogies III	XIV, 6. Recon. of opposites	

Figure 5-1—*Continued*

by the vertical line. His mental age is indicated by the other line running through the year 6 tasks. Since Kelly's chronological age is five years and three months, it is immediately evident that he has a spread of abilities ranging from year 4-6 with complete success in all areas to a high of year 8 with success in the vocabulary and verbal fluency area. It is also apparent that this child's limitations are in the visual-motor ability areas with failure on most five-year motor tasks as specified on the back of the profile form. Etiologically, this is a spastic cerebral-palsied child with a history of good academic and social progress, who now evidences strong reading readiness abilities despite his young age.

This kind of report can actually be given to the teacher working with the child, and when integrated with other relevant data, it can contribute to the development of an educational program for the child. Because it reports the IQ range by category (e.g., Kelly is "bright normal"), the profile can also be used, with consultation, directly with parents. In this way the "IQ test" becomes helpful to the teacher and parents alike, rather than merely being a confusing statistic of little use in the educational process. Profile reporting of the Wechsler Intelligence Scale for Children, the Illinois Test of Psycholinguistic Abilities, and other similar instruments should be encouraged as part of the evaluation and programming procedure.

A Psychoeducational Profile of Basic Learning Abilities

Diagnosticians and educators working with elementary-age children have long recognized the functional inadequacy of single test scores obtained from individual measures of general intellectual abilities. In order to adequately program for the prevention and remediation of serious learning disabilities, a more meaningful differential diagnosis of basic learning abilities is required. Such a diagnosis demands a thorough evaluation of the learner in terms of his specific strengths and weaknesses and their educational implications.

The purpose of the Psychoeducational Profile of Basic Learning Abilities[6] is to provide the psychologist with a developmental summary form whereby he can integrate available normative data and clinical impressions for psychoeducational programming. The Profile can be of value as a direct report in itself, in counseling with parents, and especially as a basis for consulting with teachers and other educators in educational planning and curriculum development. Although the Profile may find its greatest use in work with exceptional pupils and programs, it also has relevance to the evaluation of normal children.

RATIONALE

Since 1905 when Binet applied his newly developed scales to the problem of differentiating learning ability in Paris school children, the search has continued for more useful tests. The serious limitations inherent in reporting multiple abilities through a single score were immediately recognized; Binet soon stressed the importance of recognizing judgment, reasoning, initiative, invention, comprehension, and adaptation as essential aspects of intellectual capability.[7] A few years later, Spearman demonstrated the two-factor nature of general and special abilities with

[6]Adapted with minor editorial changes from R. E. Valett, "A Psychoeducational Profile of Basic Learning Abilities," *Journal of School Psychology*, Vol. IV, No. 2 (Winter, 1966), pp. 9-24; and R. E. Valett, *A Psychoeducational Profile of Basic Learning Abilities* (Palo Alto, Calif.: Consulting Psychologists Press, 1966).

[7]Binet and Simon, *op. cit.*

the specification of several group ability factors.[8] Thurstone's specification of the "primary mental abilities" of number, word fluency, verbal meaning, memory, reasoning, spatial perception, and perceptual speed had an immediate effect on the objective testing movement but has not been greatly utilized in clinical evaluations.[9] Wechsler's Intelligence Scale for Children has attempted to report given ability factors through a standardized profile that has distinctive educational implications although the rationale has never been adequately clarified.[10] In 1963 the author developed a clinical profile for the Stanford-Binet (L-M) (the first model in this chapter) based on logical constructs following Binet's original conceptual model.[11]

All of these instruments are inadequate *by themselves* for the evaluation of learning disabilities. What is needed is a broader model for the development of more meaningful evaluation procedures.

The work of Piaget has documented the developmental progression of learning abilities through the basic stages of sensorimotor intelligence and egocentric thinking to the rational coordination of early conceptual awareness and the later appearance of formal operational thought.[12] Cronbach has pointed out that "Intellectual development consists of the mastery of one concept after another, through pertinent experience—each stage prepares for the next."[13] The developmental tasks in each stage of human growth, together with their educational implications, have been aptly specified by Havighurst.[14] The reality of differential abilities at different developmental stages has been researched by Gesell and his collaborators, who have provided us with much of our normative data.[15, 16] More recently, Wallach has summarized research findings that "...support the generalization that whatever is being assessed by 'intelligence' tests is structurally or qualitatively different in infancy, early childhood, and middle childhood."[17]

The continuing researches of Guilford on the structure of intellect appear to offer us a promising model for meaningful evaluation.[18, 19] With the discovery of concrete, symbolic, semantic, and social types of intelligence, together with many classes of abilities by which these types are expressed, the necessity for differentiation and educational planning becomes more urgent. Recently, Frostig has suggested a functional evaluation and reporting of learning abilities in the areas of intellectual development, motor coordination, language development, social development, and perceptual abilities.[20] The author, among others, has attempted

[8]C. Spearman, *The Abilities of Man* (New York: The Macmillan Company, 1927).

[9]Thurstone, *op. cit.*

[10]Littell, *loc. cit.*

[11]Valett, *op. cit.*

[12]J. Piaget, "Principal Factors Determining Intellectual Evaluation from Childhood to Adult Life," *Factors Determining Human Behavior* (Harvard Tercentenary Publications, Cambridge, Mass.: Harvard University Press, 1937), pp. 32-48.

[13]L. Cronbach, *Educational Psychology* (New York: Harcourt, Brace & World, Inc., 1963). p. 338.

[14]R. Havighurst, *Developmental Tasks and Education* (Chicago: University of Chicago Press, 1948).

[15]A. Gesell, *The First Five Years of Life* (New York: Harper & Row, Publishers, 1940).

[16]A. Gesell and F. Ilg, *The Child from Five to Ten* (New York: Harper & Row, Publishers, 1946).

[17]M. Wallach, "Research on Children's Thinking," *Child Psychology*, NSSE Yearbook 62, Part I (Chicago: University of Chicago Press, 1963), p. 269.

[18]Guilford, *op. cit.*

[19]J. P. Guilford, "A Revised Structure of Intellect," *Rep. Psychological Laboratory No. 19* (Los Angeles: University of Southern California, School of Education, 1962), I.

[20]M. Frostig, "Education of Children with Learning Difficulties," *Distinguished Lectures in Special Education* (Los Angeles: University of Southern California, School of Education, 1962), I.

to emphasize some of the curriculum implications of psychological practice on the part of the school psychologist as related to the problem of differential diagnosis.[21]

The rationale for a profile of basic learning abilities is rooted in research, practice, and various conceptual models. Of necessity, such a profile must specify the major learning abilities of concern together with the specific tasks and available developmental data. In addition, the profile must also allow for the integration of clinical impressions and stimulate the consideration of relative educational implications.

THE BASIC LEARNING ABILITIES

Various tests and evaluation procedures have been selected in five major areas of learning abilities specified as motor integration and physical development, perceptual abilities, language, social-personal adaptivity, and general intellectual functioning. These classifications were selected because they appear to be logical constructs with a sound rationale and with distinctive educational implications.

Under each major classification a number of basic learning abilities have been listed. Some of these abilities, e.g., walking, are self-apparent, and the profile rating is determined by considering the reported time of accomplishment relative to normative expectancy. However, most of the basic learning abilities are not so apparent and must be profiled on the basis of assessment data derived from certain tests evaluated by the examiner. The tests listed are not all-inclusive but have been selected on the basis of widespread clinical use and available norms. The classification of perceptual abilities is the most extensive because of its great importance in early childhood learning.

Both the classifications and learning abilities have been arranged in a developmental sequence with tests and normative data scheduled for easy profiling. Placement of tests was an arbitrary decision relative to the conceptual model, and it is realized that multiple-placement might have been a more valid, but also a more confusing procedure. The test references (see pages 84-86) provide the source of each item listed. In actual practice it is assumed that the examiner will use only those tests of concern, or substitute other tests according to the need at hand. It must be emphasized, however, that although the entire profile will rarely be used, it is essential that some evaluation be made in each of the major classification areas if a meaningful profile of learning abilities is to result. This would preclude, for instance, the validity of reporting general intellectual functioning alone as a sound basis for understanding learning abilities or for educational planning.

SCORING PROCEDURES

Scoring the Profile (Fig. 5-2) is necessarily a subjective procedure based on clinical experience and the objective awareness of available norms for developmental abilities and tests. The Profile does, however, provide for the integration of all available data for use in consultation and educational programming. In general, marks should be placed on the Profile approximating standard score accomplishment for each ability evaluated. Placement within the middle 68% of statistical "normality" is judged accordingly and indicated on the Profile. "Very weak"

[21]R. E. Valett, The Practice of School Psychology: Professional Problems (New York: John Wiley & Sons, Inc., 1963), Ch. 12.

and "very strong" markings reflect extremely slow (low, late, etc.) or extremely early (fast, high, etc.) accomplishment respectively of the bottom and top 2% of the population. "Weak" and "strong" markings indicate accomplishment within one to two standard deviations (about 14%) above or below normal expectancy. Although actual use will vary according to the examiner, the following recommended scoring procedures can serve as guidelines.

I. Motor Integration and Physical Development

A. If the task has been accomplished within the norm specification, it is marked plus in the response column; if not accomplished by the time indicated, a minus is scored in the response column, and the actual time is written in on the line listing the task.

B. When the task has been accomplished within normal limits, the "normal" column is marked with a heavy red dot. Marks outside the normal range are subjectively placed dependent upon the examiner's clinical appraisal of the extent of the deviation.

C. With multiple task items such as footedness, the Profile marking is determined by the judgmental averaging of "kicks," "stepping forward," and "stepping backward." The notation of developmental anomalies, traumatic incidents, and significant childhood diseases (e.g., meningitis, etc.) should be made under the related health comments section.

II. Perceptual Abilities

A. Right and left auditory acuity should be indicated audiometrically if possible. A 0 to 15 decibel loss is marked as "normal" on the Profile, while a 15 to 30 decibel loss is "weak," and below this level is "very weak." A red "R" should be marked on the Profile to indicate right ear performance; mark a red "L" to indicate left ear performance.

B. Tactile abilities are indicated by having the subject grasp a hidden object from a bag, box, or sack and then correctly name the object. Aphasic and language-deficient subjects can indicate their cognitive awareness of the object by pointing to pictures of the objects spread before them. Actual Profile markings in this area are highly dependent upon clinical impressions and should include appropriate notations on the record as needed.

C. Multiple-choice, standardized items should be clearly checked. For instance, a ten-year-old child obtaining a score of 7 on the visual memory WISC picture completion test would have the number 7 checked, the 6½ norm group circled or otherwise marked, the response column indicating a plus at this level, and a Profile marking of "very weak" relative to age expectancy.

D. Visual-motor skill accomplishment should contain frequent notations. For example, if a child has below normal performance on specific maturation and coordination tests, distortion, rotation, dissociation, poor angulation, etc., should be recorded. If Frostig visual perception age equivalent scores are available, these should be written in the response column and the Profile marked relative to age expectancy.

E. The conceptual level of visual-motor coordination is reflected in the primary academic performance of writing. Approximate grade placements for spelling and arithmetic should always be indicated. Handwriting evaluation is entirely judgmental and should be supported through work samples.

III. Language

A. Articulation and speech performance are clinical judgments based on qualitative evaluation of fluency and vocabulary items as well as on other tests. Reading vocabulary and comprehension are profiled on the basis of grade-level achievement relative to age-grade expectancy; in the evaluation of learning disorders these tests provide highly significant information and should always be included.

B. Psycholinguistic abilities should indicate corresponding language ages in the response column with profiling relative to expectancy. Other language test results and available reports, such as those from speech correctionists, should be noted.

IV. Social-personal Adaptivity

A. An estimated profile marking of the Spraings' Behavior Rating Scale is based on subjective appraisal of over-all performance. This is also true for marking the test behavior item under personality integration and for appraisal of ego functioning. Because considerable subjective judgment is required in this area, it is usually important to comment on those aspects of social-personal behavior requiring further consideration than can be indicated on this limited Profile.

V. General Intellectual Functioning

A. WISC and Binet IQ's are entered as indicated with no marking in the norm or response columns. Profiling is done on the basis of 15 points per standard deviation. Other special intelligence measures may be entered in the comments section.

A CASE ILLUSTRATION

A case illustrating the actual clinical use of the Profile is shown in Figure 5-2. Behavioral observations, significant developmental and case history notes, and functional test scores are entered on the Profile in the most appropriate way. Tests not listed on the Profile, but used, are also entered. Clinical impressions are important, too, since they are usually of great significance in follow-up consultation and educational planning.

In this case the major psychoeducational problem was differentiation between mental retardation and relatively severe emotional disturbance and the implications of either for learning. The graphing and brief qualification of the results of the examination present a vivid picture of relative strengths and weaknesses. The line graph across the Profile is usually done in red so that it can be quickly perceived from the gray ground. A brief summary interpretation of the findings with pertinent recommendations can be written in immediately to complete the report, or a more formal typed report (*Fig.* 5-3) can be prepared if desired.

If a copy of the completed Profile is provided to the teacher who will be working with the child, it can become the basis for meaningful consultation between teacher and psychologist. It cannot be emphasized too strongly that use of the Profile does *not* take the place of consultation; on the contrary, the Profile stresses the need for meaningful follow-up discussion and planning between teacher and psychologist. This is the only process whereby crucial findings and implications of the psychological examination can be brought to educational fruition.

A PSYCHOEDUCATIONAL PROFILE OF BASIC LEARNING ABILITIES

BASIC LEARNING ABILITIES AND TESTS	TEST RECORD		PROFILE				
	Response + or −	Norm	Very Weak −2SD	Weak −1SD	Normal +1SD	Strong +2SD	Very Strong

I. MOTOR INTEGRATION AND PHYSICAL DEVELOPMENT

A — Sitting		9 mos.					
B — Crawling		10-12 mos					
C — Walking *"slow"*		18-24 mos	?				
D — Running/Throwing		2½-4 yrs					
E — Skates/Jumps Rope		5-6 yrs					
F — Bicycles/Dances *fearful*		7-8 yrs	●				
G — Finger localization		5 yrs					
H — Handedness: Throws_____ Cuts_____		2-5 yrs					
Points_____ Draws_____							
I — Eyedness: Telescope_____ Hole_____		5 yrs					
J — Footedness: Kicks_____		5 yrs					
Steps F._____ Steps B._____							
K — Directionality: Turns Right_____		5 yrs					
Turns Left_____							
Gives Right Hand_____							
Shows Left Foot_____							
L — Crayon — Pencil		2-5 yrs					

RELATED HEALTH COMMENTS: *Enuretic under stress.*
Good general physical health.
Poor physical coordination.

II. PERCEPTUAL ABILITIES

A —AUDITORY							
1. Acuity: R_____ L_____							
2. Functional Response:_____		2 yrs up		*appears normal*			
Loud Sound Blks_____ Soft S.B._____							
Matching Loud Blks_____ Mat. Sft. B._____							
Bell_____ Music Box_____							
3. Memory & Attention (Digits & Sentences)							
a. 4-7_____ 6-3_____ 5-8_____		2½ yrs					
b. 6-4-1_____ 3-5-2_____ 8-3-7_____		3 yrs					
c. E: "I want you to say something for me. Say, 'big boy.'							
Now say, 'I am a big boy.' Now say . . .		4 yrs					
"We are going to buy some candy for mother."							
"Jack likes to feed little puppies in the barn."							
d. WISC DS: Five Points_____		5½ yrs					
e. WISC DS: Six Points_____		6 yrs					
f. WISC DS: Seven Points_____		6½ yrs					
g. 3-1-8-5-9_____ 4-8-3-7-2_____ 9-6-1-8-3_____		7 yrs					
h. Reversed 2-9-5_____ 8-1-6_____ 4-7-3_____		7 yrs					
i. WISC DS: Eight Points_____		7½-8½ yrs					
j. WISC DS: Nine Point_____		9½-10½ yrs					
k. WISC DS: Ten Points_____		11½-13½ yrs					
l. WISC DS: Eleven Points_____		14½ yrs					
4. Receptive Conceptualization							
a. Picture recognition:		2½ yrs up					
"Show me the picture of the thing we use to eat our cereal."							
"Which thing does mother need to fix your hair?"							
"Can you find something that goes on your foot?"							
b. Three Commissions		4½ yrs					

Figure 5-2

BASIC LEARNING ABILITIES AND TESTS	TEST RECORD		PROFILE				
	Response + or —	Norm	Very Weak −2SD	Weak −1SD	Normal +1SD	Strong +2SD	Very Strong

II. PERCEPTUAL ABILITIES (continued)

B — TACTILE — *appears normal* —

Verbal or Picture Identification:
1. Spoon	2. Crayon	3. Pencil	4 yrs	— — — — — —
4. Watch	5. Nail	6. Key	4 yrs	— — — — — —
7. Rubber band	8. Shoestring		4 yrs	— — — — — —
9. Block	10. Button		4 yrs	— — — — — —
11. Envelope	12. Cloth		6 yrs	— — — — — —
13. Nickel	14. Sponge		6 yrs	— — — — — —
15. Paper clip	16. Bolt		6 yrs	— — — — — —

C — VISUAL — *appears normal*

1. Acuity: R _____ L _____
2. Discrimination:
   - a. Basic Forms — 2½ yrs
   - b. Picture Discrimination — 3½ yrs
   - c. Discrimination of Forms — 4 yrs
   - d. Pictorial Similarities and Differences I — 4½ yrs
   - e. Pictorial Similarities and Differences II — 5 yrs
   - f. Concepts — 5 to 6-9 yrs
   - g. Reversals and left-right tendency — 5-9 & up
   - h. Size Gradations — 6 & up
3. Memory:
   - a. Delayed Response — 2 yrs
   - b. Picture Memories — 3 yrs
   - c. Naming objects from Memory — 4 yrs
   - d. Picture Completion (WISC) ⑤ — *inattentive*
     - 6 — 5½ yrs
     - 7 ___ 8 ___ 9 ___ — 6½-7½-8½
     - 10 ___ 11 ___ — 9½-10½
     - 12 ___ 13 ___ — 11½-14½
4. Conceptual Organization (Hooper VO Raw Score) _____
5. Figure-Ground Contrast _____ — 5-6 yrs

D — VISUAL-MOTOR SKILLS

1. Maturation and Coordination:
   - a. Copy Circle — 3 yrs
   - b. Vertical Line — 3 yrs
   - c. Cross Lines — 4 yrs
   - d. Square — 5 yrs — *Dissociation*
   - e. B. Figs. A — + — — 6 yrs — *circles*
     - F. 1 — + — — 6 yrs — *dissociation*
     - F. 4 — — — 6 yrs — *distortion, rotation*
     - F. 5 — — — 6 yrs
   - f. Triangle — + — 6 yrs — *angulation*
   - g. Diamond — — — 7 yrs
     - B. F. 8 — — — 7 yrs — *pointed curves*
   - h. B. F. 6 — + — — 8 yrs
   - i. B. F. 2 — + — 10 yrs
   - j. B. F. 7 — + — — 10 yrs — *distortion*
   - k. B. F. 3 — — 11 yrs
   - (l. B. F. 1 pairs) — (1/3 adults)

Immature and distorted visual-motor skills, lacking integration.

Figure 5-2—Continued

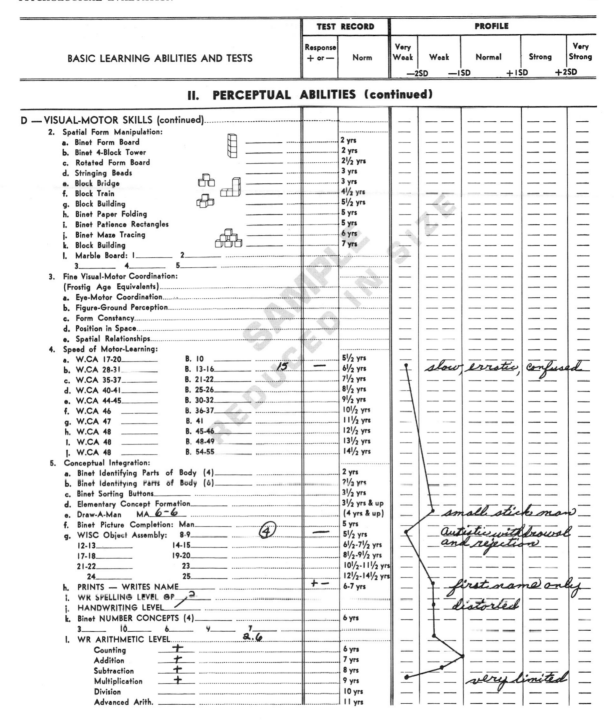

BASIC LEARNING ABILITIES AND TESTS	TEST RECORD		PROFILE				
	Response + or −	Norm	Very Weak	Weak	Normal	Strong	Very Strong
				−2SD	−1SD	+1SD	+2SD

II. PERCEPTUAL ABILITIES (continued)

D — VISUAL-MOTOR SKILLS (continued)

2. Spatial Form Manipulation:
   - a. Binet Form Board — 2 yrs
   - b. Binet 4-Block Tower — 2 yrs
   - c. Rotated Form Board — 2½ yrs
   - d. Stringing Beads — 3 yrs
   - e. Block Bridge — 3 yrs
   - f. Block Train — 4½ yrs
   - g. Block Building — 5½ yrs
   - h. Binet Paper Folding — 5 yrs
   - i. Binet Patience Rectangles — 5 yrs
   - j. Binet Maze Tracing — 6 yrs
   - k. Block Building — 7 yrs
   - l. Marble Board: 1 ___ 2 ___ 3 ___ 4 ___ 5 ___

3. Fine Visual-Motor Coordination:
   (Frostig Age Equivalents)
   - a. Eye-Motor Coordination
   - b. Figure-Ground Perception
   - c. Form Constancy
   - d. Position in Space
   - e. Spatial Relationships

4. Speed of Motor-Learning:
   - a. W.CA 17-20 ___ B. 10 ___ 5½ yrs
   - b. W.CA 28-31 ___ B. 13-16 ___ 15 — 6½ yrs — *slow, erratic, confused*
   - c. W.CA 35-37 ___ B. 21-22 ___ 7½ yrs
   - d. W.CA 40-41 ___ B. 25-26 ___ 8½ yrs
   - e. W.CA 44-45 ___ B. 30-32 ___ 9½ yrs
   - f. W.CA 46 ___ B. 36-37 ___ 10½ yrs
   - g. W.CA 47 ___ B. 41 ___ 11½ yrs
   - h. W.CA 48 ___ B. 45-46 ___ 12½ yrs
   - i. W.CA 48 ___ B. 48-49 ___ 13½ yrs
   - j. W.CA 48 ___ B. 54-55 ___ 14½ yrs

5. Conceptual Integration:
   - a. Binet Identifying Parts of Body (4) ___ 2 yrs
   - b. Binet Identifying Parts of Body (6) ___ 2⅓ yrs
   - c. Binet Sorting Buttons ___ 3½ yrs
   - d. Elementary Concept Formation ___ 3½ yrs & up
   - e. Draw-A-Man MA 6-6 ___ (4 yrs & up) *small stick man*
   - f. Binet Picture Completion: Man ___ 5 yrs
   - g. WISC Object Assembly: 8-9 ___ ④ — 5½ yrs *autistic withdrawal and rejection*
     - 12-13 ___ 14-15 ___ 6½-7½ yrs
     - 17-18 ___ 19-20 ___ 8½-9½ yrs
     - 21-22 ___ 23 ___ 10½-11½ yrs
     - 24 ___ 25 ___ 12½-14½ yrs
   - h. PRINTS — WRITES NAME ___ + − 6-7 yrs *first name only*
   - i. WR SPELLING LEVEL GP 2 ___
   - j. HANDWRITING LEVEL ___ *distorted*
   - k. Binet NUMBER CONCEPTS (4) ___ 6 yrs
     - 3 ___ 10 ___ 6 ___ 9 ___ 7 ___
   - l. WR ARITHMETIC LEVEL ___ 2.6
     - Counting + 6 yrs
     - Addition + 7 yrs
     - Subtraction + 8 yrs
     - Multiplication + 9 yrs *very limited*
     - Division ___ 10 yrs
     - Advanced Arith. ___ 11 yrs

Figure 5-2—Continued

BASIC LEARNING ABILITIES AND TESTS	TEST RECORD		PROFILE				
	Response + or −	Norm	Very Weak −2SD	Weak −1SD	Normal +1SD	Strong +2SD	Very Strong

II. PERCEPTUAL ABILITIES (continued)

D — VISUAL-MOTOR SKILLS (continued)

  6. Analysis and Synthesis:

WISC Block Design	4		5½ yrs					
5	6		6½-7½ yrs					
9-10 ⑫	13-15		8½-9½ yrs			+		
16-20	21-24		10½-11½ yrs					
29-30	32-33	34-35	12½13½14½					

III. LANGUAGE

A — BASIC EXPRESSIVE FLUENCY *hesitant and withdrawn*

  1. Binet Picture Vocabulary (3) — 2 yrs
  2. Binet Picture Vocabulary (8) — 2-6 yrs
  3. Binet Naming Objects (5) — 2-6 yrs
  4. Binet Picture Vocabulary (10) — 3 yrs
  5. Binet Response to Pictures — 3-6 yrs
  6. Binet Picture Vocabulary (14) — 4 yrs
  7. Binet Definitions — 5 yrs

B — VOCABULARY KNOWLEDGE

  1. Binet Vocabulary (6) — 6 yrs
  2. WISC Vocabulary (18) — 6½ yrs
  3. WISC Vocabulary (21-22) — 7½ yrs
  4. Binet Vocabulary (8) — 8 yrs
  5. WISC Vocabulary (25-26) — 8½ yrs
  6. WISC Vocabulary (28-29) — 9½ yrs
  7. Binet Vocabulary (11) — 10 yrs
  8. WISC Vocabulary (32-33) — 10½ yrs
  9. WISC Vocabulary (36-37) — 11½ yrs
  10. WISC Vocabulary (39) — 12½ yrs
  11. WISC Vocabulary (43-44) — 13½ yrs
  12. WISC Vocabulary (45-46) — 14½ yrs

C — CONCEPTUALIZATION (WISC Similarities)

  3   4   6 — 5½-6½-7½
  7   8   9 — 8½-9½-10½
  10   11-12 — 11½-12½
  13 — 13½-14½

D — WR READING VOCABULARY
  Level

E — GRAY ORAL READING COMPREHENSION
  Level

F — ARTICULATION AND SPEECH *delayed, very quiet, hesitant*

G — PSYCHOLINGUISTIC ABILITIES (Language Ages)

  1. Auditory Decoding
  2. Visual Decoding
  3. Auditory Vocal Association
  4. Visual Motor Association
  5. Vocal Encoding
  6. Motor Encoding
  7. Auditory Vocal Automatic
  8. Auditory Vocal Sequential
  9. Visual Motor Sequential

Slow development in early childhood.

Figure 5-2—*Continued*

BASIC LEARNING ABILITIES AND TESTS	TEST RECORD		PROFILE				
	Response + or −	Norm	Very Weak −2SD	Weak −1SD	Normal +1SD	Strong +2SD	Very Strong

IV. SOCIAL-PERSONAL ADAPTIVITY

A — SOCIAL AGE *Questionable Validity 10.0* + ?

B — SPRAINGS' BEHAVIOR RATING SCALE

C — SOCIAL JUDGMENT AND INTERPRETATION *general* +

WISC Picture Arrangement: 4 — 5½ yrs
7-9 __ 14-16 __ 22-23 __ 6½-7½-8½
25-26 __ 27-28 __ 9½-10½
29 __ 30 __ 11½-12½
32-33 __ 34-35 __ 13½-14½

D — PERSONALITY INTEGRATION
1. Test Behavior *immature withdrawal* −
2. Ego Functioning:
   a. Incomplete Sentences
   b. Rorschach (or _____)
   c. Values/Interests
   d. Self Concept *very inadequate*

E — COMMENT: *Overprotected early childhood. Bizarre mannerisms. Swims, enjoys model car building. Plays baseball and basketball.*

V. GENERAL INTELLECTUAL FUNCTIONING

A — GENERAL INFORMATION (WISC)
5 __ 7 __ 8 __ 5½-6½-7½
10 __ 11 __ 13 __ 8½-9½-10½
14 __ 17 __ 11½-12½
19 __ 19 __ 13½-14½

B — PRACTICAL KNOWLEDGE & COMPREHENSION (WISC)
5 __ 6 __ 8 __ 5½-6½-7½
9 __ 11 __ 12 __ 8½-9½-10½
13 __ 15 __ 16 __ 11½-12½-13½

C — ARITHMETIC REASONING
3 __ 4 __ 5 __ 5½-6½-7½
7 __ 8 __ 9 __ 8½-9½-10½
10 __ 11 __ 12 __ 11½-12½-14½

D — WISC: PERFORMANCE SCALE IQ *67*
VERBAL SCALE IQ
FULL SCALE IQ

E — BINET: MENTAL AGE
IQ

F — COMMENT: *Raven Progressive Matrices – below 5th percentile 1947 A, A_B, B   simplifies designs. Potential estimated as borderline to dull normal.*

Figure 5-2—Continued

84

PROGRAMMING LEARNING DISABILITIES

TEST REFERENCES FOR PSYCHOEDUCATIONAL PROFILE

I. Motor Integration

   A. Arnold Gesell, *et al.*, *The First Five Years of Life* (New York: Harper & Row, Publishers, 1940), p. 67.
   B. Arnold Gesell and Frances Ilg, *The Child from Five to Ten* (New York: Harper & Row, Publishers, 1946), p. 231.
   C. Gesell, *et al.*, *op. cit.*, pp. 70-72.
   D. *Ibid.*, pp. 82-86. Gesell and Ilg, *op. cit.*, p. 232.
   E. *Ibid.*, p. 232.
   F. *Ibid.*
   G. Clinical test.
   H. Gesell, *et al.*, *op. cit.*, p. 95.
   I. *Ibid.*
   J. *Ibid.*, pp. 95-98.
   K. *Ibid.*, pp. 99-100.
   L. *Ibid.*, pp. 89-91.

II. Perceptual Abilities

   A. Auditory.
     1. Audiometric test results.
     2. Else Haeusserman, *Developmental Potential of Preschool Children* (New York: Grune & Stratton, Inc., 1958), pp. 151-159.
     3. a. Lewis Terman and Maud Merrill, *Stanford-Binet Intelligence Scale: Manual for the Third Revision Form L-M*, "Repeating 2 Digits" (Boston: Houghton Mifflin Company, 1960), p. 70.
       b. *Ibid.*, "Repeating 3 Digits," p. 73.
       c. *Ibid.*, "Memory for Sentences I," p. 78.
     d-f. David Wechsler, *Manual: Wechsler Intelligence Scale for Children* (New York: The Psychological Corporation, 1949), p. 113.
     g-h. Terman and Merrill, *op. cit.*, p. 88.
     i-l. Wechsler, *loc. cit.*
     4. a. Haeusserman, *op. cit.*, pp. 140-141.
       b. Terman and Merrill, *op. cit.*, p. 80.
   B. Tactile.
     1-16. Haeusserman, *op. cit.*, pp. 200-201 (adapted).
   C. Visual.
     1. Snellen chart.
     2. a. Haeusserman, *op. cit.*, Test 10, pp. 145-146.
       b. Terman and Merrill, *op. cit.*, pp. 74-75.
       c. *Ibid.*, p. 78.
       d. *Ibid.*, p. 79.
       e. *Ibid.*, p. 82.
       f. Haeusserman, *op. cit.*, Test 37, pp. 195-200.
       g. *Ibid.*, Test 40, pp. 204-206.
       h. *Ibid.*, Test 21, pp. 160-163.
     3. a. Terman and Merrill, *op. cit.*, pp. 67-68.
       b. *Ibid.*, pp. 72-73.
       c. *Ibid.*, pp. 76-77.
       d. Wechsler, *loc. cit.*

4. H. Elston Hooper, *Hooper Visual Organization Test; Manual* (Redondo Beach, Calif.: Psychological Service Center of the South Bay, 1958), p. 3.

5. Hortense Barry, *The Young Aphasic Child: Evaluation and Training* (Washington, D. C.: The Volta Bureau, 1961), p. 9.

D. Visual-Motor Skills.

1. a,b,c,

d,f,g. Gesell, *et al., op. cit.*

e,g,k. Lauretta Bender, "Standardization of the Gestalt Functions in a Performance Test for Children," Ch. 11, *A Visual Motor Test and Its Clinical Use* (New York: American Orthopsychiatric Association, 1938), p. 135.

2. a,e,h,

i,j. Terman and Merrill, *op. cit.*, "Year Levels."

f,g,k. Marshall Hiskey, *Manual: Nebraska Test of Learning Aptitude* (Lincoln, Neb.: University of Nebraska, 1955), p. 46f.

l. A. Strauss and N. Kephart, *Psychopathology and Education of the Brain-injured Child*, Vol. II (New York: Grune & Stratton, Inc., 1959), pp. 152-156.

3. Marianne Frostig, *Developmental Test of Visual Perception* (Palo Alto, Calif.: Consulting Psychologists Press).

4. Wechsler, *loc. cit.*

5. a,b,c,

f. Terman and Merrill, *op. cit.*, "Year Levels."

d. Haeusserman, *op. cit.*, Test 28, pp. 174-175.

e. *Manual; Goodenough-Harris Drawing Test* (New York: Harcourt, Brace & World, Inc., 1963).

g. Wechsler, *loc. cit.*

h,i,   Joseph Jastek, *Manual; Wide Range Achievement Test* (Wilming-
j,l   ton, Dela.: Guidance Associates, 1946). (Handwriting judgment must be made by teacher.)

k. Terman and Merrill, *op. cit.*, "Year Levels."

III. Language

A. Basic Expressive Fluency.
1-6. Terman and Merrill, *op. cit.*, "Year Levels."

B. Vocabulary Knowledge.
1-12. From Binet L-M and WISC scales as indicated.

C. Conceptualization.
WISC Similarities Test.

D. Wide-range Reading Vocabulary.
Jastek, *loc. cit.*

E. Gray Oral Reading Level.
William Gray, *Gray Oral Reading Tests* (Indianapolis, Ind.: The Bobbs-Merrill Co., Inc., 1963).

F. Articulation and Speech.
Judged by examiner from all language tests.

G. Psycholinguistic Abilities.
James McCarthy and Samuel Kirk, *Examiner's Manual; Illinois Test of Psycholinguistic Abilities* (Urbana, Ill.: Institute for Research on Exceptional Children, 1961).

IV. **Social-Personal Adaptivity**

    A. Social Age.
       Edgar Doll, *Manual; Vineland Social Maturity Scale* (Minneapolis, Minn.:
       Educational Test Bureau of American Guidance Service, 1947).
    B. Spraings' Behavior Rating Scale.
       Violet Spraings, Educational Psychologist, Northern California School for
       Cerebral Palsied Children, Berkeley, Calif.
    C. Social Judgment and Interpretation.
       WISC Picture Arrangement Test
    D. Personality Integration (Clinical appraisal).
       1. Behavioral observation during test.
       2. a,c. Robert E. Valett, "Diagnostic Interview," *The Practice of School
           Psychology* (New York: John Wiley & Sons, Inc., 1963), pp. 116-118.
         b. Projective tests results as selected by examiner.
         d. Clinical judgment based on all tests.

V. **General Intellectual Functioning**

    From WISC or Binet L-M Scales as indicated.

PROFILE REPORT

Name: John Doe   *Date examined:* July 24, 1964
Address: 1341 X Street   *Date of birth:* October 23, 1955
Nationality: Native-born white   *Age:* 9-9
School: Berry Street Elementary   *Grade:* 3
Reason for referral: Psychological evaluation for possible placement in the new program
             for the educationally handicapped.

Summary of Findings and Recommendations

This boy is handicapped by a severe emotional disturbance of an autistic nature that has drastically interfered with his ability to relate to his environment. His perception of events is distorted and he tends to withdraw rather than struggle to maintain productive contact. He lacks social experience and self-confidence and remains psychologically dependent upon his mother. Functionally, the child is operating on a moderately retarded level with academic achievement about three years below age expectancy and at least one year below estimated general ability.

John's relative strengths are his abilities in arithmetic, general perceptual awareness, willingness to respond to "nonpersonal" materials, and his interests in model cars and some physical activities.

It is recommended that he be placed in a class for the educationally handicapped as an emotionally disturbed child. Emphasis should be placed on developing and strengthening nonthreatening and meaningful contacts with his environment. The use of concrete materials and an experimental educational program relevant to his primary psychological needs will have to be evolved from consultation sessions between teacher and psychologist. He will require much individual psychological support from his teacher at first and should only gradually be introduced to the more involved group activities. The parents should be referred for psychological counseling and for participation in the therapy group.

Figure 5-3

Perhaps the greatest value of the Profile is that it does place major importance on the consultation and planning function of the school psychologist. It also is very helpful as a means of profiling retest results at a later time. These results, if entered in a different color, may portray many significant differences of considerable educational value.

(It may be of interest to know that John was placed as recommended, and through consultation and planning, a program for him was developed. Within a year he showed significant psychological and social gains and is now well on the way to achieving better personal integration and improved academic performance.)

EDUCATIONAL IMPLICATIONS

The basic underlying assumption for educational programming is that if a child is significantly weak in a basic learning ability, something can be done about it. Usually corrective or remedial education of some type is called for, although certain educational programs, of necessity, may be more preventive than remedial in nature.

As stated before, the most important use of the Profile will be in developing a meaningful educational program relative to the child's needs and outstanding abilities. This is generally accomplished by consultation between psychologist and teacher at which time specific plans are made. Follow-up with educational modification and later reevaluation is also a necessary part of the program. Since teachers and others immediately concerned often request references for program consideration, some of these have been listed below.

I. Motor Integration and Physical Development

    A. Physical therapy and medical treatment

    B. Remedial and adaptive physical education and training, such as advocated by Kephart[22]

II. Perceptual Abilities

    A. Medical treatment

    B. Developmental and readiness programs such as Kephart,[23] Frostig,[24] Goldstein and Levitt,[25] and Continental Press[26]

    C. Remedial basic academic programs, such as Fernald's kinesthetic methods,[27] Cuisenaire arithmetic aids,[28] and programmed reading[29]

[22]N. Kephart, *The Slow Learner in the Classroom* (Columbus, Ohio: Charles E. Merrill Books, Inc., 1960).

[23]*Ibid.*

[24]M. Frostig and D. Horne, *The Frostig Program for the Development of Visual Perception* (Chicago: Follett Publishing Company, 1964).

[25]H. Goldstein and E. Levitt, *A Simplified Reading Readiness Program* (Urbana, Ill.: R. W. Parkinson and Associates, 1964).

[26]Reading Readiness Series (Pasadena, Calif.: The Continental Press, Inc.).

[27]G. Fernald, *Remedial Techniques in Basic School Subjects* (New York: McGraw-Hill Book Company, 1943).

[28]Cuisenaire Company of America, 9 Elm Avenue, Mount Vernon, N.Y.

[29]M. Sullivan and C. Buchanan, *Programmed Reading* (Manchester, Mo.: Webster Division, McGraw-Hill Book Company, 1964).

III. Language

    A. Speech therapy

    B. Developmental language programs in the classroom

    C. Remedial language approaches for aphasoid and dyslexic children[30]

IV. Social-personal Adaptivity

    A. Pupil and parent counseling and guidance

    B. Parent education programs

    C. Psychiatric treatment

    D. Pupil programming for social success and participation in school and community activities

    E. Social studies units on the development of social judgment; use of materials such as Basic Social Studies Discussion Pictures,[31] Bullis stories,[32] SRA guidance aids,[33] and role playing situations

V. General Intellectual Functioning

    A. Medical treatment as necessary

    B. Environmental manipulation, such as early preschool programs and compensatory education[34]

    C. Conceptual development units in primary grades, such as Continental Press Thinking Skills[35]

The Psychoeducational Prescription

The last model for psychoeducational evaluation is an outline summary form on which the examining psychologist can report his findings and impressions in a prescriptive manner (*Fig. 5-4*). In most cases the brief prescriptive report suffices to identify and place the child in the appropriate learning situation and also serves as the base for follow-up consultations. This is only the beginning, however, because the evaluative process must be an ongoing, cooperative venture between teacher and psychologist.

It will be noted that the prescription contains an extensive section, labeled "Psychodiagnostic Impressions," that covers the six major areas of the basic learning abilities. This is a *learning systems* evaluation rather than the usual *test* evaluation. In other words, the psychologist reports his impressions by integrating and relating his observations and test data. This, in turn, results in a professional judgment of the pupil's over-all performance. For example, the examiner may decide to check the average column in gross motor development if his impression is that these skills are normal for the age of the child; this conclusion may be based purely on observation and clinical judgment, or it could depend on some standardized motor evaluation tests such as the Lincoln-Oseretsky Motor Devel-

---

[30]H. Barry, *The Young Aphasic Child: Evaluation and Learning* (Washington, D.C.: The Volta Bureau, 1961).

[31]Basic Social Studies Discussion Pictures (Evanston, Ill.: Harper & Row, Publishers).

[32]H. Bullis and E. O'Mallery, *Human Relations in the Classroom, Course I and II* (Wilmington, Dela.: The Delaware State Society for Mental Hygiene, 1947).

[33]Guidance Materials (Chicago: Science Research Associates, Inc.).

[34]N. Sullivan, "Making History in Prince Edward County," *Saturday Review* (Oct. 17, 1964).

[35]Thinking Skills (Pasadena, Calif.: The Continental Press, Inc.).

PSYCHOEDUCATIONAL PRESCRIPTION

Pupil's name _____ _____ Birth date _____

Address _____ _____ Telephone _____

Parents' names _____

School _____ Date examined _____

Examiner _____ Referred by _____

Reasons for referral _____

_____

Psychological tests and instruments used _____

_____

PSYCHODIAGNOSTIC IMPRESSIONS

Learning Area	Per-formance Level	Very Weak	Weak	Aver-age	Strong	Very Strong
Gross Motor Development Developmental skills, self-identification, muscular strength, etc.						
Sensory-Motor Integration Balance, motor accuracy, directionality, laterality, etc.						
Perceptual-Motor Skills						
Auditory: association, decoding, memory, etc.						
Visual: coordination, discrimination, etc.						
Visual-Motor: coordination, speed, integration						
Language Development*						
Vocabulary—fluency						
Reading						
Writing						
Spelling						

*Important to indicate performance level in this area, especially for children of elementary school age.

Figure 5-4

Conceptual Skills*						
Arithmetic						
General information						
Classification-comprehension						
Social Skills						
Ability to relate						
Self-control and attention						
Anticipatory response and foresight						
Self-concept						

Comments:

FUNCTIONAL GENERAL INTELLIGENCE

Functional Classification (IQ range plus/minus five points)	Check one	Educational Placement Program Implications
Gifted (130 plus)		Gifted class
Bright normal/superior (115-129)		Advanced
High average (110-114)		Regular
Average (90-109)		Regular
Low average (85-89)		Remedial-basic
Borderline retarded/slow learning (70-84)		Educable mentally retarded?
Mildly retarded (55-69)		Educable mentally retarded
Moderately retarded (40-54)		Trainable mentally retarded?
Severely retarded (25-39)		Trainable mentally retarded

Comments:

*Important to indicate performance level in this area, especially for children of elementary school age.

Figure 5-4—*Continued*

PSYCHOEDUCATIONAL PRESCRIPTION AND RECOMMENDATIONS

Special Class Placement

_____Gifted.

_____Educable mentally retarded.

_____Trainable mentally retarded.

_____Educationally handicapped.

_____Compensatory education.

_____Aurally handicapped.

_____ Visually handicapped.

_____Orthopedically handicapped.

_____Speech handicapped.

_____Remedial physical education.

Comments:

Recommended Educational Interventions

_____Remedial education.

_____Special tutoring.

_____Flexible scheduling.

_____Modified day attendance.

_____ Systematic exemption contract.

_____Suspension.

_____Referral to state residential schools, centers, or private agencies

_____Exemption or exclusion.

_____Medical evaluation and management.

_____Specific behavior modification.

_____Counseling.

_____Parent education and family therapy.

_____Play or recreation therapy.

_____Psychotherapy.

Comments:

Other Recommendations

Figure 5-4—Continued

opment Scale. The performance level (PL) column may or may not be filled in to indicate the grade level or other statistic if a normative score is available. The asterisk marking language and conceptual skills serves as a reminder that in most cases it is important to indicate performance level in these areas if learning, disabilities for elementary-aged children are of prime consideration. For instance, some reading tests, such as the Wide Range or Gilmore, may be used, and the grade placement scores written in accordingly.

The second major part of the model is concerned with functional general intelligence as assessed during the examination. Although intellectual potential may be estimated under the comments section, it is important that the actual operational intelligence be recorded here since educational placement and programming must begin with *where the child is* as against *where he might be.* The IQ should be reported by range with the appropriate classification checked and comments noted regarding intellectual strengths and weaknesses. There is also space to mark placement and programming recommendations.

The last, and by far the most important section of the model is entitled "Psychoeducational Prescription and Recommendations." The first part concerns special class placement. The most appropriate special class for the child should be checked and pertinent comments should be written in the space provided. For example, the psychologist might check "Educationally handicapped" and write in the specification, "self-contained perceptual-motor class." The psychologist should then present the child's special learning needs and programming recommendations in as simple and concrete a manner as possible. (The recommendations might contain references to programmed materials and aids for use by the teacher in remediating any diagnosed learning disability.) As an illustration, the psychologist could recommend that a child placed in an educationally handicapped class for perceptual-motor disabilities be given some special remediation in auditory decoding. Since most teachers would require more definitive information as to how to provide such remediation, the psychologist might wish to include actual illustrations of appropriate resource materials with the report for teacher consideration. A sample programming recommendation might read: "It is recommended that remediation exercises in auditory decoding, such as those suggested on the enclosed psychoeducational resource program number 23 from *The Remediation of Learning Disabilities,* be selected and adopted." (*Fig. 5-5.*) Such a direct approach to psychoeducational prescription provides a sound basis for later consultation with the teacher and parent concerned.

It is recognized that the psychoeducational prescription is dependent upon the professional administration and interpretation of a number of pertinent psychological tests. In most cases the initial test battery is limited by time requirements and seldom extends beyond two hours in length. Since the primary purposes of the initial psychological evaluation are the identification of learning disorders and the outlining of preliminary programming recommendations, tests should be selected that will sample the range of learning disabilities and will lend themselves to prescriptive insights and interpretations. A highly recommended initial test battery is composed of the following tests:

1. A perceptual-motor skills sample (Kephart, etc.)—including the Draw-a-Man test (*Fig. 5-6*).
2. The Stanford Binet (L-M) or Wechsler Intelligence Scale for Children.
3. The Bender Visual-Motor Gestalt Test.

PERCEPTUAL-MOTOR SKILLS

Auditory Decoding

DEFINITION: The ability to understand sounds or spoken words.

ILLUSTRATION: Pupil can follow simple verbal instructions, can indicate by gesture or words the meaning or purpose of auditory stimuli, such as animal sounds, nouns, or verbs.

EDUCATIONAL RATIONALE: Children need to be taught to listen carefully and to understand and respond to oral stimulation and instructions. Training activities should stress behavioral responses and simple "yes-no" answers rather than long verbal replies.

SUGGESTED PROGRAM ACTIVITIES

1. Sound Identification

   a. Matching: Place picture of train, cow, dog, gun, etc., on chalkboard; teacher then says sound ("choo-choo," "moo," etc.), and child points out appropriate picture. Use *The Sound Says* and *Mr. Farmer Says* for additional matching exercises.

   b. Tone matching: Teach children to match step bells or piano notes by holding hands high for high notes, squatting for low notes, etc.

   c. Instrument sounds: Arrange pictures of musical instruments and use records or actual instrument to teach sound. Play sound on tape or record and have child point out appropriate picture.

   d. Noises: Child turns his back while teacher claps hand, blows whistle, hits with hammer, crumples paper, etc. Child then turns around and duplicates noise.

   e. Tapping: With child's back turned, teacher taps glass, box, can, drum, etc. Child turns around and points out object tapped.

   f. Contrasting sounds: Teacher walks noisily; then tiptoes, rapidly-slowly; talks in high voice, low voice. Child then duplicates sounds by name—loud, fast, high, etc.

2. Understanding Questions

   a. "Yes or no": Child responds to questions with a "yes" or "no" or nods head accordingly. Verbs—"Do birds crawl?" "Do cars move?" "Do worms walk?" etc. Sex—"Is a boy a man?" "Are girls females?" "Is John a woman?" etc. Purpose—"Are crayons to color?" "Are chairs to fly?" "Is food to eat?" "Are bicycles to ride?" "Are pencils to paint?" "Are shoes to wear?" etc.

   b. "Alike or different": Teacher instructs pupil to indicate if the second word is the *same* or *different* than the stimulus word: "dog—fog," "shush—slush," "ape—ape," "coat—boat," "throw—threw," etc.

   c. "True or false": Read a story or textbook assignment aloud. Prepare a series of true or false questions to be presented in spelldown fashion.

   d. "Clues": Arrange assorted objects or pictures on table. Teacher says, "What is big, round and bounces," ". . . small, long and sharp?" etc. Child points out object.

3. Understanding and Following Directions

   a. Action records: Play rhythm and activity records such as *Dance-a-Story* and teach children to carry out directions.

   b. Charades: Children divide into teams and select names of books, movies, events (Pinocchio, Mary Poppins, Halloween, etc.) to *act out* for the other side to guess. Show how to open the door, cut with a knife, sweep the floor, etc.

   c. Simple directions: "Open the door." "Walk around the room." "Find me the arithmetic book on the second shelf." "Put your hand on your head and skip to the desk and back," etc.

   d. Book exercises: "Locate page 320." "Show me the third paragraph on this page." "Point out the first word in the last paragraph on page 1."

   e. Sounds and voice training exercises: Teach lessons from *Play It by Ear—Auditory Training Games* from the John Tracy Clinic (also for direct use with parents as a source of homework exercises).

   f. Drawing and marking exercises: Prepare special ditto work sheet and record instructions for listening post use; i.e., "Mark the first circle in the top row," etc.

   g. Speech games: Play "Speecho" and other speech discrimination games.

Figure 5-5 (Copyright 1967, by Fearon Publishers.)

h. Symbol association: Arrange mixed letters, numbers, and simple words in chalk tray. Teacher says "a," "l," "cat," etc., and child points out symbol. "Show me the letter that comes before "N." "Give me the number that comes after 14," etc. Use phonetic records and formal phonic training program.

SAMPLE PROGRAM

Program A requires the pupil to follow simple directions which are read to the child.

Exercise B is an illustrative series of discriminating questons which can be played with picture cards; the cards are placed by the child on the "yes," "no," or "don't know" piles as the questions are asked by the teacher.

Project C requires fine motor response in carrying out detailed oral instructions.

Activity D calls for the child to discriminate whether the "sh" sound comes at the initial, medial, or final position in words as said by the teacher. The pupil indicates position by pointing out the man's place in the front, middle, or rear of the train.

All programs should be modified or extended to meet the needs of individual pupils.

REFERENCES

1. Related Programs
   a. *Listen* and *These Are Sounds About You* (Record and filmstrip), Guidance Associates, Pleasant-ville, N.Y.
   b. *What's Its Name: A Guide to Speech and Hearing Development,* Palfrey's School Supply Co., 7715 E. Garvey Blvd., South San Gabriel, Calif.
   c. Ronnei, Eleanor C., *Learning To Look and Listen,* 1951, Bureau of Publications, Teachers College, Columbia University, New York, N.Y.
   d. *Who Said It?* (Record #703), Educational Activities, Inc., P.O. Box 392, Freeport, N.Y.
   e. Lowell, Edgar, and Stoner, Marguerite, *Play It by Ear—Auditory Training Games* (Sound section), 1963, John Tracy Clinic, 806 W. Adams Blvd., Los Angeles, Calif. 90007
   f. Barry, Hortense, "Discrimination," *The Young Aphasic Child: Evaluation and Training,* 1961, pp. 32-34, Alexander Graham Bell Association for the Deaf, Inc., Washington, D. C.

2. Instructional Materials
   a. Hand Trap Set, #M386, Creative Playthings, Princeton, N.J.
   b. *Mr. Sound Says,* #49N4645, *The Farmer Says,* #49N508, Sears, Roebuck & Co.
   c. Wood Recorder, #Q338, Step-Bells, #AM366, Creative Playthings
   d. *Poems Children Enjoy,* Palfrey's School Supply Co.
   e. Basic Set of Word-making Cards, Word making Production, P.O. Box 305, Salt Lake City, Utah
   f. Speecho—a Phonetic Game, Palfrey's School Supply Co.
   g. Sound and Articulation Game, Palfrey's School Supply Co.
   h. *Dance-a-Story* (Record), Educational Record Sales, 500 S. Douglas Street, El Segundo, Calif.
   i. *Sounds for Young Readers* (Phonetic and auditory discrimination sounds, record), Educational Record Sales

3. Further Evaluation
   a. Wepman Auditory Discrimination Test
   b. Valett, Robert E., *Developmental Survey of Basic Learning Abilities* (Auditory Discrimination Section), Consulting Psychologists Press, Palo Alto, Calif.
   c. Illinois Test of Psycholinguistic Ability: Auditory Decoding Subtest

4. General References
   a. Kirk, Samuel, "Children with Auditory Handicaps," *Education of Exceptional Children,* 1962, pp. 151-166, Houghton Mifflin Co., Boston, Mass. 02107
   b. Montessori, Maria, "Exercise for the Discrimination of Sounds," *The Montessori Method,* 1964, pp. 203-214, Shocken Books, Inc., New York, N.Y. 10016

Figure 5-5—*Continued*

PERCEPTUAL-MOTOR SKILLS

Pupil's Name

PSYCHOEDUCATIONAL RESOURCE PROGRAM NUMBER **23**

Auditory Decoding

1. Color the car.
2. Draw a circle around the boy.
3. Draw a line from the car to the tree and from the tree to the boy.

A

YES	NO	DON'T KNOW

 Are pencils to write with?

 Do arrows grow?

 Are snakes animals?

 Do apples rot?

B

Figure 5-5—Continued

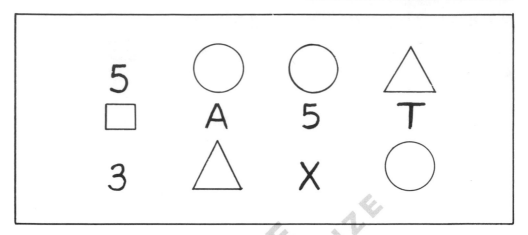

1. Color the upper triangle red.

2. Circle the number 5 on the second row.

3. Draw a line through the second circle from the left in the top row.

C   4. Color the top half of the number 3 black.

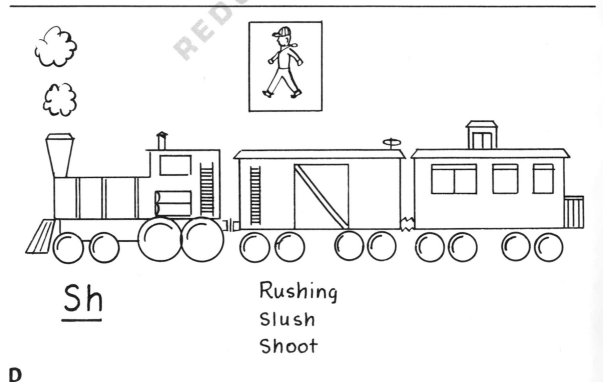

Sh

Rushing
Slush
Shoot

D

Figure 5-5—Continued

PERCEPTUAL-MOTOR SKILLS SAMPLE*

Code: 1 = poor, 2 = fair/average, 3 = good

Pupil's name _____ _____ Birth date _____ Age _____

School _____ Date _____

---

1. Walking Board

 A. Forward _____ B. Backward _____ C. Sideways _____

2. Jumping

 A. Both feet _____ C. Left foot _____ E. Alternate hop _____

 B. Right foot _____ D. Alternate skip _____ F. Double alt. hop _____

3. Identification of Body Parts—"Touch your . . ."

 A. Shoulders _____ D. Ankles _____ G. Eyes _____

 B. Hips _____ E. Ears _____ H. Elbows _____

 C. Head _____ F. Feet _____ I. Mouth _____

4. Imitation of Movements—"Do what I do . . ."

 A. _____ C. _____ E. _____ G. _____

 B. _____ D. _____ F. _____ H. _____

5. Obstacle Course—Spatial Orientation

 A. Step over knee-high yardstick. _____

 B. Step under shoulder-level yardstick. _____

 C. Squeeze between two chairs. _____

6. Angels in the Snow—"Move just your (and replace) . . ."

 A. Right arm _____ D. Both arms _____ G. RA—RL _____

 B. Right leg _____ E. Both legs _____ H. RA—LL _____

 C. Left leg _____ F. LA—LL _____ I. LA—RL _____

7. Chalkboard—Laterality

 A. Centered circle _____ C. Lateral lines _____

 B. Double circles _____ D. Vertical lines _____

8. Ocular Pursuits (thumbtack on pencil)

 A. Lateral _____ D. Rotary _____ G. Visual acuity R_____ L_____

 B. Vertical _____ E. Mono—LE _____ H. Eyedness: Hole _____

 C. Diagonal _____ F. Mono—RE _____ I. Telescope _____

*Modified for use with ages 6–9 after Newell C. Kephart, *The Slow Learner in the Classroom* (Columbus, Ohio: Charles E. Merrill Books, Inc., 1960), pp. 120–155.

Figure 5-6

9. Kraus-Weber—Muscular Performance

    A. Holding sit-ups_____ B. Leg-ups_____ C. Floor touch_____

10. Visual-motor Skill

    A. Bender-Gestalt or Gesell Copy Forms   Age_____

    B. Gray Oral Reading   Grade Placement_____

11. Pupil Self-awareness

    A. How did you do in school this year?

    B. What did you enjoy most in school?

    C. What are you best in?

    D. What do you need more help in?

    E. What do you dislike in school?

12. Draw-a-Person

    A. Standard score (IQ)_____ MA_____

    B. Associations:

13. Handedness

    A. Writing name_____ Drawing_____

    B. Handing objects_____

    C. Scissors_____

14. General Behavior and Observations

15. Writes Name	**Writes Address**

16. Summary and Recommendations

Examiner_____

Figure 5-6—Continued

4. The Wide Range Achievement Test.
5. The Gilmore or Gray Oral Reading Test.

The experienced examiner will recognize that this battery covers the entire range of developmental skills, perceptual-motor tasks, cognitive functioning, language skills, and school achievement performance. All of these tests are standardized except for the sample of perceptual-motor skills, which must be selected by the examiner. A perceptual-motor skills sample form similar to that presented in Figure 5-5 should be developed and used for instant recording of the child's responses; attached to the psychoeducational prescription form, such a sample is also of great practical value as a programming aid and as a basis for later consultation between teacher and psychologist.

6

A Developmental Task Approach to Early Childhood Education[1]

What should preschool and pre-primary children be taught? What are they capable of learning? These are two basic questions of age-old concern to educators that have come under consideration again because of recent research findings in developmental psychology. With the growth of preschool programs and early childhood education projects, many attempts are being made to apply recent research results to the creation of meaningful classroom educational programs.

The goal of most new programs is the early identification of the child's developmental level and needs for the purposes of correct school placement and educational programming. It is generally assumed that the educational program or curriculum in the preschool, kindergarten, and transitional first grades is one that has been created to meet the educational needs of children at specified stages of growth and development.

[1]Robert E. Valett, "A Developmental Task Approach to Early Childhood Education," *Journal of School Psychology*, Vol. V, No. 2 (Winter, 1967), pp. 136-147, updated.

The purpose of this chapter is to examine some of the implications of developmental programming in the public schools, to suggest specific developmental tasks for inclusion in such programs, and to consider some of the related problems inherent in such programs.

A Developmental Concept

The prevailing view of leading psychologists and educators is that human growth and development can be significantly furthered through sound educational experiences at an early age. Any level of physiological growth and maturation has implications as to the behavioral expectations of a child. Likewise, the extent and richness of experiential exposure and stimulation has implications as to what might reasonably be expected from the child and his school program. Human intelligence, abilities, and achievement are greatly influenced by the culture of the society and the educational opportunities available to the individual during his early years of life.

Longitudinal research by Bloom has shown conclusively that half of all growth and intelligence present at 17 years takes place before the age of 5, and the next 30 per cent is achieved between 5 and 8.[2] Certainly then, what happens to the young child is of critical importance in affecting his ability and motivation to learn. A child's capabilities vary tremendously from infancy to eight years of age, however, with each stage having implications for the development of cognitive processes and educational programs. The work of Piaget, for instance, has documented the development of children's thinking from the early stages of sensorimotor organization and preoperational thought to the beginning of concrete-operational thinking (about seven years of age) that precedes the later period of more formal cognitive operations.[3] Although Piaget's developmental stages imply genetic limitations to learning and thinking processes, they present many possibilities for the organization of educational programs geared to the cognitive level of the child.

Several notable beginnings have been made in attempting to bridge the gap between developmental psychology and educational practice. The importance of providing specific perceptual training as part of a program for the development of sensorimotor intelligence in handicapped children has been discussed by Wolinsky.[4] The use of sequentially organized perceptual training materials and programs in the stimulation of cognitive development of normal preschool children was recently defended by Hunt in his comments on the Montessori method.[5] A step forward in the meaningful evaluation of developmental skills in preschool children for the purpose of determining school readiness and behavioral grouping has been taken by Ilg and Ames.[6] Certainly one of the first major attempts to apply the insights of developmental psychology to educational programming has

[2]B. S. Bloom, *Stability and Change in Human Characteristics* (New York: John Wiley & Sons, Inc., 1964).

[3]J. H. Flavell, *The Developmental Psychology of Jean Piaget* (Princeton, N.J.: D. Van Nostrand Co., Inc., 1963).

[4]Gloria F. Wolinsky, "Piaget's Theory of Perception: Insights for Educational Practices with Children Who Have Perceptual Difficulties," *Training School Bulletin*, Vol. LXV (1965), pp. 12-260.

[5]J. M. Hunt, "Introduction to the Montessori Method," in Maria Montessori, *The Montessori Method* (New York: Schocken Books, Inc., 1964).

[6]Frances L. Ilg and Louise Bates Ames, *School Readiness: Behavior Tests Used at the Gesell Institute* (New York: Harper & Row, Publishers, 1964).

been made by Educational Testing Service in conjunction with the First-grade Project in New York City Schools;[7] this is a direct attempt to develop intelligence through the provision of lessons and exercises around specific developmental concepts ranging from auditory discrimination and attention through the higher levels of general knowledge and developing imagination. Since the beginning of Project Head Start, many school systems have also been experimenting with preschool and kindergarten programs with varied attempts to adapt theory to the practical demands of the classroom; a recent report by Bereiter and Engelmann supports the effectiveness of direct instruction with preschool disadvantaged children and concludes that a structured approach may be superior to a non-directive activity program.[8] In all of these programs, increasing attention has been given to the role of the teacher in both the evaluation and instructional guidance of young minds.

Teacher Involvement in Developmental Programming

Perhaps the primary requisites for teachers of preschool and young primary children are sound training in the developmental needs of children and a conviction of the importance of early childhood education. The teacher should be able, as Bruner says, to "... translate the way of thought of a discipline into its Piagetian (or other) equivalent appropriate to a given level of development and take the child onward from there."[9] To accomplish this, however, constant involvement in the ongoing evaluation and programming of pupils is required. Meaningful appraisal of pupil characteristics and abilities, therefore, is a continual process demanding teacher awareness of developmental tasks and the ability to guide the young child onward through a program of sequential developmental experiences.

Such a program need not be formal and highly directive, but it does require organization and the provision of learning materials and opportunities for creative development. The teacher must be involved in direct and systematic appraisal of her pupils and in the development of a follow-up educational plan geared to the individual needs of each child. Because of the teacher's time limitations, developmental task surveys or rating forms can serve as a useful guide in pupil evaluation and class planning. Since basic sensorimotor skills and concrete operations are fundamental to the development of more formal academic abilities, it is essential that careful evaluation be made of these areas.

One classification and arrangement of basic developmental tasks for teacher use has been made by the author.[10] Selected tasks in the areas of motor integration and physical development, tactile discrimination, auditory discrimination, visual-motor coordination, visual discrimination, language development and verbal fluency, and conceptual development have been arranged on an ascending scale of difficulty from two through seven years of age. Developmental norms have been listed from varied studies and resources and provide the teacher with a frame of reference for her evaluation. This survey can be made directly by the teacher involved and in as much detail as may be required. The major value to the

[7] *From Theory to Classroom* (Princeton, N.J.: Educational Testing Service, 1965).

[8] C. Bereiter and S. Engelmann, "Observations on the Use of Direct Instruction with Young Disadvantaged Children," *Journal of School Psychology*, Vol. IV (1966), pp. 55-62.

[9] J. S. Bruner, "The Growth of Mind," *American Psychologist*, Vol. XX (1965), pp. 1007-1017.

[10] R. E. Valett, *The Valett Developmental Survey of Basic Learning Abilities* (Palo Alto, Calif.: Consulting Psychologists Press, 1966).

teacher of such a survey is that it offers direct clues for educational programming. For instance, if a pupil lacks successful accomplishment in one or more areas of developmental tasks, this may indicate distinct limitations to further learning, and the educational program should then be developed accordingly; children should be taught any basic skills they are lacking that might reasonably be expected of them in terms of their total development.

AN ILLUSTRATION

By seven years of age most children have accomplished the developmental tasks shown in Figure 6-1. The scores indicated are for a grossly immature seven-year-old child who needs specific educational help in many areas. This boy is awkward, has difficulty in following directions, lacks spontaneous language, has few language concepts, and is easily confused; however, he has good visual discrimination and visual-motor coordination. Incidentally, his IQ on the Wechsler Intelligence Scale was 83 (with a high-scaled score of 14 on Block Design), and he obtained an IQ of 100 on the Leiter International Performance Scale.

It can be seen that such a survey does help to pinpoint areas of strengths and weaknesses and can, therefore, be very helpful to the teacher in planning for the needs of the child. Examination of the results suggests, for example, that this child could profit from training in:

1. Dressing and buttoning.
2. Jumping, skipping, and adaptive physical education exercises.
3. Word-naming and basic language development.
4. Body part and self-identification exercises.
5. Color training.
6. Simple counting.
7. Elementary concept development of big and little, first and last, loud and soft, etc.

In working on such basic skills as these, the teacher will become aware of related areas of difficulties and will be able to evolve a truly meaningful program for the individual child. With teacher involvement in the developmental evaluation and programming of children, the need for supporting consulting and referral services becomes essential.

Some Educational Implications

A developmental task approach to early childhood education with continual teacher involvement in evaluation and programming assumes that teachers can be trained to perform such functions; it also assumes that teacher time can be organized to allow these responsibilities to be carried out. An in-service training program would, of necessity, require the cooperative services of primary curriculum personnel, school psychologists, and elementary guidance and special education personnel. Through the use of theory presentations, discussion groups, demonstrations, and practical workshops, teachers could become sufficiently skilled. Although the allocation of teacher time may be a more complex problem, this, too, can be resolved through the use of paid teacher aides, parent and student volunteers, and team teaching; in addition, early-late schedules, preschool screening, and other modifications in school organization would help to provide time for these basic functions.

Such a program implies that the random, heterogeneous grouping of young children in schools is educationally unsound. Since the developmental approach focuses on specific behavioral characteristics of concern for given age levels, the logical result for school organization is that children can best be grouped on the basis of developmental level and needs. Single test scores such as IQ's are therefore of little value in working with the majority of young children unless such information is supplemented by reference to growth levels and educational needs. In a similar way, the reporting of developmental age levels alone has limited value for curriculum implementation and individual programming. For instance, although it may be helpful for purposes of class placement to know that a child is at a "five-year" developmental age according to the Ilg and Ames school readiness criteria, it is more helpful to know the *pattern* of strengths and weaknesses and then to create an educational program to help the child accomplish those crucial developmental tasks that are of unique significance to him.

This approach to early childhood education also implies that certain developmental tasks are of such crucial importance that until they are successfully accomplished, the child is handicapped in his future "academic" learning. Accordingly, the curricula must be concerned with the provision of primary experiences in developmental areas. Of special concern is the importance of emphasizing the meaningfulness of basic physical-motor experiences, auditory discrimination, visual-motor coordination, and particularly, language development programs, if the child is to be adequately prepared for later conceptual development and training. Thus, the need for special training and activity centers within the classroom assumes new importance. For instance, mats, physical development equipment, and perceptual training materials become an essential part of the total program. More specifically, regarding language development, intensive verbal stimulation through human contact and attention, including word naming and object classification, field trips, activities supplemented by listening posts with tapes, records, and other material aids, is more readily understood and acknowledged as a most crucial part of any formal early educational program.

Undoubtedly, one of the most important implications of a developmental program is the need for supportive consultation services. With adequate consultation from school psychologists, curriculum coordinators, and elementary guidance personnel, the teacher can be most effective. Without such consultive services, it is impossible to establish a developmental program. Because of his training in child growth and development and psychoeducational evaluation, the school psychologist becomes a primary consultant in teacher training, programming for individual growth needs, and in following through on parent and pupil referrals received from teachers for purposes of further study, counseling, placement, special treatment, or referral as may be necessary. If the psychologist is not trained in early childhood curricula, however, it is essential that some curriculum consultant be intimately involved in the entire program. Only through the cooperative efforts of teacher, principal, psychologist, and curriculum personnel can a developmental program evolve that is of sound educational value to the child and all concerned.

VALETT DEVELOPMENTAL SURVEY OF BASIC LEARNING ABILITIES

A. MOTOR INTEGRATION AND PHYSICAL DEVELOPMENT

1	+	Unwrap this piece of candy and eat it.	(2V)
2	+	Crawl on your hands and knees.	(2V)
3	+	Run in a circle.	(2½V)
4	−	Take off your coat (sweater, etc.).	(3V)
5	−	Put it back on.	(3V)
6	+ −	Cut this paper in two with these scissors.	(3V)
7	−	Button your coat (dress, etc.) for me.	(4V)
8	+	Throw me the ball.	(4V)
9	−	Skip around me.	(5V)
10	+ −	Draw a picture for me—any picture will do like a house or a person or anything you want.	(5V)
11	+ −	Bounce this ball for me.	(6G)
12	+ −	Show me how you jump rope.	(6V)
13	−	Can you ride a scooter (wagon, tricycle, sled, skates)?	(6V)
14	+ −	Do what I do (imitates examiner).	(6K)
15	−	Can you ride a bicycle?	(7V)
16	−	Bend over and touch the floor.	(7K)
17	−	Lie down, put your feet together, lift them up straight, and put them down slowly.	(7V)

RELATED HEALTH COMMENTS:

B. TACTILE DISCRIMINATION

Present indicated items together in a cloth bag. Have child alternate hands in obtaining objects. Say "Put your hand in this bag and find me the ____."

18	+	Dog and <u>doll</u>	(2–3Va)
19	+	<u>Car</u> and airplane	(2–3Va)
20	+	Nail – <u>spoon</u> – penny – bolt	(4Va)
21	+	Nail – spoon – <u>penny</u> – bolt	(4Va)
22	−	Crayon – <u>pencil</u> – stick – nail	(5Va)
23	−	<u>String</u> – rubber band – ribbon – bolt	(5Va)
24	+ −	<u>Bolt</u> – nail – tack – crayon	(6Va)
25	−	Cloth – <u>leather</u> – sponge – paper	(6Va)
26	−	<u>Envelope</u> – paper – sandpaper – block	(7Va)
27	−	<u>Little ball</u> – medium ball – big ball – block	(7Va)
28	−	Little sandpaper circle – <u>large sandpaper circle</u> – little cardboard circle – large cardboard circle.	(7Va)

Obviously did not know names of objects.

Figure 6-1

C. AUDITORY DISCRIMINATION

29	+	Play with this rattle.	(2Va)
30	+	Play with this bell.	
31	+	Play with this music toy.	
32	+	Put the ball on the chair.	(2G)
33	+	Put the ball on the table.	
34	+	Give me the ball.	
35	+	Show me the picture of the thing we use to eat our cereal. (spoon)	(2½ H)
36	+	Which thing does mother need to fix your hair? (brush)	
37	+	Can you find something that goes on your foot? (shoe)	

Present pictures of cow, dog, and cat; then hide (examiner's) lips and mouth and say:

38	+	Show me the cow or "moo-moo".	(2½ Va)
39	+	Show me the dog or "woof-woof".	
40	+	Show me the cat or "meow".	
41	+	Say: 4 — 7	(2½ B)
42	+	6 — 3	
43	+	6 — 4 — 1	(3B)
44	—	3 — 5 — 2	
45	+	Say: "boy".	(3G)
46	+	Say: "girl".	
47	—	Are you a little boy or a little girl?	
48	+	Say: "big boy (or girl)".	(4G)
49	+	Say: "I am a big boy (girl)".	
50	—	Now say: "We are going to buy some candy for mother".	
51	—	Say: "Jack likes to feed little puppies in the barn".	
52	—	Where do you live?	(5G)

Response: _____ *No response.* _____

53	—	Say: 9 - 6 - 8 - 1	
54	—	Say: 5 - 7 - 2 - 6	
55	—	Say these backwards: 2 - 9 - 5	(6G)
56	—	Say these backwards: 8 - 1 - 6	
57	+	Say: "Bub".	(6Va)
58	+	Say: "Tub".	
59	+	Say: "Stub".	
60	+—	Say: "Flub".	

OK on second try.

Listen to the sound at the beginning of this word and write the letter that stands for the sound:

61	—	Boy	(7Va)
62	—	Girl	
63	—	Apple	
64	—	Mother	

Verbal responses echolalic.

Figure 6-1—Continued

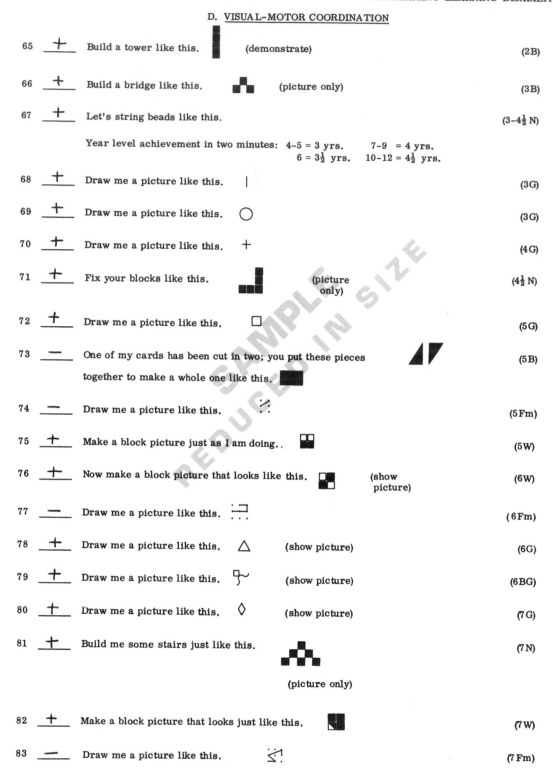

D. VISUAL-MOTOR COORDINATION

65 __+__ Build a tower like this.   (demonstrate)   (2B)

66 __+__ Build a bridge like this.   (picture only)   (3B)

67 __+__ Let's string beads like this.   (3-4½ N)

Year level achievement in two minutes: 4-5 = 3 yrs.   7-9 = 4 yrs.
                                            6 = 3½ yrs.   10-12 = 4½ yrs.

68 __+__ Draw me a picture like this. | (3G)

69 __+__ Draw me a picture like this.   ◯   (3G)

70 __+__ Draw me a picture like this.   +   (4G)

71 __+__ Fix your blocks like this.   (picture only)   (4½ N)

72 __+__ Draw me a picture like this.   □   (5G)

73 __—__ One of my cards has been cut in two; you put these pieces   (5B)
         together to make a whole one like this.

74 __—__ Draw me a picture like this.   (5Fm)

75 __+__ Make a block picture just as I am doing.   (5W)

76 __+__ Now make a block picture that looks like this.   (show picture)   (6W)

77 __—__ Draw me a picture like this.   (6Fm)

78 __+__ Draw me a picture like this.   △   (show picture)   (6G)

79 __+__ Draw me a picture like this.   (show picture)   (6BG)

80 __+__ Draw me a picture like this.   ◇   (show picture)   (7G)

81 __+__ Build me some stairs just like this.   (7N)

                          (picture only)

82 __+__ Make a block picture that looks just like this.   (7W)

83 __—__ Draw me a picture like this.   (7Fm)

Figure 6-1—*Continued*

E. VISUAL DISCRIMINATION

84   +   Show me one like this (circle).   ($2\frac{1}{2}$ H)

85   +   Show me one like this (square).

86   +   Show me one like this (triangle).

Show me an animal like this (matching):   ($3\frac{1}{2}$ Bm)

87   +   Cat   88   +   Dog

89   +   Horse   90   +   Bear

Show me one like this: (4 Bm)

91   +   ○   92   +   □   93   +   △

94   +   ○   95   +   ◇   96   +   □

97   +   ◪   98   +   ○   99   +   □

Mark the one that is different from the others: ($4\frac{1}{2}$–5 Bm)

100   —   ○○○□○   101   —   △△△△○

102   —   ⬠⬠□⬠⬠   103   —   ⅄⅄⅄⅄⅄

104   —   l l l / l   105   —   A A ᴀ A A

106   —   ⊘⊘⊘⊘⊘   107   —   d b d d d

Show me the one that looks exactly the same: (5–6 Hm)

108   +   [·]   109   —   [:]

110   —   [∴]   111   —   [::]

112   +   [⁙]   113   +   [⁚⁚⁚]

114   +   [⁛]

115   +   Place first <u>three</u> of six circles in ascending order and say: "Which comes next?"   (6 H)

                  · ● ● ● ● ●

Find one just like mine: (6 H)

      | 2 | sat | home | tac | 4 | cat |

116   +   2   117   +   tac

118   +   home   119   +   4

120   +   cat   121   +   sat

Now watch carefully, because I'm going to show and hide my card and then   ($6\frac{1}{2}$ H)
I want you to find one like it:

122   +   cat   123   +   2

124   +   sat   125   +   4

126   +   home   127   +   tac

Find one just like mine: (7 Va)

   | b | was | 9 | p | dad | d | saw | bad | 6 |

128   +   b   129   +   saw

130   +   d   131   +   dad

132   +   p   133   +   9

134   +   bad   135   +   6

136   +   was   *Good responses when able to hold materials and manipulate items.*

Figure 6-1—Continued

F. LANGUAGE DEVELOPMENT AND VERBAL FLUENCY

137 _____ Look at this pretty book and tell me what you see.   (2G)
               (Names three or more common pictures as he leafs through the book)

               What is this?   (2½ G)
138 _____ Dog
139 _____ Shoe
140 _____ Cup
141 _____ House
142 _____ Book

143 _____ What is your name — your whole name?   (3G)

144 _____ Look at this picture and tell me all about it.   (3½ B)
               (Enumerates three objects, describes, or interprets picture)

145 _____ What burns?   (4G)
146 _____ What cuts?
147 _____ What shoots?
148 _____ What sleeps?

149 _____ Brother is a boy; sister is a (   ).   (4½ B)
150 _____ Father is a man; mother is a (   ).

151 _____ What is a ball?   (5B)
152 _____ What is a hat?
153 _____ What is a stove?
154 _____ What is the opposite of "boy"?   (6D)
155 _____ What is the opposite of "up"?
156 _____ What is the opposite of "brother"?
157 _____ What is the opposite of "hot"?
158 _____ What is an apple?   (6–7 B/W)
159 _____ What is a letter?
160 _____ What is a knife?
161 _____ What does "roar" mean?
162 _____ What is a pony?
163 _____ What is Mars?
164 _____ What is a gown?
165 _____ Tell me in what way cookies and cake are alike.   (7G/Va)
166 _____ Tell me in what way cars and airplanes are alike.

No verbal responses other than echolalic.

Figure 6-1—*Continued*

G. <u>CONCEPTUAL DEVELOPMENT</u>

167 + Show me your ear.	168 + What is this (eye)?	$(2-2\frac{1}{2} B)$
169 + Show me your nose.	170 + What is this (mouth)?	
171 − Show me your knee.	172 − What is this (foot)?	
173 − Show me your elbow.	174 + What is this (head)?	
175 + Show me your big toe.	176 − Show me your little finger.	(3Va)
177 + Show me the little ball.	178 + Show me the big ball.	(3H)
179 − Show me the little dog.	180 − Show me the big dog.	
181 + Give me ONE penny.	182 + Give me ONE MORE penny.	$(3\frac{1}{2} H)$
183 + Give me TWO pennies.		(4H)
184 + Show me the red crayon.	185 − What color is this (blue)?	(4H/G)
186 + Show me the yellow crayon.	187 − What color is this (black)?	
188 + Show me the brown crayon.	189 − What color is this (green)?	
190 − Show me the purple crayon.	191 − What color is this (orange)?	
192 +− Clap your hands softly.	193 +− Clap your hands loudly.	$(4\frac{1}{2} H/V)$
194 − Stomp your feet softly.	195 − Stomp your feet loudly.	
196 − Give me four pennies.	197 − Give me three pennies.	
198 − Give me six pennies.	199 − Give me five pennies.	

      (Examiner lines up 12 pennies) $(5-5\frac{1}{2} G/Va)$

200 − Count these pennies.	201 − Show me the first penny in the line.	
202 − Show me the last penny.	203 − Show me a middle penny.	
204 − Which is bigger: 9 or 4?		$(5\frac{1}{2}-6 J/Va)$
205 − Which is more: three pieces of candy or five pieces of candy?		
206 − Is it morning or afternoon?	207 − When do you eat breakfast?	(6H)
208 − How many shoes in a pair?	209 − Show me your right hand and left foot.	(6G)
210 − Show me your left eye and right ear.		
211 − Give me a penny.	212 − Give me a nickel.	(6Va)
213 − Give me a dime.	214 − Give me a quarter.	
215 + Show me number "1".	216 + What number is this (3)?	$(6\frac{1}{2} J/Va)$
217 + Show me number "7".	218 + What number is this (10)?	
219 + Write (or print) your name for me.		$(6\frac{1}{2} J)$
220 + Write numbers for me as far as you can go (at least 20).		$(6\frac{1}{2} G/Va)$
221 + Name these letters: A U B H C M		$(6\frac{1}{2} J/Va)$
222 + Write as many of your ABC's as you can.		(7J/Va)
Add these numbers:		(7J/Va)

223 − (2 + 1)   224 − (4 + 2)   225 − (6 + 5)

Read these words: (7J)

226 + TO   227 + SEE   228 − CAT   229 + BIG

Write: (7J)

230 − CAT   231 + IN   232 − GO   233 − MAN

Figure 6-1—*Continued*

7

The Diagnostic-Prescriptive Teacher

When a child with learning disabilities is finally placed with a special education teacher, the second stage in the evaluation procedure begins. The first stage, of course, has included the initial screening, referral, and identification examinations leading to the decision that some special education is required. Although information derived from these initial evaluations is of significant value, it seldom provides the teacher who is working with the pupil with the kind of current data needed for actually programming learning disabilities. Since experience has aptly demonstrated that sufficient psychoeducational diagnostic services have never been (and probably never will be) available to special educators when they need them, it is best to train teachers in educational diagnosis so that they can continue and extend the evaluation process while working with their pupils. A second major factor is that much of the information derived from initial placement evaluations is actually irrelevant to the demands of the immediate teaching situation. In most cases the initial evaluation was done months preceding placement in a special program, and the report is usually not wholly applicable to programming the learner in his present educational setting. Consequently, the teacher is actually forced to reappraise the child and then to proceed accordingly.

In the past one of the tragic mistakes of special educators has been to assume that the learning characteristics and needs of the pupils placed with them are all relatively similar. Thus, the feeling has been that it is not necessary to develop a highly individualized educational program. Now, however, with the growing emphasis on the identification of specific learning disabilities and their prescriptive implications, it is essential that teachers become diagnosticians in their own right and that considerable time and attention be allocated to this process *before* any attempt is made to educate the child. The rationale presented in this book implies that the teacher should work from an operational frame of reference that is centered on the evaluation and programming of the basic learning abilities. Whatever the age of the child or his placement in special education, the starting point is the same. The teacher must become immediately involved in the diagnostic-evaluative process with emphasis on determining major strengths and weaknesses in the basic areas of gross motor development, sensory-motor integration, perceptual-motor skills, language development, conceptual skills, and social skills.

To accomplish this purpose the teacher needs to be provided with in-service training, appropriate diagnostic instruments, and time to do the job. In-service training should be achieved through the combined services of the school psychologist and program consultants in informal training programs and workshops. The provision of appropriate diagnostic instruments poses a more difficult problem and can best be resolved through the appointment of a joint teacher-administrator committee responsible for selecting and/or developing diagnostic-evaluation instruments for use by teachers at various instructional levels in the program (*Fig. 7-1*). This committee should also decide how and when during the school

A TEACHER DIAGNOSTIC-EVALUATION SCHEDULE

Program Level	Recommended Instruments
Preschool	Developmental Survey of Basic Learning Abilities
Kindergarten	Developmental Survey of Basic Learning Abilities Metropolitan Readiness Test
Primary	Psychoeducational Inventory Frostig Test of Developmental Perception Gilmore Oral Reading Test
Intermediate- elementary	Psychoeducational Inventory Spache Developmental Reading Scales
Junior high	Psychoeducational Inventory Wide Range Achievement Test Spache Developmental Reading Scales
Senior high	Spache Developmental Reading Scales Wide Range Achievement Test

Figure 7-1

year these evaluations are to take place. In all cases it is recommended that these instruments be used at the beginning of the school year. When possible, pupils should be brought to the teacher by their parents on an appointment basis either immediately preceding the opening of school or during the first week, which could be set aside for this purpose. This arrangement accomplishes two purposes —it provides early contacts with the parents, and it results in immediate evaluation of the pupil that can be used for early program development purposes. It must be recognized, however, that this is only the first stage of teacher involvement in the ongoing, continuous diagnostic process.

Information that is derived from the evaluative process should be directly used in educational programming and prescriptive teaching. For example, if the pupil fails a given educational task expected of his developmental stage, he should be provided with direct remedial education and ample opportunity to practice and develop proficiency in the diagnosed area of difficulty. The standard curriculum must be recognized as being of secondary importance in this regard, since prescriptive remediation based on functional evaluation should be the primary concern. Ongoing evaluation should include ample use of diagnostic and review tests provided by most publishers of curricular texts and materials; failure or difficulty in given items should cause the teacher to carefully consider the possible remedial implications involved. Of course, a record of all diagnostic-evaluation results and their prescriptive follow-up usage should be maintained in the pupil's file, which becomes of increasing value to any special educators who will be involved with the child in the future.

Although the involvement of the teacher in the diagnostic process is crucial at all stages in the education of children with learning disabilities, there are three major time periods in the educational sequence that require some special consideration: the periods of preschool, elementary school, and secondary school evaluation and programming.

The Preschool Period

Education for exceptional children and children with learning disabilities should begin at an early age. Children who are aurally handicapped or who have orthopedic disabilities commonly begin preschool special education at three years of age. Programs for the retarded and educationally handicapped are increasingly becoming available to four-year-olds. With the advent of Head Start and other compensatory education preschool programs, public awareness about the importance of early childhood education has increased. More recognition is now being given to the identification of possible physical, environmental, and specific learning disabilities in young children. Remediation of disabilities at this early stage in their development may prevent more serious handicaps in elementary and secondary school.

It can be argued, then, that preschool, primary, and kindergarten teachers must become diagnostic child development specialists concerned with the nature of the young learner and his functioning during the early formative years. Preschool teachers should become increasingly involved in evaluating the degree of pupil success in accomplishing crucial developmental tasks. To this end, the tasks need to be defined as concisely as possible for varying age groups so that the teacher can make a direct assessment. It is obvious that the usual standardized instruments have not met this need; therefore, educators must give more consideration to fundamental tasks that are relevant to the preschool experiential curriculum. This need was the prime factor in the creation of the Developmental Survey of Basic Learning Abilities, which was considered in detail in the previous chapter.

The role of preschool, primary, and kindergarten teachers in making a direct personal evaluation of at least those pupils suspected of having learning disabilities cannot be overstressed. It is not enough merely to make general observations of such children and to refer them later for more complete physical and psychological evaluation. Direct and early evaluation of specific developmental tasks is required, with some attempts at educational intervention if this is implied, prior to the time of first-grade enrollment. The child with learning problems who has had the advantage of such preschool and kindergarten attention and experience will have an immeasurably better chance for more meaningful education and remediation during his elementary school years.

The Elementary School Period

By the time the average elementary school child has been placed in a special education learning disabilities program, considerable information is available that can be used for diagnostic-remedial programming. Usually, the data includes prior teacher observation records and reports, group test results such as are derived from the Lee Clark or Metropolitan Readiness Tests, and results from various group tests of general learning ability or scholastic aptitude. Of course, much more specific diagnostic information is also available from the individual psychological examination if the child has been placed in a special education program.

Invariably, however, the teacher is faced with the dilemma of determining present functioning in the basic learning areas. To meet this need A Psychoeducational Inventory of Basic Learning Abilities[1] was developed for direct use by teachers concerned with the diagnostic evaluation of the basic learning abilities (Fig. 7-2). The Inventory begins with an operational definition of each ability and an accompanying illustration. This is followed by instructions for the evaluation of specific learning tasks. (The tasks should always be administered in an individual situation.) The Inventory is not a standardized instrument and relies entirely on the examiner's subjective judgment and experience regarding the rating to be employed and the nature of the remedial program rquired. It will be most helpful in the diagnostic-planning phase when used by the teacher in conjunction with a psychoeducational consultant, such as a school psychologist, who can follow up on the Inventory with more specialized examinations if needed.

The Inventory can be quickly mastered by an experienced teacher. All required evaluation materials are listed in the general directions for the Inventory and are easily obtainable. The pupil's written responses for the specific learning tasks should be made in the accompanying workbook. Oral responses and related observations for each task should be recorded by the evaluating teacher under the "notes" column. Tasks are listed by level of difficulty: B—beginning tasks that are generally accomplished by children in primary grades, ages 5-8; M—middle-level tasks that are successfully performed by middle elementary pupils, ages 8-10, and A—advanced tasks that are generally accomplished by upper elementary pupils, ages 10-12. Actual ratings should be checked in one of the five columns according to the scale that follows.

[1]Robert E. Valett (Palo Alto, Calif.: Fearon Publishers, 1968).

1. *VW—very weak performance:* Very little, if any, actual task achievement. Poor attention and concentration, very little effort demonstrated, little or no response or skill evident.
2. *W—weak performance:* Limited skill or response, obvious difficulty in attending to task, cautious, unsure, lacking confidence.
3. *A—average performance:* Partial accomplishment judged appropriate for mental and physiological development.
4. *S—strong performance:* Fairly good task achievement, quite responsive, confident, no lack of attention.
5. *VS—very strong performance:* High achievement and response, excellent motivation, effortless performance.

An over-all rating for each learning ability should be judged and checked on the form entitled "A Psychoeducational Evaluation of Basic Learning Abilities." For example, auditory sequencing might be rated S (strong) while the performance level column could be marked A (average); this would typify the response of an upper elementary-age pupil who was able to accomplish the advanced-level task with fair achievement although considerable time and effort may have been required for successful accomplishment. Very weak or weak ratings indicate possible learning disabilities and should become the focus of further investigation and direct remedial programming.

The diagnostic elementary school teacher will need to supplement the Inventory with other evaluative procedures. In particular, such tests as the Frostig and the Gilmore, and the Spache Reading Scales have all proven of value in that they contribute directly to prescriptive teaching and remediation.

The Secondary School Period

The young adolescent secondary school pupil with learning disabilities presents special diagnostic problems. Transition from a child-centered elementary program to a subject-centered departmentalized junior or senior high school program (with less allowance for individual differences) can be, and often is, a traumatic experience for pupils with specific learning disabilities. On this level, the teacher should begin with an evaluation of motor and perceptual skills to determine first if individual special education in these areas, or adaptive physical education, is implied. Next, diagnostic appraisal should cover basic spelling, writing, arithmetic, and reading skills. In addition, special consideration should be given to adolescent peer group pressures and concomitant motivational and affective problems that will determine much of the actual program strategy to be employed. The secondary school teacher of children with learning disabilities must be an effective counselor and must also be capable of evaluating pupil social-personal skills and problems and of programming accordingly in these areas.

In summary then, this brief discussion has shown that the secondary level diagnostic teacher proceeds in essentially the same way as her elementary school colleague, although somewhat hindered by a subject-centered teaching framework. As the diagnostic-prescriptive approach gains acceptance on all levels of education, we can hopefully anticipate a growing concern and provision for individual differences and learning disabilities in secondary school education.

A PSYCHOEDUCATIONAL INVENTORY OF BASIC LEARNING ABILITIES

GROSS MOTOR DEVELOPMENT: The development and awareness of large muscle activity. (Basic learning abilities 1-14)

Learning Ability	Illustration	Task Level	Specific Learning Task (The examiner should give the following directions to the pupil.)	Notes	Rating Scale VW W A S VS
1. **Rolling:** The ability to roll one's body in a controlled manner.	From a supine position, with arms over head, pupil can roll from back to stomach. Pupil can do sequential rolling to right and left, can roll down hill or incline.	B	Lie on your back with your arms over your head and your feet together. Roll over slowly to the right. Now roll over slowly to the left.		
		M	Put one arm straight over your head and the other arm down by your side. Roll to the right three times. Now roll to the left two times.		
		A	Do a forward somersault.		
2. **Sitting:** The ability to sit erect in a normal position without support or constant reminding.	Pupil can demonstrate proper poise in sitting at desk with feet on floor, back straight, and head and arms in proper position for work at hand.	B	Sit up straight with your feet flat on the floor and your hands folded while you count to ten.		
		M	Sit on the floor Indian-style, with your legs crossed and your arms folded, while you count to ten.		
		A	Sit up straight in your chair and let me see how long you can balance a book on your head.	Time:	
3. **Crawling:** The ability to crawl on hands and knees in a smooth and coordinated way.	With eyes fixated on target, pupil first crawls in a homolateral fashion. Pupil progresses to cross-lateral crawling program.	B	Crawl on the floor moving your arm and leg on the same side together (homolateral).		
		M	Crawl on the floor fast like a dog, moving your opposite arm and leg together (cross-lateral).		
		A	Crawl over to the wall while carrying this spoon with the bead on it between your teeth without dropping the bead.		
4. **Walking:** The ability to walk erect in a coordinated fashion without support.	With head up and shoulders back, pupil walks a specified path and walking line. Pupil can walk backward and sideways without difficulty.	B	Walk forward in a straight line putting one foot directly in front of the other. Touch the heel of one foot to the toes of the other.		
		M	Now walk backward in the same way, holding your arms out. Be sure your heels and toes are touching.		
		A	Now close your eyes, put your arms out in front of you, and walk straight to me. Remember to keep your eyes closed. (Pupil should not touch heel and toes as he walks.)		

Figure 7-2 (Copyright 1968, by Fearon Publishers.)

Learning Ability	Illustration	Task Level	Specific Learning Task (The examiner should give the following directions to the pupil.)	Notes	Rating Scale VW W A S VS
5. **Running:** The ability to run a track or obstacle course without a change of pace.	Pupil runs a straight track of easy distance without difficulty, can change direction through a simple obstacle course without stopping or significantly changing pace.	B	Run in place while I count out loud to 50.		
		M	Run around the room (or obstacle course) without falling or bumping into anything.		
		A	Run from there to here (about 50 yards) as fast as you can.		
6. **Throwing:** The ability to throw a ball with a reasonable degree of accuracy.	Pupil throws a ball to another person so that it may be caught, can throw ball accurately into box or basket.	B	Throw this texture ball to me so that I can catch it.		
		M	Throw these three paper balls into the wastebasket from here. (Distance is approximately four feet.)		
		A	Let's play catch with this softball. (Pupil should catch and throw accurately three out of five times.)		
7. **Jumping:** The ability to jump simple obstacles without falling.	Pupil can jump from chair to floor without difficulty, can jump from jumping board without falling, can jump over knee-high obstacles.	B	Jump back and forth over this line three times.		
		M	Jump rope forward.		
		A	Jump rope backward.		
8. **Skipping:** The ability to skip in normal play.	Pupil can skip, alternating feet, around circle of players, can skip rope forward both by hopping and alternate-foot skipping.	B	Skip forward in a circle as I am doing.		
		M	Skip backward in a circle as I am doing.		
		A	Skip rope forward around in a circle.		
9. **Dancing:** The ability to move one's body in coordinated response to music.	In young children, abilities are shown by free movement and eurhythmic expression. There is a progression to more formal dance steps with older pupils.	B	March in a circle and slap your sides as I clap my hands.		
		M	Dance freely to the record I am going to play. (Play music such as *The Nutcracker Suite*.)		
		A	Do any modern dance for me when I play this record. (Play any contemporary record.)		
10. **Self-identification:** The ability to identify one's self.	Pupil can identify self by name, respond to name when called, and identify self in pictures and mirrors.	B	What is your name?		
		M	Point to yourself in this mirror. (Hand mirror should reflect part of the examiner and part of the pupil.)		
		A	I am printing three names on this paper. Point to your name. (Space provided in Workbook for response.)		

Figure 7-2—Continued

Learning Ability	Illustration	Task Level	Specific Learning Task (The examiner should give the following directions to the pupil.)	Notes	Rating Scale VW W A S VS
11. **Body Localization:** The ability to locate parts of one's body.	Pupil can locate eyes, hands, mouth, hair, nose, feet, eyebrows, fingernails, shoulders, elbows, knees, back, neck, chin, forehead, wrists, arms, legs, toes.	B	Touch your eyes, nose, mouth, feet, and wrists.		
		M	Look in this mirror and point to your hair, teeth, eyebrows, and chin.		
		A	What are your eyes for? What are your hands for? What is your stomach for?		
12. **Body Abstraction:** The ability to transfer and generalize self-concepts and body localization.	Pupil can identify others by names and pictures, can locate body parts on others, generalize to pictures, complete body picture puzzles.	B	Point to the clown's nose, hands, feet, knees, hair, and elbows (see Workbook).		
		M	Draw a picture of yourself in this space (see Workbook). Draw your whole body. (Cover clown's picture in 12B.)		
		A	When you grow up, what do you think you will look like?		
13. **Muscular Strength:** The ability to use one's muscles to perform physical tasks.	Pupil can touch floor from standing position. From supine position he can sit up and touch toes, can raise legs off floor for few seconds. Pupil can do one push-up and chin self from bar.	B	Crouch down like this (demonstrate), and when I say "go," jump up and reach over your head.		
		M	Stand up with your feet together and raise your hands over your head. Now bend over and touch the floor.		
		A	Do one or two push-ups.		
14. **General Physical Health:** The ability to understand and apply principles of health and hygiene while demonstrating good general health.	Pupil has good personal health and hygiene habits—no chronic absences for health reasons, no unusual accidents or health history, and no significant physical disabilities interfering with learning.	B	What should you do if you cut your finger?		
		M	Tell me what foods should be in a balanced dinner.		
		A	Why is it important for boys and girls to get lots of exercise and sleep?		

SENSORY-MOTOR INTEGRATION: The psychophysical integration of fine and gross motor activities. (Basic learning abilities 15-21)

15. **Balance and Rhythm:** The ability to maintain gross and fine motor balance and to move rhythmically.	Pupil is able to balance on balance board or rail, can move rhythmically in playing jacks and in bouncing on trampoline or spring.	B	Stand on your tiptoes and run in a circle.		
		M	Walk forward and then backward along this line (or balance beam).		
		A	Balance yourself on one foot while standing on this brick.		

Figure 7-2—*Continued*

Learning Ability	Illustration	Task Level	Specific Learning Task (The examiner should give the following directions to the pupil.)	Notes	Rating Scale VW	W	A	S	VS
16. **Body-spatial Organization:** The ability to move one's body in an integrated way around and through objects in the spatial environment.	Pupil can run maze on playground or in classroom without bumping, can move easily through tunnels and use playground monkey bars, can imitate body positions in space.	B	Climb up on this chair and squat like the figure in this picture (see Workbook).						
		M	Crawl through my legs without touching me.						
		A	Stand up and move your arms and legs as I am doing.						
17. **Reaction-Speed Dexterity:** The ability to respond efficiently to general directions or assignments.	Pupil can attend to the teacher sufficiently to comprehend total directions. He can organize self and respond adequately to complete the given assignment within a normal time expectancy. Pupil has good attention and concentration span.	B	Make as many marks like this (/) in this box (see Workbook) as fast as you can until I tell you to stop. (Allow 60 seconds.)						
		M	Take this deck of cards. Turn all of the cards face up and group them together by aces, twos, threes, etc. Do this as fast as you can.	Time:					
		A	Go to that table and bring that book over here and open it to page 56 and point to the second paragraph on the page.	Time:					
18. **Tactile Discrimination:** The ability to identify and match objects by touching and feeling.	With hidden toys and materials, pupil can match objects with both left and right hands, name or classify materials or substances, differentiate weights, discriminate temperatures.	B	Put your hand in the bag and give me the nail. (Bag contains nail, stick, and pencil.)						
		M	Put your hand in the bag and give me the longest stick. (Bag contains 2"-long, 4"-long, and 6"-long sticks.)						
		A	Put your hand in the bag and give me the letter "A." Now give me the letter "X." (Bag contains A-B-N-M-Y-X-T.)						
19. **Directionality:** The ability to know right from left, up from down, forward from backward, and directional orientation.	Pupil can write and follow picture story or reading material from left to right, discriminate right and left body parts and those of other people, locate directions in room and school.	B	Touch the floor with your right hand. Now shake your left foot.						
		M	Put your finger on the bottom of this block. Now put your finger on the right side of the block. Now the top. Now the left side. (Use square wood building block.)						
		A	Point to the north, the south, the east, the west.						

Figure 7-2—Continued

Learning Ability	Illustration	Task Level	Specific Learning Task (The examiner should give the following directions to the pupil.)	Notes	VW	W	A	S	VS
20. **Laterality:** The ability to integrate one's sensory-motor contact with the environment through establishment of homolateral hand, eye, and foot dominance.	Pupil has consistent right- or left-sided approach in use of eyes, hands, and feet in tasks such as kicking ball, cutting paper, sighting with telescope.	hand	Hand me that pencil. Cut this paper in two. Print your first name here (see Workbook).						
		foot	Kick this paper ball. Hop across the floor on one foot. Push this brick to the wall using one foot.						
		eye	Look out the window with this cardboard telescope. Look through the hole in this card and find the pencil in my hand. Pretend that this yardstick is a rifle and show me how you would hold it and sight it to shoot a lion.						
21. **Time Orientation:** The ability to judge lapses in time and to be aware of time concepts.	Pupil is prompt in attending class, completing timed assignments, and following directions. Child is aware of day, month, year, time of day, and seasons.	B	Jump up and down as I clap my hands.						
		M	What time of the year does Christmas come? _____ Easter? _____ Halloween? _____						
		A	What time is it by this watch?						

PERCEPTUAL-MOTOR SKILLS: The functional utilization of primary auditory, visual, and visual-motor skills. (Basic learning abilities 22-36)

Learning Ability	Illustration	Task Level	Specific Learning Task	Notes	VW	W	A	S	VS
22. **Auditory Acuity:** The ability to receive and differentiate auditory stimuli.	Pupil responds functionally to watch tick, hidden sound toys, and general normal conversational directions. Pupil has no significant decibel loss.	B	Listen to this watch tick when I place it by each of your ears. As I move it away, raise your hand when you no longer hear it.						
		M	Turn your back and listen. When I am through, turn around and repeat what I did. (Tap on desk three times; cough quietly twice.)						
		A	Turn your back, listen carefully, and then repeat what I whisper. ("I like chocolate ice cream." "What day is it today?")						
23. **Auditory Decoding:** The ability to understand sounds or spoken words.	Pupil can follow simple verbal instructions, can indicate by gesture or words the meaning or purpose of auditory stimuli such as animal sounds, nouns, or verbs.	B	Point to the appropriate picture (see Workbook) as I make the sound: "meow," "choo-choo," "moo."						
		M	Answer "Yes" or "No": Do cars move? _____ Is Billy a girl? _____ Can a tree grow? _____						
		A	Color the top part of the number 8, and then draw a line from 8 to 1 without touching the number 5 (see Workbook).						

Figure 7-2—Continued

Learning Ability	Illustration	Task Level	Specific Learning Task (The examiner should give the following directions to the pupil.)	Notes	Rating Scale VW W A S VS
24. **Auditory-vocal Association:** The ability to respond verbally in a meaningful way to auditory stimuli.	Pupil can associate with verbal opposites, sentence completions, or analogous verbal responses.	B	Tell me all the things you think of when you hear the word "vacation."		
		M	Which of the following does not belong: "John, Mary, Bill, George"?		
		A	Describe the clothes I have on.		
25. **Auditory Memory:** The ability to retain and recall general auditory information.	Pupil can act out (charades) Santa Claus, simple plots of common nursery rhymes ("Jack and Jill"), can verbally relate yesterday's experiences, meals, television and story plots.	B	What is the title of your favorite song?		
		M	Tell me the sound a snake makes: _____; a train makes: _____; a sheep makes: _____.		
		A	Tell me your favorite story so that I can understand what it is about.		
26. **Auditory Sequencing:** The ability to recall in correct sequence and detail prior auditory information.	Pupil can imitate specific sound patterns, follow exactly a complex series of directions, repeat digit and letter series.	B	Listen carefully and do what I say: "Put this pencil on the floor, open the door, walk around the room, come back, and sit down."		
		M	Listen and repeat these numbers: "2-3, 5-1-8, 4-3-9-6, 7-2-5-1-9."		
		A	Listen carefully and repeat what I say: "School starts in September of each year and Halloween comes in October."		
27. **Visual Acuity:** The ability to see and to differentiate meaningfully and accurately objects in one's visual field.	Pupil sees without notable fatigue, holds material at appropriate working distance, has no significant loss of acuity on Snellen or Illiterate E chart.	B	Look around this room and tell me all the things you see.		
		M	Look through this cardboard telescope at the picture I am putting up (about 15 feet away) and tell me all about it.		
		A	Now look out the window and name all the things you can see that are as far away as possible.		
28. **Visual Coordination and Pursuit:** The ability to follow and track objects and symbols with coordinated eye movements.	With head steady, pupil can move eyes to fixate on stable objects in varied places, pursue moving objects such as finger positions, follow picture and word stories left to right without jerky movements.	B	Hold your head straight and move only your eyes. Now look at the door. Look at the ceiling. Look at the floor.		
		M	(Sit in front of pupil with a thumbtack in the eraser of a pencil; hold the pencil about 18 inches from the midline of pupil's nose.) Hold your head still and follow the thumbtack with your eyes as it moves to the left while I count to five. Now follow it to the right while I count to five. Now follow it as it moves up and down while I count to five.		
		A	Hold your head straight; put your right arm straight out in front of you, pointing your thumb up. Now look at what I tell you: "thumb-floor, thumb-window, thumb-table, thumb-ceiling."		

Figure 7-2—*Continued*

Learning Ability	Illustration	Task Level	Specific Learning Task (The examiner should give the following directions to the pupil.)	Notes	Rating Scale VW W A S VS
29. Visual-Form Discrimination: The ability to differentiate visually the forms and symbols in one's environment.	Pupil can match identical pictures and symbols such as abstract designs, letters, numbers, and words.	B	(See Workbook for all three tasks.) Look at this picture. Now mark one on this side that looks like the first picture.		
		M	Now look at this picture and mark one on this side that looks like this first picture.		
		A	Look at this picture. Now mark one on this side that looks like the first picture.		
30. Visual Figure-Ground Differentiation: The ability to perceive objects in foreground and background and to separate them meaningfully.	Pupil can differentiate picture of self and friends from group picture, differentiate objects in "front" and "back" part of pictures and mock-ups, differentiate his name from among others on paper or chalkboard, perceive simple forms and words imbedded in others.	B	(See Workbook for all three tasks.) Look at this picture. Is the dog in front of the girl? Is the tree behind the girl? Is the wagon behind the tree?		
		M	Look at this picture. Find the four hidden figures for me.		
		A	Look at these words. Tell me all the little words you can find in each of these big words.		
31. Visual Memory: The ability to recall accurately prior visual experiences.	Pupil can recall from visual cues where he stopped in book, can match or verbally recall objects removed or changed in the environment, can match briefly exposed symbols.	B	(See Workbook for all three tasks.) Look carefully at these four pictures. (Wait five seconds, then cover.) Now tell me what you saw.		
		M	Look at this picture. (Expose #1 only for three seconds, keeping others covered. Then cover #1 and uncover the others.) Now I will cover this picture and I want you to find it among these others.		
		A	Look at the word picture. (Follow same procedure as in 31M.) Now I will cover the picture and I want you to find it among these others.		
32. Visual-Motor Memory: The ability to reproduce motorwise prior visual experiences.	Pupil can draw designs and symbols following brief exposure, can reproduce letters, numbers, simple words on demand, can portray prior objects or events through gestures or drawings, can reproduce varied patterns and identify hidden materials.	B	(See Workbook for all three tasks.) Look at this picture. (Expose for ten seconds and cover.) Now draw it here. (Point to space in Workbook.)		
		M	Look at this picture. (Expose for ten seconds and cover.) Now draw it here.		
		A	Look at this picture next. (Expose for ten seconds and cover.) Now draw it here.		

Figure 7-2—Continued

Learning Ability	Illustration	Task Level	Specific Learning Task (The examiner should give the following directions to the pupil.)	Notes	Rating Scale VW W A S VS
33. **Visual-Motor Fine Muscle Coordination:** The ability to coordinate fine muscles such as those required in eye-hand tasks.	Pupil can write legibly, trace, and imitate precise body movements without difficulty, can cut, can manipulate, and can judge fine physical responses without gross errors.	B	Untie your shoelaces. Now tie them for me.		
		M	Print or write your whole name for me (see Workbook).		
		A	Look at this picture (see Workbook) and then draw one just like it in the empty box.		
34. **Visual-Motor Spatial-Form Manipulation:** The ability to move in space and to manipulate three-dimensional materials.	Pupil can build block houses and designs, can draw three-dimensional pictures, complete shop and craft projects, integrate form and space puzzles.	B	(See Workbook for all three tasks.) Look at this picture of a book on a table with a pencil across the top. Take this pencil and book and fix them like the picture.		
		M	Look at this picture of the six coins with a pencil across them. Take these coins and this pencil and fix them like the picture.		
		A	Here is a picture of a paper airplane. You copy me, and we will make one together.		
35. **Visual-Motor Speed of Learning:** The ability to learn visual-motor skills from repetitive experience.	Pupil can respond with increasing speed to rote learning tasks such as copying digit or letter sequences, spelling, specific arithmetic processes, and gross motor skills such as jumping over a rope.	B	In the space provided (see Workbook), make as many marks like this (X O +) in that order, as quickly as you can, until I tell you to stop. (Allow 60 seconds.)	Number:	
		M	Take these bolts, washers, and nuts. Put a washer and nut on each bolt like this (demonstrate) as fast as you can. (Use three half-inch bolts, washers, and nuts.)	Time:	
		A	Look at these boxes (see Workbook). Each number has a letter. Look at the numbers and write in the letters that go in the boxes. When you have finished, tell me what it says.	Time:	
36. **Visual-Motor Integration:** The ability to integrate total visual-motor skills in complex problem solving.	Pupil can play complex team sports, swim, draw accurate pictures including people, may play musical instrument, write extended letters, move freely about neighborhood and community.	B	(See Workbook for all three tasks.) Draw a picture of your family.		
		M	Look at this first picture. Now mark each of the following boxes that has a part of the design in the first picture. (Demonstrate by marking first box.)		
		A	Complete the sentence; then copy it on the lines provided.		

Figure 7-2—Continued

LANGUAGE DEVELOPMENT: The current functional stage of total psycho-linguistic development. (Basic learning abilities 37-43)

Learning Ability	Illustration	Task Level	Specific Learning Task (The examiner should give the following directions to the pupil.)	Notes	Rating Scale VW W A S VS
37. **Vocabulary:** The ability to understand words.	Pupil has a basic receptive vocabulary in accord with chronological age and educational opportunity.	B	(See Workbook for all three tasks.) Point to the house (woman, rocket, telephone) for me.		
		M	Point to the helmet (skull, juggler, planet) for me.		
		A	Tell me the names of these objects. (Point to kangaroo, television, motorcycle, telescope, stethoscope.)		
38. **Fluency and Encoding:** The ability to express oneself verbally.	Pupil can communicate verbally, has average fluency of speech without undue hesitation or stuttering, uses coherent sentence structure.	B	Listen carefully and then repeat after me: "Georgie Porgie, pudding 'n pie, kissed the girls and made them cry."		
		M	Tell me all of the things you would like to have for your birthday or for Christmas.		
		A	Describe to me in detail what you would like to do next summer during your vacation.		
39. **Articulation:** The ability to articulate words clearly without notable pronunciation or articulatory problems.	Pupil uses words with correct pronunciation of initial, medial, and final sounds.	B	Repeat after me: "brother," "girl," "snake," "chair," "sled," "train," "rate," "blush."		
		M	Good! Now repeat these words: "yellow," "anything," "spring," "fresh," "music," "twins," "drum."		
		A	Now repeat this: "Rub-a-dub-dub, three men in a tub! And who do you think they be?"		
40. **Word Attack Skills:** The ability to analyze words phonetically.	Pupil can make proper phonetic associations, break down words phonetically, recognize component words.	B	(See Workbook for all three tasks.) Look at these words. Now draw a circle around those words that begin with the sound "ch." Now circle those words that begin with "fl."		
		M	Look at all these words again. Draw a line under all the little words you can find that are part of a bigger word. (Demonstrate using the word "beep.")		
		A	Look how the word "band" is created when you add "b" to "and." Now make four other words by adding different letters to "and."		

Figure 7-2—Continued

Learning Ability	Illustration	Task Level	Specific Learning Task (The examiner should give the following directions to the pupil.)	Notes	Rating Scale VW W A S VS
41. **Reading Comprehension:** The ability to understand what one has read.	Pupil can recall story and paraphrase plot, can explain or relate meaningfulness of what has been read.	B	(See Workbook for all three tasks.) Read this sentence and do what it says.		
		M	Read this sentence to yourself. Now tell me what the snake's name is. What is the turtle's name?		
		A	Now read this story aloud. Tell me who this story is about. What did he do in the winter? What happened when he awoke?		
42. **Writing:** The ability to express oneself through written language.	Pupil can write simple sentences and communicate ideas through paragraph, letter, story, or essay.	B	(See Workbook for all three tasks.) Write your name here. Now copy these two words.		
		M	Copy this sentence.		
		A	Now write this sentence: "The old man caught a big fish."		
43. **Spelling:** The ability to spell in both oral and written form.	Pupil spells within general age expectancy.	B	Tell me how you spell these words: "in" "man" "boy" "house" "person" "Christmas"		
		M	Now write these words for me: "go," "girl," "arm," "watch," "circle," "picnic," "airplane."		
		A	Now write this sentence for me: "The jet airplane circled in the sky."		

CONCEPTUAL SKILLS: The functional level of concept attainment and general reasoning ability. (Basic learning abilities 44-49)

Learning Ability	Illustration	Task Level	Specific Learning Task	Notes	Rating Scale VW W A S VS
44. **Number Concepts:** The ability to count and use simple numbers to represent quantity.	Pupil can count forward and backward to 100, count by twos, group simple quantities upon request.	B	(See Workbook for all three tasks.) Look at these pictures. Put your finger on the picture with the most pumpkins. Now put your finger on the picture with the least number of cats.		
		M	How many pumpkins are there all together? ___ How many cats are there all together? ___		
		A	How many different groups of things are there? ___ How many different sets of things are there? ___		

Figure 7.2—*Continued*

Learning Ability	Illustration	Task Level	Specific Learning Task (The examiner should give the following directions to the pupil.)	Notes	Rating Scale VW W A S VS
45. **Arithmetic Processes:** The ability to add, subtract, multiply, and divide.	Pupil can demonstrate knowledge of basic processes within expectation of his chronological age.	+	(See Workbook for all four tasks.) Do these addition problems for me. (Ans: 5, 10, 17, 52)		
		−	Good! Now do these subtraction problems. (Ans: 4, 4, 7, 64)		
		×	Very good! Now do these easy multiplication problems. (Ans: 16, 72, 477, 345)		
		÷	Fine! Now do these division problems for me. (Ans: 2, 3, 11, 13)		
46. **Arithmetic Reasoning:** The ability to apply basic arithmetic processes in personal and social usage of problem solving.	Pupil can purchase goods and account for funds, knows coinage and exchange, can calculate time differentials, understands weights and measures.	B	(See Workbook for all three tasks. Read problems orally and have pupil follow in Workbook.) At 4¢ each what would two pencils cost? (Ans: 8¢) Bill receives 60¢ allowance every Friday night. If he saved his money for three weeks, how much would he have altogether? (Ans: $1.80)		
		M	If Joe played football for one and three-quarters hours, how many minutes did he play altogether? (Ans: 105) If one-quarter of a pound of butter costs 21¢, how much would you have to pay for one pound? (Ans: 84¢)		
		A	How many quarts are there in two and one-half gallons of ice cream? (Ans: 10) If eight-inch bricks are used to build a curb line four yards long, how many bricks will be needed. (Ans: 18)		
47. **General Information:** The ability to acquire and utilize general information from education and experience.	Pupil is aware of major local and national current events, knows local geography, has concept of city, state, and nation.	B	What is the name of your closest grocery store? Tell me how to get there.		
		M	Tell me what you know about the country of South Viet Nam.		
		A	Explain to me what a city council does.		
48. **Classification:** The ability to recognize class identities and to use them in establishing logical relationships.	Pupil can sort objects by classification, recognize subclasses, verbalize common elements in class identity.	B	(See Workbook for all three tasks.) Look at these pictures and put a circle around the object that is the smallest in real life. Now draw lines under the two objects that are bigger in real life than the others.		
		M	Now put an X on all those objects that have a similar function or purpose. What is that purpose?		
		A	To what classification would these objects belong? dog _____ man _____ ice cream _____ flower _____		

Figure 7-2—Continued

Learning Ability	Illustration	Task Level	Specific Learning Task (The examiner should give the following directions to the pupil.)	Notes	Rating Scale VW W A S VS
49. **Comprehension:** The ability to use judgment and reasoning in common sense situations.	Pupil responds to factual reasoning when situation is explained to him. He can recognize alternatives in situations and can judge actions accordingly. Pupil can identify logical reasons for given actions.	B	If a house were to catch fire, what do you think might happen?		
		M	What happens to rivers in the spring of the year? Why?		
		A	Explain to me how baseball is played. What are some of the rules of the game?		

SOCIAL SKILLS: The skills involved in social problem solving. (Basic learning abilities 50-53)

Learning Ability	Illustration	Task Level	Specific Learning Task	Notes	Rating Scale VW W A S VS
50. **Social Acceptance:** The ability to get along with one's peers.	Pupil can relate meaningfully to others and is accepted in both one-to-one and group situations.	B	Do you have friends? Tell me some of their names.		
		M	Tell me how you play with other children before and after school, during recess, and on weekends. Do you belong to any clubs, gangs, groups, or organizations?		
		A	What are good manners? When and how should you use them?		
51. **Anticipatory Response:** The ability to anticipate the probable outcome of a social situation by logical inference.	Pupil can predict the consequences of his own behavior and that of others in given situations.	B	What may happen to a child who runs into the street?		
		M	George always takes his arithmetic homework home with him, but he hardly ever does it. What do you think might happen to him?		
		A	Tell me some of the things you think might happen to boys and girls who get married too young.		
52. **Value Judgments:** The ability to recognize and respond to moral and ethical issues.	Pupil has a sense of right and wrong, controls own actions, demonstrates proper behavior.	B	Diane found a five-dollar bill on the floor near the classroom door. What should she do with it?		
		M	What do you believe is the most important thing in the world?		
		A	What does "justice" mean to you?		
53. **Social Maturity:** The ability to assume personal and social responsibility.	Pupil is socially mature and independent, demonstrates appropriate citizenship, and assumes social responsibility.	B	Do you think children should have certain chores to do or should be expected to help around the house in some way? Why? What kind of chores?		
		M	Tom was riding his bicycle when he saw two men carrying guns and wearing masks going in the front door of a store. What should he do?		
		A	What do you think are some of the responsibilities of a good citizen?		

Figure 7-2—Continued

A PSYCHOEDUCATIONAL EVALUATION OF BASIC LEARNING ABILITIES

	Performance Level	Learning Disabilities			Learning Strengths	
Name_____ Date_____ _____Age_____ Evaluator_____		Very Weak	Weak	Average	Strong	Very Strong
		0 5		25	75	95 100
GROSS MOTOR DEVELOPMENT						
ROLLING (controlled)						
SITTING (erect)						
CRAWLING (smoothly)						
WALKING (coordinated)						
RUNNING (course)						
THROWING (accurately)						
JUMPING (obstacles)						
SKIPPING (alternately)						
DANCING (eurythmy)						
SELF-IDENTIFICATION (name/awareness)						
BODY LOCALIZATION (part location)						
BODY ABSTRACTION (transfer/generalization)						
MUSCULAR STRENGTH (sit-, leg-ups/bends)						
GENERAL PHYSICAL HEALTH (significant history)						
SENSORY-MOTOR INTEGRATION						
BALANCE AND RHYTHM (games/dance)						
BODY-SPATIAL ORGANIZATION (mazes)						
REACTION-SPEED DEXTERITY (motor-accuracy)						
TACTILE DISCRIMINATION (object identification)						
DIRECTIONALITY (right-left/etc.)						
LATERALITY (hand-eye-foot)						
TIME ORIENTATION (lapse and concept)						
PERCEPTUAL-MOTOR SKILLS						
AUDITORY: ACUITY (functional hearing)						
A—DECODING (following directions)						
A—VOCAL ASSOCIATION (imitative response)						
A—MEMORY (retention)						
A—SEQUENCING (patterning)						
VISUAL: ACUITY ("Snellen")						
V—COORDINATION AND PURSUIT (tracking)						
V—FORM DISCRIMINATION (association)						

Figure 7-2—Continued (Copyright, 1967, by Fearon Publishers.)

	Performance Level	Learning Disabilities			Learning Strengths	
		Very Weak	Weak	Average	Strong	Very Strong
		0 5	25		75	95 100
V—FIGURE/GROUND (differentiation)						
V—MEMORY (visual recall)						
VISUAL-MOTOR: MEMORY (designs)						
VM—FINE MUSCLE COORDINATION (designs)						
VM—SPATIAL-FORM MANIPULATION (blocks)						
VM—SPEED OF LEARNING (coding)						
VM—INTEGRATION (draw-a-man)						
LANGUAGE DEVELOPMENT VOCABULARY (word knowledge)						
FLUENCY AND ENCODING (use and structure)						
ARTICULATION (initial/medial/final)						
WORD ATTACK SKILLS (phonic association)						
READING COMPREHENSION (understanding)						
WRITING (expression)						
SPELLING (oral/written)						
CONCEPTUAL SKILLS NUMBER CONCEPTS (counting)						
ARITHMETIC PROCESSES (+ − × ÷)						
ARITHMETIC REASONING (problem solving)						
GENERAL INFORMATION (fund of knowledge)						
CLASSIFICATION (relationships)						
COMPREHENSION (common sense reasoning)						
SOCIAL SKILLS SOCIAL ACCEPTANCE (friendship)						
ANTICIPATORY RESPONSE (foresight)						
VALUE JUDGMENTS (ethical-moral sense)						
SOCIAL MATURITY (gross problem solving)						

Figure 7-2—Continued

8

The Development of Sensory-Motor
and Perceptual Skills

In recent years increasing emphasis has been placed on the organization of systematic sensory-motor and perceptual training programs as a fundamental part of special education. With the growing awareness that children's abilities develop in a progressive manner as a result of the interplay of maturation and experience, attempts are now being made to provide the child with a healthful early environment, proper stimulation, and appropriately planned educational experiences. It has finally been recognized by most educators that much prior preparation and development are necessary before a child can successfully learn typical school subjects requiring reading, writing, and arithmetic. Evidence has shown that most children with specific learning disabilities have, or had, some sensory-motor and/or perceptual dysfunction requiring remediation. In the author's opinion sensory-motor and perceptual skills are primary developmental requisites to higher forms of learning—before man walks, he must crawl; before understanding what he hears, he must learn to attend and listen; before reading, he must discriminate visually and aurally; before speaking he must babble; before conceptualizing, he must meaningfully relate varied experiences; and before reaching social maturity, he must struggle through stages of self and social awareness.

With the specification of the author's developmental task approach to the programming of basic learning abilities,[1] a number of questions have been raised. The most important question concerns the validity of the rationale for sensory-motor (in this reference also including gross motor skills) and perceptual training as part of special education programs: Do sensory-motor and perceptual skills actually contribute to the development of higher learning processes, such as reading and cognitive ability? If so, how much emphasis should be placed on these skills? Other important questions concern the actual development of an educational program: How should the program units and lessons be organized, and what should the role of parents and supplemental therapy programs be?

Theory and General Research

The rationale for teaching sensory-motor and perceptual skills is based on theoretical formulations, clinical and educational experiments and practice, and research findings. It is important to consider a few of the most outstanding works that have had significant impact on this movement. Certainly, much of the work today is rooted in the theories and reeducational procedures formulated by Séguin[2] and Itard[3] in their attempts to use sensory-motor methods to teach the "unteachable." Over half a century ago Montessori formulated a theoretical rationale for using sensory-motor and perceptual techniques and developed a teacher's handbook of great practical value.[4] A major breakthrough came with the publication of the work of Strauss and Lehtinen in which both theoretical and practical implications for the special education of brain-injured children were presented relative to physiological and psychological studies.[5]

A number of general studies have made contributions to the developing theory and rationale of special training. A prominent psychologist, D. O. Hebb, has presented a neuropsychological theory that helps to explain the role of purposeful action in sensory-motor training activities and is based on the idea that any frequently repeated stimulation leads to the gradual development of "cell assemblies" in the brain. When cell assemblies are repeatedly activated as a result of a specific motor response, they tend to become associated with that activity; this, in turn, may eventuate in neurological growth and learning.[6] In 1966 Rosenzweig published extensive data that would also support this theory. His research with rats showed that measurable changes occurred in the brain as a consequence of experience, and he concluded that "studies also show that differential growth of cortical regions can be induced by specific programs of experience."[7] In generalizing this research to humans, it is felt that it may be possible to develop general

[1] R. E. Valett, *The Remediation of Learning Disabilities* (Palo Alto, Calif.: Fearon Publishers, 1967).

[2] E. Séguin, *Idiocy: and Its Treatment by the Physiological Method* (Albany, N.Y.: Brandon Printing Co., 1947).

[3] J. Itard, *The Wild Boy of Averon* (New York: Appleton-Century-Crofts, 1962).

[4] M. Montessori, *Dr. Montessori's Own Handbook* (New York: Schocken Books Inc., 1966).

[5] A. Strauss and L. Lehtinen, *Psychopathology and Education of the Brain-injured Child* (New York: Grune & Stratton, Inc., 1947).

[6] D. O. Hebb, *The Organization of Behavior: A Neurological Theory* (New York: John Wiley & Sons, Inc., 1949).

[7] M. Rosenzweig, "Environmental Complexity, Cerebral Change, and Behavior," *American Psychologist*, Vol. XXI, No. 4 (April, 1966), p. 102.

abilities by enriching environments and by stimulating total growth of the brain. Further, it is thought that specific skills might be developed through special programming that would affect specific cerebral areas.

Much of this work can be understood in a psychoeducational schema as presented by Piaget's theory of perception.[8] The theory shows perceptual activity as an intimate part of the sensory-motor period and total sensory-motor intelligence, with "intelligence" (or cognitive thought) not resulting until the child frees himself from the immediacies of perceptual and motor activity so that he is able to concentrate on activities involving higher mental processes. Wolinsky elaborates on the educational implications with the statement that "The sensory-motor stage, with its carefully analyzed stage sequences of development (Piaget, 1937, 1945, 1946), presents a unique opportunity for curriculum development. Earlier it was noted that perception is tied up with sensory-motor activity and as such is basically not an act of intelligence. It might be said that possibly, what is seen in the behavioral activity of a brain-injured child is the activity of a child who has not completed the sensory-motor stage in certain areas and who is attempting to build acts of intelligence on a structure that is not yet free of the demands of a sensory-motor period."[9]

With recognition of the probability that cerebral functioning can be enhanced by psychoeducational programming, new impetus has been given to the development of educational therapy and rehabilitation approaches. A number of these new approaches have already begun to have some implications for educational and therapeutic practice. For example, following a review of studies that are relevant to the practice of physical therapy by Granit, Fay, Hagbarth, Rood, and others, Semans concluded that "...it is possible by utilizing various types of sensory stimuli to influence motor response by sensory impulses at spinal levels, at brain stem levels through the reticular facilitatory, and inhibitory systems, and by sensation reaching the cortex through reticular ascending pathways...increased understanding of the physiological mechanisms of sensation, both on and below the level of consciousness, and the role of sensory input in directing motor response should be of great value...."[10]

Such a point of view on the part of therapists and special educators should stimulate applied experiments in sensory-motor and perceptual training curricula and individually prescribed instruction. One notable example of such an approach, which has resulted in much controversy, is the "neurological organization" habilitation program of the Institutes for the Achievement of Human Potential. The basic rationale for this widely known program involving specific educational and physical therapy is the assumption of cerebral change as a result of programmed sensory-motor and perceptual training that is effective in brain-damaged individuals because of the "...anatomic and basic functional symmetry of the brain which makes possible *transfer of function* from a particular area in one cerebral hemisphere to its exact counterpart in the contralateral hemisphere."[11] This program, as well as many others, proceeds on the basis of providing frequent and specific

[8]G. Wolinsky, "Piaget's Theory of Perception: Insights for Educational Practices with Children Who Have Perceptual Difficulties," *Training School Bulletin*, Vol. LXII, No. 1 (May, 1966), p. 20.

[9]*Ibid.*

[10]S. Semans, "Physical Therapy for Motor Disorders Resulting from Brain Damage," *Rehabilitation Literature*, Vol. XX, No. 4 (April, 1959), p. 102.

[11]*A Summary of Concepts, Procedures, and Organization*, pamphlet (Philadelphia: The Institutes for the Achievement of Human Potential, n.d.), p. 5.

training of ontogenetic developmental patterns, which means programming the child through the early developmental stages of gross motor, sensory-motor, and perceptual skill acquisition. That this theory has gained some scientific acceptance and respectability is attested to by the statement of Ayres that "The effectiveness of the principle of following ontogenetic developmental patterns in neuromuscular training has long been recognized as empirically sound . . . following the principle of ontogenetic development requires maturation and integration at each step. Maturation and integration are dependent upon the principle of repetition, for repeated and prolonged motor output in given positions or motions is required. Because of the necessity of requiring repeated motor output, activities play not only the important role of purposefulness for the central nervous system, but also of providing interest during therapy."[12] This is an important statement because it takes note of the value of purposeful activity and interest in sensory-motor training, which is the motivational key to success and may in and of itself justify the activity.

Psychoeducational Research

With this background of theory and general research, it would be expected that a number of educational research designs would have been formulated and subjected to specific investigation and hypothesis testing. The actual availability of applied research results from well-developed and controlled studies in special education or allied fields is, however, most limited. Very few studies have been conducted on a longitudinal basis with an adequate number of subjects, and many of the other available studies have been questioned on the grounds of faulty research design. Whatever limitations there may be, it is important to recognize that some studies have been done in the area of sensory-motor and perceptual training and that a number of tentative conclusions have been made. The general conclusion is well summarized by Frostig's statement that "Without good motor coordination, a child is handicapped not only on the playground, but may also be retarded in all his learning. Moreover, difficulties in motor coordination influence also the perceptual development, as discussed by Kephart and others."[13] The following studies by Painter, Richardson, McConnell, Fowler, and Doman, *et al.* certainly support this point of view.

1. *Sensory-motor and perceptual training:* Painter conducted a study with a small number of children to determine what effect a rhythmic and sensory-motor activity program would have on the motor and spatial abilities of kindergarten children. The educational program involved an integrated sensory-motor skills training session lasting one-half hour and extending over twenty-one days. The program itself consisted of direct teaching of visual dynamics, auditory dynamics, dynamic balance, spatial awareness, tactual dynamics, body awareness, rhythm flexibility, and unilateral and bilateral movements. The structured program resulted in significant and specific changes in skills as compared to the control group, and so the generalization

---

[12]A. Ayres, "Occupational Therapy for Motor Disorders Resulting from Impairment of the Central Nervous System," *Rehabilitation Literature*, Vol. XXI, No. 10 (1960), p. 306.

[13]M. Frostig, "Education of Children with Learning Difficulties," in E. Frierson and W. Barbe (eds.), *Educating Children with Learning Disabilities* (New York: Appleton-Century-Croft, 1967), p. 388.

was made that such a program was preventative of more serious learning disabilities.[14]

2. *Tactile training and language skills:* An indication of the interest of the medical profession in this field is attested to by the work of Richardson on early language training with preschool children. This project cited evidence that "Skill acquired by practice in differentiating solid objects by touch transfers to a visual identification test; that children given tactile training perform significantly better in visual identification than those trained in other ways."[15] This conclusion has many practical implications for pre-language training of children with learning disabilities.

3. *Sensory-perceptual training and the culturally disadvantaged:* After a recent research project involving 121 culturally deprived Negro children, McConnell concluded that a 15- to 20-minute structured sensory-perceptual training period daily, together with specific language instruction periods, "... may be expected to combat in an effective way the sociologically induced mental retardation of such children."[16]

4. *Sensory-motor training and cognitive growth:* In his excellent review of experimental work done in the field of cognitive learning in early childhood, Fowler discussed a number of important studies on motor development and its effect on cognitive growth. His conclusions can be construed as being supportive of the value of sensory-motor training. He points out that many existing studies are inadequate because they do not provide a long enough training period "... to permit mastery of complicated patterns of skills and to accumulate really significant quantities of knowledge. Limited training periods do not allow sufficient time for the conceptual transformation of stable schema."[17] In other words, sensory-motor training programs must be carried on over a long period of time in order for the skills learned to have any effect on total cognitive growth.

5. *Sensory-motor training and mobility effectiveness:* One of the most widely known and controversial studies of the effect of specific sensory-motor training on the mobility skills of children with severe brain damage has been reported by Doman, *et al.* In this study covering a two-year period, 76 children were programmed through specific crawling, creeping, and body activity patterns supplemented by sensory stimulation activities and dominance training. The results were reported without comparison to the usual research control groups. They were felt to be better than previous clinical results from work with such children and "... sufficiently encouraging to warrant an expanded and continued study of these procedures."[18] The authors also

[14]G. Painter, "The Effect of a Rhythmic and Sensory-Motor Activity Program on Perceptual-Motor Spatial Abilities of Kindergarten Children," *Exceptional Children*, Vol. XXXIII, No. 2 (Oct., 1966), pp. 113-116.

[15]S. Richardson, "Early Language Training for the Preschool Retarded Child" (Paper presented at the annual convention of The American Association of Mental Deficiency, Kansas City, Mo., May, 1964).

[16]F. McConnell, "A Method Emphasizing Sensory-perceptual and Language Training for the Culturally Disadvantaged Preschooler" (Paper presented at the 45th Annual International Convention of the Council on Exceptional Children, St. Louis, Mo., March 31, 1967).

[17]W. Fowler, "Cognitive Learning in Infancy and Early Childhood," *Psychological Bulletin*, Vol. 59, No. 2 (1962), pp. 116-152.

[18]R. Doman, *et al.*, "Children with Severe Brain Injuries: Neurological Organization in Terms of Mobility," *The Journal of the American Medical Association*, Vol. 374 (Sept. 17, 1960), pp. 257-262.

stated that "We think that many additional techniques may be developed which could speed the process of habilitation of children with severe brain injuries and perhaps increase the number of types of brain injuries which can be treated."[19]

Because of the widespread favorable publicity (*Life*,[20] and *Readers' Digest*[21]), the general public and parents of handicapped children are more aware of the Doman-Delacato program for neurological organization than of any other sensory-motor training program. Since this program is a highly specific one that has been used in some special education situations, and because many parents and teachers continually request information and professional opinion regarding the value of the neurological organization program, it will be considered in some depth.

The Doman-Delacato Neurological Organization Program

Considerable interest and some research has been generated by the neurological organization theory of Delacato and its stated implications for educational programming. Although most of this theory and the resulting remedial practices stem from premises and sensory-motor training procedures cited earlier, Delacato has integrated them into a systematic program that supposedly also has relevance to the development of higher language skills such as reading.[22] The actual training program varies according to the individual's needs, but group approaches have also been used in formal school settings. In order to consider the limited research available, it is essential to have some concept of the over-all training program and activities themselves. In a general review of the neurological organization program Freeman presents the following overview and concludes that the validity of the objections and the claimed results cannot be established at present.

The hypothesis providing the basis for the methods of the institutes follows the principle that "ontogeny recapitulates phylogeny" and that failure to pass properly through a certain sequence of developmental stages in mobility, language, and competence in the manual, visual, auditory, and tactile areas reflects poor "neurological organization" and may indicate "brain damage." Unlike conventional methods which are said to be "symptomatic," we reach the brain itself by pouring into the afferent sensory system . . . all of the stimuli normally provided by his environment but with such intensity and frequency as to draw, ultimately, a response from the corresponding motor systems. In more severe cases of brain damage, patterns of passive movement are imposed which have as their goal "the reproduction of normal activities which would have been the product of the injured brain level had it not been injured." Several people are required to manipulate repeatedly the extremities and head of the child with "brain damage," in positions determined by the theory and which will not be fully presented here. This manipulation is usually carried out for five minutes at least four times each day, seven days a week. Additional techniques may include: sensory stimulation (not unique with this system of therapy); rebreathing of expired air with a plastic face mask for 30 to 60 seconds once each waking hour (alleged increase vital capacity and stimulate cerebral blood flow); restriction of fluid intake, salt, and sugar (alleged to decrease cerebrospinal fluid production and cortical irritability); early learning of reading (beginning at age 2, if possible); and techniques which are aimed at establishing uniform cortical hemispheric dominance (latter including restrictions on hand use, eye use, or exposure to music; sleep and rest positioning; and visual and gait training). A controversial element of the theory is that enhancement of one function will result in improvements in other areas (e.g., gains in mobility patterns will, without special attention to speech, lead to improvement in expressive language.)[23]

[19]*Ibid.*
[20]*Life*, Vol. 55 (Aug. 23, 1963), pp. 31-36.
[21]Marilyn Segel, "Run Away Little Girl," *Reader's Digest*, Vol. 45 (Nov., 1966), pp. 259-300.
[22]C. Delacato, *Neurological Organization and Reading* (Springfield, Ill.: Charles C. Thomas, Publisher, 1966).
[23]Roger Freeman, "Controversy over 'Patterning' as a Treatment for Brain Damage in Children," *Journal of the American Medical Association*, Vol. 202, No. 5 (Oct. 30, 1967), p. 385.

A few research studies have been made on the neurological organization program. For example, Mariam made a comparative study of the reading disability of 203 neurologically organized and neurologically disorganized fifth-grade children and found that 140 of the group, or 69% were poorly organized, with 137 of these having some type of laterality problem and 63 of the 137 having poor crawling patterns. She concluded that there ". . . is more than a chance relationship between lateral dominance and general neurological development and reading disability."[24] A doctoral study by Miracle on the linguistic effects of neuropsychological techniques in treating a selected group of retarded readers incorporated much of Delacato's training program and concluded that "The utilization of neurological training seems to be of far greater value in helping retarded readers than does reading remediation as given by this writer [Miracle]."[25] Recently, Kershner attempted to determine the effects of a structured program of physical activities upon the physical and intellectual development of trainable mentally retarded children using 14 experimental subjects and 16 control subjects. No significant difference was found in motor skill development although there was a significant difference on the Peabody Picture Vocabulary Test in favor of the experimental group.[26] One of the more extensive studies frequently quoted in the literature is the doctoral research of Robbins on the general validity of Delacato's theory of neurological organization. Robbins utilized 126 second-grade pupils in experimental and control situations that included a three-month specific training program with Delacato methods. The results did not show any significant relationships between training procedures and lateral development or reading, and Robbins concluded that "Since the central concept of the theory—the relationship between neurological organization and reading—has not been supported by the findings, the entire theory is suspect."[27]

SAMPLE CASES

Although the limited research available is inadequate to arrive at any reliable conclusion for the practice of special education, the fact remains that this method of sensory-motor training has many strong adherents and is rapidly spreading throughout the country. Much of this program's strength stems from the claimed behavioral changes in individual children who had not profited under regular special education or related therapy programs. In order to consider this in some perspective, the author has reported objectively on his visitations with four exceptional children who were participating in the neurological organization program. It must be recognized that these reports and conclusions are judgmental opinions based on the author's observations, review of available data, and experience as an educational psychologist and special educator.

1. *Dean:* A nine-year-old third grader with autistic mannerisms, Dean was observed from 8 to 9:30 A.M. in his home. Training began with patterning on the high table; the author, a member of a five-person team, manipulated

[24]S. Mariam, "A Comparative Study of the Reading Disability in Neurologically Organized and Neurologically Disorganized Fifth-grade Children," in C. Delacato, *op. cit.*, pp. 75-108.

[25]B. Miracle, "The Linguistic Effects of Neuropsychological Techniques in Treating a Selected Group of Retarded Readers," in C. Delacato, *op. cit.*, pp. 156-179.

[26]J. Kershner, "Doman-Delacato's Theory of Neurological Organization Applied with Retarded Children," *Exceptional Children*, Vol. XXXIV, No. 6 (Feb., 1968), pp. 441-450.

[27]M. Robbins, "A Study of the Validity of Delacato's Theory of Neurological Organization," *Exceptional Children*, Vol. XXXII, No. 8 (April, 1966), pp. 517-523.

the left arm for a five-minute period. Dean showed little resistance to the rhythmic movements of the patterners. Immediately thereafter, the mother had Dean creep on his stomach up and down the hallway for approximately ten minutes. Then there was a ten-minute period of cross-lateral crawling on all fours, following a taped-track on a rug that was marked for his hands. Next, the mother made a large maze on a chalkboard, and Dean traced this very well while working on the floor. This exercise was followed by having him trace a few cursive words written on the chalkboard. An eye coordination exercise was next. A short two-by-four with small pegs in a number of holes was held in front of his mouth; he jumped one peg over the other down the length of the board. Then a few minutes were spent in a tactile development exercise in which Dean felt different-textured materials and used a paper bag to search for the "heads" or "tails" side of various coins. The final exercise was the alternate stimulation of both eyes by a one-second exposure of a flashlight in the eye, which was repeated several times.

Dean remained cooperative throughout most of the program, but he began to balk somewhat about 9:00 A.M. by pouting, crying, and asking to play games. During the crawling exercise, his mannerisms were ritualistic—it was necessary for him to lick his hand in a certain way as he moved along. Eye contact was indirect and speech lacked fluency and clear articulation. During the period, his little brother and sister watched and urged him on at his tasks. This boy has received speech therapy in the schools but has never been in a special education class. His parents report significant changes in his motor and perceptual skills since beginning this program.

2. *Roberto:* An eight-year-old educable mentally retarded child, Roberto was not attending school but was being patterned throughout the day by his parents and volunteers. The patterning began on the high table with the use of an inclined board that lifted the boy's body up and permitted the workers to take him through a series of swimming-like movements. This was followed with a regular patterning period in which the author manipulated the left leg as a member of the team. Following this activity, Roberto spent about ten minutes creeping back and forth through a creeping box following a small pull-toy pulled by one of the volunteers. During the remainder of a 45-minute observation period, he was engaged with a volunteer in playing with toys and using hand lotion, at which time he spontaneously said, "I have some lotion."

Roberto appeared active and happy and was obviously pleased with the attention he was getting. His mother felt he would profit more at home for the time being, since the EMR program would not be able to give him the individual attention she felt he required.

3. *Lori:* A small, attractive seven-year-old girl, Lori has a diagnosis of severe mental retardation. During the observation, Lori was patterned by the team on a high table with a textured surface for greater stimulation. The author, as a member of the team, turned Lori's head, but there was difficulty in manipulating the child, who tended to resist erratically. Lori then spent about ten minutes creeping back and forth across the room after a pull-toy; her creeping pattern was obviously very poor.

Lori has never been in a public school program, although she has spent three years in the Easter Seal preschool program. She is very uncoordinated, has no speech, and is not toilet trained. However, after being on the program for the past year, she is now beginning to focus on interesting things, is making progress in toilet training, and has definitely improved in strength and the ability to creep across the floor.

4. *Doug:* Doug is eight and one-half years old and is currently in a primary class for the educationally handicapped. This boy has a long history of neurological difficulty and has been on the patterning program for about nine months as an after-school supplement to the EH program.

He was quite responsive and was patterned for the usual five minutes with the author manipulating the left arm. No resistance was evoked, and the mother indicated that the child had been taking swimming lessons and was doing quite well. Some time was then spent on back and forth creeping through a creeping box with a roped top through which he could be observed. The mother also presented a number of small nuts and bolts used in a visual-motor program that reportedly has produced significant results. Doug was restricted from exposure to music while at home in an effort to reduce stimulation of the subdominant side of the brain.

Doug performed his exercises without urging, and his mother appeared pleased at his performance and progress. Doug's mother is a graduate social worker who has spent considerable time in working directly with handicapped children.

OTHER FACTORS

In addition to the specific comments made on each child, several other factors need to be taken into consideration. All of these children were on a sensory-stimulation program that ranged from unstructured play with selected games and toys to direct tactile stimulation, including the rubbing of their skins. Several times a day the children were "masked" by having a plastic bag placed over their nose and mouth for a minute or two, resulting in forced breathing of carbon dioxide, which supposedly stimulates their brain cells. All of the children were restricted in part or whole from musical stimulation in the belief that musical perception is a function of the subdominant cerebral hemisphere and such stimulation interferes with the development of neurological dominance and laterality. These children were also receiving special reading exercises of a sight-word exposure type several times throughout the day. It must be recognized, too, that each of these children was programmed several times daily with the help of many different volunteers (approximately 70 persons per child) who would come into the home once a week for a short period of time. Although the program varies for each child, and this observational report does not adequately present the scope and sequence of activities involved, it is felt to be sufficient for the purpose at hand.

PROGRAM ASSETS

Anyone who has visited children like those described, or who has carefully considered all of the data available, would find it nearly impossible to state categorically that the neurological organization program is without value. In considering these four children, it is felt that the following represent some of the values of the program.

1. *Interpersonal awareness:* As a result of much attention, stimulation, and structured interaction with numerous persons, there is no doubt but that

these children are more aware of themselves in relation to their environment and other people. It would appear that both social skills and total personality development might well occur as a result of such positive and rewarding interaction.

2. *Motor skill proficiency:* There is no reason to doubt that these children improved significantly in various skills, such as crawling, balancing, and visual-motor tasks, and in physical strength. After all, most persons engaged in regular, systematic, motor exercises improve their performance with practice and effort; this can also be expected of children with these specific motor disabilities.

3. *Family integration:* From observable and reported evidence, it appears that there has been a reduction of anxiety and frustration in many of the families involved in this program. As one mother said, "It is a relief to know that we did not cause our child's handicap through mismanagement in his early years and that something can be done about it." The relief from feelings of guilt and anxiety, together with a sense of purposeful involvement with the child, has made for a more livable family situation.

PROGRAM LIMITATIONS

Most of the scientific criticisms of this program are available in previously cited articles and will not be repeated here. Within the context of immediate concern, however, there are at least three major areas that must be construed as containing valid objections.

1. *Vague objectives:* With most of these children, the parental objectives seemed confused. It appears that for many parents, the long-range goal is perceived to be the achievement of normal behavior or near-normal behavior and the concomitant enrollment in regular or special school programs. The underlying rationale of Delacato's neurological organization program leads parents to develop a pseudoreligious belief system in which they become unrealistically concerned about actual cerebral development and neurological organization. This commitment to the development of physiological wholeness, even though the theory of neurological organization lacks sufficient scientific substantiation, precludes focusing on the specification of immediate and short-term behavior goals and the accompanying developmental tasks for *their own extrinsic value*. For example, parents must accept the importance of providing crawling, balancing, and selected visual-motor tasks because these are basic performance skills and goals in their own right.

2. *Harmful aspects:* Several aspects of the program appear to be potentially harmful to the child. Although there is no evidence of actual physical harm or disability resulting from the program, this could be a possible result when, for instance, there is forced head manipulation during patterning of a multihandicapped and resisting child.

   The psychological limitations appear to be greater than the physical, however. Of primary concern are the great demands of time and energy made on many severely handicapped children with the expectation that they conform to the regimen and behave accordingly. The author is of the opinion that such a restrictive program may actually hinder greater development that might result from participation in music, art, crafts, and related physical development programs such as swimming and tumbling, all of which also demand time and energy from the child. Some families have even gone so far as to restrict the child from public school attendance because of the time demands of patterning. It would appear that any child capable of being in any school program should be there where he will have other social and achievement demands made of him that are essential to his total growth and development.

3. *Family restrictions:* If the entire family routine and existence is built around one family member, some serious problems may develop. Restrictions on social participation, musical activities, and time limitations can, even in the best-intended families, result in serious management problems leading to feelings of rejection or alienation on the part of children and parents alike. Although, as has been previously stated, family integration can be furthered by the presence of a handicapped child, it must be recognized that the opposite can also be true. This is especially disconcerting because the family routine is organized around a program in which the measure of a child's progress (evaluation on the Doman-Delacato Developmental Profile) is accepted as the sole criterion by the parents without concern for the lack of scientific validation.

The Doman-Delacato neurological organization program has been reviewed in some detail as an example of a sensory-motor training approach that is currently being used in some special education classes as well as by private therapists and parents. Many of the remedial procedures employed in this program, such as large muscle and sensory stimulation activities can be found in the curricula for the retarded and in Montessori-type schools. There are other similar and widely used programs, such as the perceptual-motor approach advocated by Kephart,[28] the visual perception program developed by Frostig,[29] or Barsch's Movigenics curriculum.[30] The one common element in all of these approaches is an emphasis on the importance of systematically planning gross motor skill activities and on integrating them into a combined sensory and perceptual training curricula as a fundamental prerequisite to achieving academic proficiency.

Program Development and Organization

The parent, teacher, and related professional working with exceptional children who have learning disabilities require guidance and direction in the organization and development of sensory-motor and perceptual training programs. The following recommendations and suggestions for the establishment and operation of such programs summarize the presented data and are offered as a basis for practical program planning.

1. It is recommended that special education programs be organized around the teaching of specific developmental tasks in areas of basic learning abilities. Teachers and others involved should carefully define abilities, disabilities, and the sequential task levels for programming purposes. Related concepts and the instructional rationale should be understood by all those working with the child. It is especially important that all persons working in the program have a positive commitment to a philosophy of growth and human

[28]N. Kephart, *The Slow Learner in the Classroom* (Columbus, Ohio: Charles E. Merrill Books, Inc., 1962).

[29]M. Frostig, *The Frostig Program for the Development of Visual Perception* (Chicago, Ill.: Follett Publishing Company, 1964).

[30]R. Barsch, *Achieving Perceptual-Motor Efficiency* (Seattle, Wash.: Special Child Publications, 1967).

development that stresses the primary role of special education in helping the handicapped child to reach his potential.

2. The training objectives need to be defined in clearly understood behavioral terms. Within the school setting, educational objectives should be related to the instructional program through the development of individual daily lesson plans. Weekly lesson plans and long-range goals also need to be specified by teachers and parents alike, with frequent reexamination of the specified goals and the accompanying educational program.

Within the classroom, structured time periods need to be set aside for working with children who have similar sensory-motor or perceptual problems. For example, a teacher may organize a sensory-motor activity period for four or five children with similar motor problems according to the following daily routine:

Obstacle course creeping	5 minutes
Balance beam activities	3 minutes
Jumping board	2 minutes
Jump rope activities (to music)	3 minutes
Ball bouncing	3 minutes
Sit-ups and push-ups	3 minutes
Form tracing (designs, letters, words)	4 minutes

A program such as this could extend over a considerable period of time and could be modified as necessary to meet the needs of individual group members. The group program should also be supplemented by individual training periods concentrating on the more pronounced learning disabilities that require special attention.

3. The training program must provide for the direct evaluation and reevaluation of sensory-motor and perceptual skills by the special education teacher responsible for the remediation. The teacher should be trained in the use of specific sensory-motor and perceptual scales, inventories, tests and related diagnostic instruments, such as reading tests, that will be directly used in constructing the remedial program. Prior to beginning remedial work, time must be allowed for evaluation of pupils and subsequent consultation with curriculum and psychological personnel.

4. Special education personnel should be fully aware of the extrinsic value of remedial activities used in the sensory-motor training program. Although it is hoped that many of the training activities will have transfer value to the development of higher-order language and cognitive skills, it is important to recognize that "Improvement of a child's general feeling about himself by raising his aspiration level through the enhancement of his motor functioning is justifiable in itself, disregarding any direct relationships between movement and thinking."[31] The sensory-motor and perceptual training program should be accepted as providing meaningful activities for the child that have value as motivational and achievement programs in their own right. Training activities must be planned according to individual need, however, and should not be pressed beyond the point of the child's frustration tolerance or pursued at the expense of related remediation needs of equal value.

[31]B. Cratty, *Developmental Sequences of Perceptual-Motor Tasks: Movement Activities for Neurologically Handicapped and Retarded Children and Youth* (Freeport, Long Island, N.Y.: Educational Activities, Inc., 1967), p. 3.

5. Sensory-motor and perceptual training programs should be planned and carried out on a systematic and regular daily basis with full recognition by the child of the importance of practice and successful achievement of the activity. The purpose of the activity should be explained as clearly as possible in order to obtain the child's full cooperation and commitment.

6. Sensory-motor and perceptual training activities should be integrated into regular school units as much as possible. In addition to individualized and small group prescriptive teaching, there should be opportunities for the development of related skills through participation in music and dance programs, drama, arts and crafts, remedial and adaptive physical education, and through widespread contact with regular children wherever possible. Children with learning disabilities in sensory-motor areas should be attending school with as few restrictions as possible.

7. Parents must be involved in the evaluation and training of children with sensory-motor and perceptual problems. Teachers, psychologists, and curriculum consultants should be expected to work closely with parents in the development of home training and prescriptive approaches to supplement the school program. Special attention should be given when working with parents to help them recognize that "... it is of prime importance, when considering gross motor delay, that the therapeutic program outlined should follow sequential patterns based on normal motor development ... in helping a child move up the developmental ladder, it is important to start a remedial program at a level preceding his present functioning. In this way, we successfully stimulate activity in which both parent and child can achieve a measure of success early, thus preventing discouragement on both sides."[32]

The actual program of parental involvement should be determined by the special teacher who should begin with an explanation of her evaluation of the child and the special class training routine. Home prescriptions for learning should then be given for limited periods of time on a daily basis; they can be modified with time and experience. As an example, a family might spend two 15-minute periods daily in routine jump rope, throwing, balancing, and vocabulary discrimination and reinforcement activities. In addition, interested parents could participate in special sensory-motor and perceptual training tutoring activities with assigned children within the classroom setting.

8. Sensory-motor and perceptual training programs should be developed on an eclectic and pragmatic basis. Training activities should be used if they prove of empirical value, regardless of the source of the method or the theoretical rationale involved. Special education teachers should be expected to refine, adapt, and create their own methods relevant to the needs of the child being worked with.

9. All people directly involved in the training of children with sensory-motor and perceptual problems should be experimentally minded and research oriented. Ideally, they should be involved in an ongoing evaluation of new research and in continual applied research and pilot projects of their own. Emphasis should be placed on new hypothesis formulation, testing, and refinement as it relates to the immediate instructional program.

[32]N. D'Wolf and E. Donnelly, "Home Developmental Guidance Program for Cerebral Dysfunction: Physical Therapy and Cerebral Palsy," *Clinical Pediatrics*, Vol. 5, No. 6 (June, 1966), pp. 351-352.

10. Teachers and psychoeducational consultants must be involved in the ongoing process of curriculum organization and development. The formulation of model lesson plans as proposed by Sutphin[33] and others, and the systematic recording of individual learning prescriptions and approaches should be encouraged. In-service training should provide for the total professional involvement of the teacher in the planning, organization, and evaluation of sensory-motor and perceptual training programs.

An attempt has been made here to consider the importance of providing special instruction for sensory-motor and perceptual disabilities. It is felt that the planning and organization of this instruction must involve parents as well as teachers and consultants. Further, the program must be recognized as part of a broader program that includes language development, conceptual-cognitive skills, and social skills, all of which are dependent upon successful attainment of the more basic learning abilities.

[33]F. Sutphin, *A Perceptual Testing-training Handbook for First-grade Teachers* (Winter Haven, Fla.: Winter Haven Lions' Research Foundation, Inc., 1964).

9

Prescriptive Programming

Successful programming begins with careful diagnosis and task analysis and proceeds through the selection and development of appropriate learning experiences for the individual pupil. The goal of prescriptive programming is to provide remediation of specific learning disabilities and, through successful accomplishment of sequentially selected and increasingly difficult tasks, to prepare the pupil to cope with regular curicular demands insofar as this may be possible.

When the diagnostic teacher has completed her own appraisal of the pupil, she is ready to plan his prescriptive learning program. After a review of the psychologist's psychoeducational prescription and report, together with all supplementary educational and health records, the teacher should integrate all prior data with her own appraisal for immediate planning purposes. The guiding principle in starting work with a child with learning disabilities is to build on his strengths in order to motivate him by initial achievement and to increase his self-confidence. This also enables the teacher to develop a positive relationship with the child without the complications that might possibly stem from beginning failure and frustration if areas of difficulty were immediately programmed.

Once a sound working relationship between teacher and pupil has been established, the second step is to broaden the prescriptive program slowly to include some areas of difficulty. It is best to begin this stage by selecting one or two minor disabilities for programming; the teacher can move into these following a short period of successful work with more easy lesson assignments. In this way it is usually possible to transfer or generalize positive feelings to other learning abilities that may generate more anxiety and frustration. For example, let us consider the profile presented in Figure 9-1. This profile was completed by a teacher who had just finished administering the Psychoeducational Inventory, which was presented in Chapter 7. With this beginning diagnostic information on Jerry, who was nearly ten years old, we can immediately see that he has few strengths and many disabilities. It appears, however, that Jerry has relatively fewer visual and visual-motor problems, and his visual acuity is judged to be strong. Therefore, the teacher could begin programming in those areas. Or, useful programming information could be obtained from reviewing the actual learning tasks that Jerry successfully accomplished on the Psychoeducational Inventory, and then the teacher could begin work with similar types of programming tasks. Another suggested approach would be to start some remedial work on gross motor and sensory-motor skills, such as skipping, body abstraction, and body-spatial organization. From there the teacher would be able to move into areas of more pronounced difficulty, such as directionality and specific language abilities.

The Daily Lesson Assignment

When programming learning disabilities, the teacher must develop individual learning assignments that are highly prescriptive in design. A model lesson plan should be written to the student in words that he can understand. The purpose, of course, is to provide directions and accompanying learning materials that are based on individual pupil needs and that afford a high probability of successful accomplishment.

One such prescriptive approach to daily lesson assignments is shown in Figure 9-2. The teacher prescribes lessons in one or more of the six major learning areas of gross motor development, sensory-motor integration, perceptual-motor skills, language development, conceptual skills, and social skills according to the following guidelines:

1. The daily learning assignments are written or typed out by the teacher for each of her pupils on the day preceding the expected accomplishment of the lesson.
2. The teacher must be selective in assigning appropriate learning tasks. The 53 basic learning abilities are listed along the left side of the form. The ability areas selected for the day's program can be underlined and usually should include at least one ability in each major area.
3. The teacher assigns tasks and related materials in the designated ability area in instructions that the pupil can understand. Instructions must be relevant to the teaching goal or objective and should contain specific references to materials to be used, including book titles, page numbers, workbooks, dittoed material, games, etc. It is also useful to designate any time limitation and whether the task is a group or an individual activity.

A PSYCHOEDUCATIONAL EVALUATION OF BASIC LEARNING ABILITIES

Name JERRY B.
Date 1-19-68   Age 9-11
Evaluator S. M.

	Performance Level	Learning Disabilities			Learning Strengths	
		Very Weak	Weak	Average	Strong	Very Strong
		0 5	25		75	95 100
GROSS MOTOR DEVELOPMENT						
ROLLING (controlled)				✓		
SITTING (erect)				✓		
CRAWLING (smoothly)			✓			
WALKING (coordinated)			✓ →	✓		
RUNNING (course)				✓		
THROWING (accurately)				✓		
JUMPING (obstacles)				✓		
SKIPPING (alternately)			✓ →	✓		
DANCING (eurythmy)						
SELF-IDENTIFICATION (name/awareness)				✓		
BODY LOCALIZATION (part location)				✓		
BODY ABSTRACTION (transfer/generalization)			✓			
MUSCULAR STRENGTH (sit-, leg-ups/bends)				✓		
GENERAL PHYSICAL HEALTH (significant history)			✓			
SENSORY-MOTOR INTEGRATION						
BALANCE AND RHYTHM (games/dance)				✓		
BODY-SPATIAL ORGANIZATION (mazes)			✓			
REACTION-SPEED DEXTERITY (motor-accuracy)			✓			
TACTILE DISCRIMINATION (object identification)				✓		
DIRECTIONALITY (right-left/etc.)		✓ →	✓			
LATERALITY (hand-eye-foot)			✓ →	✓		
TIME ORIENTATION (lapse and concept)			✓			
PERCEPTUAL-MOTOR SKILLS						
AUDITORY: ACUITY (functional hearing)				✓		
A—DECODING (following directions)				✓		
A—VOCAL ASSOCIATION (imitative response)				✓		
A—MEMORY (retention)			✓			
A—SEQUENCING (patterning)			✓			
VISUAL: ACUITY ("Snellen")					✓	
V—COORDINATION AND PURSUIT (tracking)				✓		
V—FORM DISCRIMINATION (association)				✓		

Figure 9-1 (Copyright 1967, by Fearon Publishers.)

	Performance Level	Learning Disabilities			Learning Strengths	
		Very Weak	Weak	Average	Strong	Very Strong
		0 5	25		75	95 100
V—FIGURE/GROUND (differentiation)			✓—	✓		
V—MEMORY (visual recall)				✓		
VISUAL-MOTOR: MEMORY (designs)				✓		
VM—FINE MUSCLE COORDINATION (designs)				✓		
VM—SPATIAL-FORM MANIPULATION (blocks)				✓		
VM—SPEED OF LEARNING (coding)		✓————		✓		
VM—INTEGRATION (draw-a-man)			✓			
LANGUAGE DEVELOPMENT VOCABULARY (word knowledge)				✓		
FLUENCY AND ENCODING (use and structure)			✓			
ARTICULATION (initial/medial/final)				✓		
WORD ATTACK SKILLS (phonic association)			✓			
READING COMPREHENSION (understanding)	1.4		✓			
WRITING (expression)		✓				
SPELLING (oral/written)	1.2	✓				
CONCEPTUAL SKILLS NUMBER CONCEPTS (counting)				✓		
ARITHMETIC PROCESSES ($+-\times\div$)	2.6	✓—	✓			
ARITHMETIC REASONING (problem solving)		✓				
GENERAL INFORMATION (fund of knowledge)			✓			
CLASSIFICATION (relationships)				✓		
COMPREHENSION (common sense reasoning)			✓			
SOCIAL SKILLS SOCIAL ACCEPTANCE (friendship)				✓		
ANTICIPATORY RESPONSE (foresight)			✓—	✓		
VALUE JUDGMENTS (ethical-moral sense)		✓—✓				
SOCIAL MATURITY (gross problem solving)				✓		

Figure 9-1—Continued

DAILY LESSON ASSIGNMENTS

Name_____   Date_____

	Pays Attention (starts work)	Works Hard (good posture and attitude)	Completes Work (neatly done)	Accuracy			Special Behavior Award (1 to 3 bonus points)
				Fair some correct	Good most correct	Exc. all correct	
Points Earned							

Gross Motor Development

Rolling
Sitting
Crawling
Walking
2 Running
Throwing
Jumping
Skipping
Dancing
Self-identification
Body localization
Body abstraction
3, 4 Muscular strength
1 General physical health

Beginning time: 10:00
1. Do daily physical fitness routine.
2. Run around the outdoor track three times.
3. Cross the parallel ladder three times.
4. Do ten pull-ups.

Points Earned							

Sensory-Motor Integration

Balance and rhythm
Body-spatial organization
Reaction speed-dexterity
1 Tactile discrimination
2 Directionality
Laterality
3 Time orientation

Beginning time: 12:30
1. Review the beaded alphabet (lower case).
2. Play the Twister Game with Kent and Scotty.
3. Listen to the record, Telling Time--Facts and Fun with Clock Face.

Figure 9-2

	Pays Attention (starts work)	Works Hard (good posture and attitude)	Completes Work (neatly done)	Fair some correct	Accuracy Good most correct	Exc. all correct	Special Behavior Award (1 to 3 bonus points)
Points Earned							

Perceptual-Motor Skills

Auditory: Acuity
A-Vocal association
1 A-Decoding
A-Memory
A-Sequencing
Visual: Acuity
V-Coordination and pursuit
V-Form discrimination
3 V-Figure/ground
V-Memory
Visual-Motor: Memory
2 VM-Fine muscle coordination
4 VM-Spatial-form manipulation
VM-Speed of learning
VM-Integration

Beginning time: 12:00
1. Listen to a story told to the class by the teacher.
2. While listening to the story, color abstractly on 12" x 18" manila paper.
3. Do the Frostig Figure-ground exercise, number 24.
4. Finish the "Bee Puzzle" from the Sunday newspaper (shapes and puzzle completion).

Points Earned						

Language Development

1-3 Vocabulary
Fluency and encoding
6 Articulation
7 Word attack skills
Reading comprehension
5 Writing
4 Spelling

Beginning time: 8:40
1. Do the Sullivan Workbook Series #1, pp. 32-42.
2. Write answers to the Sullivan questions, pp. 32-42, on lined paper.
3. Review Dolch Basic Sight Words with the aide (5 min.).
4. Take the Reading Road to Spelling, Book I, test on p. 29.
5. Do Noble's Book Exercise, Book 3, p. 17.
6. Use the Phono Wheel to work on blends and initial consonants (5 min.).
7. Listen to the tape, "Listen and Learn with Phonics."

Figure 9-2—Continued

	Pays Attention (starts work)	Works Hard (good posture and attitude)	Completes Work (neatly done)	Fair some correct	Accuracy Good most correct	Exc. all correct	Special Behavior Award (1 to 3 bonus points)
Points Earned							

Conceptual Skills

<u>2</u> Number concepts
<u>1 Arithmetic processes</u>
   Arithmetic reasoning
   General information
<u>3 Classification</u>
   Comprehension

Beginning time: 10:30
1. Complete the exercises in Science Research Associates Book IV, pp. 78-79.
2. Use the filmstrip, "Meeting Math--Pulling Together, #1-B," (a self-programmed filmstrip).
3. Use the Magna Board and make groups of 10 similar class items.

Points Earned							

Social Skills

   Social acceptance
   Anticipatory response
<u>1,2 Value judgments</u>
   Social maturity

Beginning time: 11:10
1. Listen to the filmstrip and recording, "Rudyard Kipling--Elephant's Child."
2. Discuss story read by teacher from <u>Tensions Our Children Live With</u>. (Story should be selected by the teacher to meet the needs of the group at that time.

Citizens' Council Code Awards

Respects Others' Rights (lines up, takes turns, does not hit) _____

Respects Others' Property (helps keep school clean, does not destroy or take things) _____

Attempts To Understand Others' Feelings (does not call names, is courteous and kind) _____

Tries To Be a Good Neighbor (cooperates, raises hand, helps others) _____

Total Points Earned Today_____

Figure 9-2—*Continued*

4. Teachers are encouraged to think in terms of selecting beginning, middle-level, or advanced educational tasks. In general, pupil performance on the Psychoeducational Inventory can be used as a starting point. If, for instance, a child demonstrated great difficulty in accomplishing middle-level tasks, these could be used as a beginning for educational programming. Other tasks on a similar level and ideas for other appropriate instructional materials could be selected from a reference such as *The Remediation of Learning Disabilities*. A 15- to 20-minute work period for each task is sufficiently long for most children with learning disabilities and tasks should be selected that can be completed in that time. Whenever possible, the beginning time should be indicated for each assignment to help provide order and sequence for the learner and the class-room situation.

5. Upon completion of the prescriptive "Daily Lesson Assignment" form, the teacher should clip it to the outside of a large manila envelope labeled with the pupil's name and the heading, "Today's Work." The teacher should put all ditto sheets, workbooks, and related teaching materials necessary to complete the lesson assignments into the envelope and place it on the corner of the pupil's desk where he can expect to find it every morning.

6. Daily lesson assignments should also include occasional work at one or more "learning centers" situated throughout the room. In general, the learning centers should contain highly motivational material and should only be used by assignment or permission. The centers can be used for individual project work, with the pupil being allowed privileged access to them upon completion of his regular lesson assignment. Specific suggestions for each center are listed in Chapter 10.

7. Because of the great importance of developing sound habits of attention and motivation for continued learning, a specific reinforcement system has been built into the daily lesson assignment. Under this system pupil performance is evaluated immediately following completion of the assigned learning task or at the end of the scheduled work period. (The rationale and application of these behavior modification approaches are considered in detail in Chapter 11.)

It is quite apparent that this prescriptive approach to lesson planning requires time from the teacher and ample resource material for program reference. It is also obvious, however, that specific instructions, concrete goals, and individual records all lead to more meaningful evaluation. For children with specific learning disabilities a daily prescriptive approach such as this is essential if remediation is to be relevant and effective.

Long-range Planning

Some comparatively long-range teaching plans need to be considered by professionals working with pupils with learning disabilities. For programming consideration these can be thought of in two major phases. Phase one consists of weekly objectives and includes weekly schedules. Phase two involves semester and yearly plans and recommendations for programming based on teacher experience.

Weekly lesson plans and class program schedules can be extremely helpful to the teacher as over-all guides for where she has been and where she is going. They do not supplant the daily lesson plan assignment, but they do supplement it in a useful way. Weekly plans must provide for the transition and integration of daily plans on a prescriptive basis. Two different examples of common approaches to weekly programming are presented here. The first focuses on the extension and integration of daily plans for the individual pupil (*Fig. 9-3*). In this illustration the basic skill area is listed on the left, and daily activities are indicated for each area. This teacher used *The Remediation of Learning Disabilities* as a programming guide, and the number and letter references refer to the resource programs and activities in this handbook. Six 15-minute work periods are planned daily for Eric, who is with the teacher a total of 90 minutes. This type of plan is to be used by the teacher and not by the student directly; essentially it consists of professional notes that help to relate daily activities into a broader plan with consistent goals. (This teacher elected to omit social skills for this particular pupil and to substitute a combination of language and perceptual-motor skills.)

The weekly class schedule represents a second common approach to lesson planning (*Fig. 9-4*). This plan has been developed by a resource class teacher who sees children individually or in small groups. Programming is accomplished by blocking off given times each day of the week and then carrying through from day to day with a series of related assignments.

Long-range programming also needs to provide for periodic progress reporting and reconsideration of proper pupil placement and educational goals. In most cases the traditional report card system of assigning letter grades or percentage ratings is of little value in working with children with learning disabilities. A descriptive interpretation of the pupil's general progress is required so that it can be meaningfully reported and discussed with the pupil himself, his parents, new teachers, and consultants. The "Pupil Progress Report by Teacher" helps to meet this need, and if completed in midyear and followed up with a case conference, can be an important contribution to the ongoing programming plan (*Fig. 9-5*). Jerry, who is nearly ten years old, is seen by his teacher as having a number of specific learning disabilities. The report focuses on concrete behaviors of concern to the educational situation and so becomes a basis for planning the next step.

The Resource Program

Most teachers beginning work in the field of learning disabilities are not acquainted with resource programs and materials available to them. It is primarily the responsibility of the psychoeducational consultant or program supervisor to inform the teacher of resource programs and materials available for specific remedial purposes and to aid her in selecting and obtaining them. The school psychologist can help significantly by including sample resource program materials in his report. The teacher will need concrete help in selecting and developing appropriate learning tasks for the child. For example, consider some of the possible programming implications from the Pupil Progress Report on Jerry (*Fig. 9-5*). Under the Sensory-Motor Integration section the teacher has indicated that Jerry exhibits confusion in directionality. The next problem, then, is to consider what specific directionality skills have been learned and what new skills need to be taught or reinforced. Resource program ideas such as the following from the author's *The Remediation of Learning Disabilities* can help the teacher decide where to begin teaching directionality (*Fig. 9-6*).

By asking the pupil to perform these skills the teacher might discover that Jerry has few directional problems in body orientation and that he has the most difficulty in applying directional concepts to his environment. Through consideration of the suggested psychoeducational resource program and worksheet the teacher may be able to explore the problem and find ideas for developing more detailed lesson plans.

The Specific Learning Task

The most difficult and by far the most important step in programming learning disabilities is the actual selection and development of the specific learning task to be taught. Selection of the task presupposes that it is appropriate for the pupil and that its probability of successful accomplishment is high. Specific learning tasks may be selected from commercially prepared materials and programs, or they may be developed by the teacher to meet special needs. Two approaches commonly used by teachers in developing specific learning task lessons will be considered here.

The first is a highly specific lesson plan on auditory-sequencing for use by the teacher (*Fig. 9-7*). This plan clearly specifies the learning area and basic learning ability of concern, as well as the specific learning tasks to be taught. The beginning, middle, and advanced stage activities offer a series of increasingly difficult tasks.

A second approach involves independent work by the student (*Fig. 9-8*). This program on reading comprehension is complete in itself since the purpose of the assignment is clear to the pupil and the entire lesson is self-contained—it can be accomplished in one work period and provides varied practice. The particular lesson presented here was designed for use with an upper elementary-age pupil with comprehension problems.

Both approaches to selecting and developing specific learning tasks for pupils with special difficulties should be used. It will always be necessary for the teacher to become directly involved with her pupils and to present and relate lesson content and material. At the same time, self-programmed material should be developed by the teacher as necessary or purchased commercially when new programs appear that may be adapted for use with specific disabilities.

INDIVIDUAL WEEKLY LESSON ASSIGNMENTS

Pupil's name __Eric__ _____ Week __October 7-11, 1968__

Skills	10/7 Monday	10/8 Tuesday	10/9 Wednesday	10/10 Thursday	10/11 Friday
Gross Motor Development	#13:* 1a. Crouch and jump 1c. Foot push 1e. Arm circles	#13: 1b. Pole hang 1f. Torso 1g. Standing run	#7: 1a. Jumping together 1b. Jumping line 1c. One foot jump	#7 and #13: Review all skills practiced this week. Play hopscotch.	#12: Angels in the Snow
Sensory-Motor Integration	#15: Play Blockhead game.	#19: Ditto off mittens. Child colors all those he could wear on his dominant hand.	#16: Use Twister game.	#17: Sort buttons. (Record time.)	#21: 1f. Bouncing 1g. Jumping
Perceptual-Motor Skills	#23: Listen to tape directions. Do what they say on a ditto sheet.	#24: 3e. Listening post reports: Listen to taped story and answer questions about it.	#33: Bead stringing "G" Sewing card "D" [teacher-made projects].	#32: 1a. Show designs for 5 seconds, remove, and have child reproduce.	#33: Typing letter sequences [a teacher innovation].
Language Development	#39: Give child six word cards. Child reads these into tape recorder. Replay. Discuss pronunciation. Teacher says correctly. Repeat. Add more words.		#40: 1a. Vowels and consonants.	#40: Play lake game.	#41. 1a. Meaningful vocabulary. Choose words. Make manuscript and cursive cards for matching.
Conceptual Skills	#45: SRA-V, p. 54	#46: 1a. Money use in a grocery store situation.	#47: 2a. Take walk around school yard. Discuss perceptions.	#48: The Classification Game.	#48: Look for magazine pictures of items that have similar functions.
Language and Perceptual-Motor Skills	#42 and #43: "It, sit." Cursive tracing and then copying.	#42 and #43: Continue from yesterday. Use chalkboard and paper.	#42 and #43: Rainbow writing practice. [Teacher's own technique.] Test.	#38: 1b. Use Peabody kit pictures.	#30: 1b. Visual perception skills and figure-ground perception filmstrips.

*The numbers and letters refer to resource programs and activities in *The Remediation of Learning Disabilities*.

Figure 9-3

WEEKLY CLASS

For week ending _____

Times	8:45-9:45	9:15-11:30	
Pupils	Dean, Phillip	Bruce	
Monday	1. Rolling and Crawling: Valett 1, 3 2. PLDK: Lesson 10 3. CP: Selected visual-form discrimination sheets 4. Play-doh—work with alphabet letters missed	1. Reading: "Funny Bunny," pp. 27-30, and worksheet 2. Vocabulary review on tape 3. Math: Level IV, pp. 271-3 4. PLDK: Lesson 10 5. Filmstrip on weather	
Tuesday	1. Motor skills: Jensen, p. 29 2. PLDK: Lesson 11 3. Continue CP materials 4. Cuisenaire rod play 5. Alphabet puzzles 6. Parquetry designs	1. Word study: "Little White House," pp. 114-115 2. Selected spelling assignment 3. Math: Level IV, pp. 273-4 4. Beginning sounds tape 5. Filmstrip on clay modeling	
Wednesday	1. Walking and Self-identification: Valett 4 and 10 2. PLDK: Lesson 12 3. Poetry on tape 4. Sullivan prereading exercises 5. Block designs	1. Reading workbook test 2. Word analysis: "Little White House," p. 120 3. Tape: "Ned and Nod" 4. Math: Level IV, p. 275 5. Figure discrimination worksheet	
Thursday	1. Running and Self-identification: Valett 5 and 10 2. PLDK: Lesson 13 (taped story) 3. Frostig: Selected eye-motor worksheets	1. Reading: "Something for Betty," pp. 32-34 2. Reading workbook, p. 18 3. Math: Level IV, p. 276 4. Vocabulary, spelling, and writing assignment 5. Record: *Sound of P* 6. Filmstrip: *Wheels and Axles*	
Friday	1. Throwing: Valett 6 2. CP: Figure discrimination worksheets 3. PLDK: Free play with language puppets 4. Puzzle play	1. Word attack material, pp. 134-6 2. "Little White House" worksheet 3. Figure discrimination worksheets 4. Math: Taped combinations	

Program materials code: Jensen—*A Guide to Movement Exploration*
Sullivan—*Sullivan Programmed Reading Series*
Valett—*The Remediation of Learning Disabilities*

Figure 9-4

SCHEDULE

10:00–11:15	11:15–12:00	1:00–2:00
Daniel, Paul	Michael, Gordon	Richard, Terry
1. Cut out and assemble movable figures 2. Reading: Sullivan, Book 1	1. Rhythm exercises 2. Reading: Sullivan, Book 4 3. Read a short story and check comprehension 4. Use ditto sheets on "ill," "all," "ell"	1. Balance beam exercises 2. Reading: Selected from Sullivan 3. Vocabulary tape on "Little White House" 4. Taped story: "Ned and Nod"
1. Story tape: "Ned and Nod" 2. Reading: Sullivan, Book 1 3. CP: Directions and visual perception worksheets	1. Gross motor exercises 2. Reading: Sullivan, Book 4 3. Phonics tape: Blends 4. Taped story for comprehension 5. Reading workbook	1. Balance beam exercises 2. Spelling: Typed list review 3. Taped vocabulary review 4. Selected visual-motor exercises 5. Writing: Plastic overlay and grease pencil
1. Reading: Sullivan, Book 1 2. Math: Tape on combinations 3. CP: Visual perception worksheets	1. Balance beam exercises 2. Reading: Sullivan, Book 4 3. Vowel Lotto game	1. Reading: Selected from Sullivan 2. Taped poetry 3. Cuisenaire rod exploratory play 4. Tracing exercises
1. Reading: Sullivan, Book 1 2. Poetry tape 3. Blocks puzzle	1. Rhythm exercises 2. Reading: Taped short story, comprehension lessons	1. Reading: Selected from Sullivan 2. Frostig visual perception Figure D 3. Record: *Sounds*
1. Consonant Lotto game 2. Magic cards	1. Physical fitness: Exercise record 2. Selected reading games 3. Play games: Take, and a free choice	1. Reading: Selected from Sullivan 2. Spelling test 3. Free play with Play-doh

PLDK—*Peabody Language Development Kit, Level 1*
CP—*Continental Press*
Frostig—*The Frostig Program for the Development of Visual Perception*

WEEKLY CLASS SCHEDULE — *Continued*

For week ending_____

Times	1:30-2:15	2:15-2:55
Pupils	Stephanie	Sandra
Monday	1. Self-identification exercises 2. Selected Sullivan readings 3. Spelling drill 4. Correct math paper 5. Filmstrip: *My Eyes*	1. Selected visual training exercises 2. Filmstrip: *My Body*
Tuesday	1. Sullivan reading 2. Taped vocabulary drill from "Far and Near" 3. Finish math assignment 4. Type spelling words 5. Read-discuss booklet: "My Body"	1. Short story for comprehension 2. Cut out and assemble puppets 3. Balance beam exercises 4. Read-discuss: "My Body"
Wednesday	1. Sullivan reading 2. Write spelling words on board 3. Taped story: "Ned and Nod" 4. Discuss: "My Body"	1. Use visual-motor worksheets 2. Balance beam exercises 3. Taped story: "Ned and Nod" 4. Discuss: "My Body"
Thursday	1. Sullivan reading 2. Write and type spelling words 3. Phonics tape on beginning sounds and blends 4. Discuss: "My Body"	1. Selected visual training exercises from Frostig 2. Balance beam exercises 3. Discuss: "My Body"
Friday	Club meeting for all pupils (social skills discussion)	Go Fish game

Figure 9-4—*Continued*

Note to teacher: First, on the form entitled, "A Psychoeducational Evaluation of Basic Learning Abilities," evaluate *present* functioning in the basic learning abilities by marking the performance level. Then, in January and June at the end of each school semester, complete the "Pupil Progress Report," indicating the present educational program and progress to date. Make two copies of that report. Place the original in the special cumulative record folder. Send the carbon to the office of the director of special education for inclusion in the pupil's central file.

PUPIL PROGRESS REPORT BY TEACHER

Pupil's Name Jerry B.   *Birthdate* 2-26-58   *Grade* Intermediate

Address 42 Menalto St., Sacramento, Calif.   *Telephone* educationally handicapped

GROSS MOTOR DEVELOPMENT   (Programs and progress in motor activities, physical education, general health, etc.)

Sitting posture needs to improve. Needs to practice crawling pattern, walking backward, and jumping rope backward. In all other gross motor activities he does well. Participates well in physical education. His general health appears good.

SENSORY-MOTOR INTEGRATION   (Programs and progress in motor integration, art, music, etc.)

Jerry has difficulty imitating body positions in space. He is confused in directionality and laterality. He has little awareness of seasons, months, etc. He cannot tell time.

PERCEPTUAL-MOTOR SKILLS   (Programs and progress in perceptual skills, including listening, attention and memory, fine muscle coordination.)

Auditory memory and sequencing is weak. Response is very slow. He is very observant of the things around him. He has difficulty seeing small words in larger ones but is able to see hidden pictures in diagrams. Visual-memory is good. Speed of learning is slow. He is very proud of neat papers--both written or art assignments.

Copyright 1967, by Fearon Publishers.

Figure 9-5

LANGUAGE DEVELOPMENT   (Programs and progress in language usage, including functional level of reading, writing, and spelling.)

Wide Range Achievement Test Reading Grade Placement 1.4, Spelling 1.2; word attack skills very weak. He cannot distinguish the sound of "w" from "r," or "f" from "v." He has difficulty building words when given the ending, e.g. -an, man. Comprehension fair when he can read the material.

CONCEPTUAL SKILLS   (Programs and progress in arithmetic understanding, social studies, fund of information, concept development.)

Wide Range Arithmetic 2.6. Counts fairly well. Addition and subtraction weak. Does not understand other processes. Arithmetic reasoning very weak. Has some difficulty with classification.

SOCIAL SKILLS   (Programs and progress in social and personal development, including self control, responsibility, and general behavior.)

Lacks self-confidence. Has been able to dodge responsibility by saying "I don't know" or "I don't understand." Still does some name calling but becomes very upset if others do this to him. Seems to have several friends in his neighborhood. Is frequently in trouble on the bus. Still tries to get by with the least amount of effort on his part. Can do very well when he wants to.

GENERAL COMMENTS

Continue in his present program and school placement.

What recommendations do you have regarding educational placement and programs for this pupil for the forthcoming semester or year?

Signed: _____*Susan Monroe*_____   ___Educationally Handicapped___
                              Teacher   Type of Special Class

___*John M. Warren* Taft_____   ___1-4-68___
        Principal   School   Date

Figure 9-5—Continued

SENSORY-MOTOR INTEGRATION

PSYCHOEDUCATIONAL RESOURCE PROGRAM NUMBER **19**

Directionality

DEFINITION: The ability to know right from left, up from down, forward from backward, and directional orientation.

ILLUSTRATION: Pupil can write and follow picture story or reading material from left to right, discriminate right and left body parts and those of other people, locate directions in room and school.

EDUCATIONAL RATIONALE: Since many learning and problem-solving situations require directional orientation, it is important that these skills be specifically taught if necessary. Such instruction should begin with body orientation and proceed to object relationships and concrete applications.

SUGGESTED PROGRAM IDEAS

1. Body Orientation
   a. Hand and foot identification: Place red ribbon or bracelet on right hand and leg. "Simon says touch the floor with your right hand." "Shake your left foot." "Touch your right foot," etc.
   b. Other body parts: Teach right and left ears, fingers, toes, shoulders, ankles, knees, legs, arms, elbows, wrist, teeth, sides of body. Play body identification games such as follow-the-leader.
   c. Music and rhythm: Play marching music and give commands: "Stamp your left foot." "Slap your right side," etc.
   d. Tracing: Trace and cut out right and left hands and feet. Color or paint, and place on bulletin board for constant reference.
   e. Whole body movement: Give directions: "Move over to the left of John." "Sit in the chair to the right of my desk." "Crawl under the first table to the left of the door," etc.
   f. Finger localization: Ditto off standard left and right hand designs. Give directions: "Color the left finger green." "Place a ring on the right first finger." "Put an x on the left thumbnail." "Place your left thumb on your right little finger," etc.
   g. Body imitation: Teach pupil to *name* what body part teacher or other pupil is moving and then to duplicate the movement ("left thumb," etc.).

2. Object Relations
   a. Paper marking: Teach marking and drawing on right, left, middle, top, and bottom parts of paper according to directions.
   b. Alternate commands: Instruct pupil to respond with the opposite direction: "Raise your right hand" (left). "Grasp your left shoulder" (right), etc.
   c. Sorting games: Have children sort right and left gloves, shoes, paper hand and foot outlines, up and down objects (birds, submarines, etc.).
   d. Dressing: Have children put on right or left shoe, glove; untie and tie shoelaces; place things in pockets, etc.
   e. Up-down/above-below: Teach concepts and practice placing the book *up* on the shelf, putting the paper *down* in the basket, tossing the ball *above* the head, crawling *below* the table, etc.
   f. Map directions: Teach north, south, east, west. Locate and mark sides of the room. Generalize to school layout. Play games with children placing themselves according to map directions: "Billy go north of Mary."
   g. Jump to music: "Jump in—jump out—jump north—jump south," etc.
   h. General objects: Teach right-left discrimination of animals, cars, buildings, trains, theaters, etc.
   i. Drawing: Place x mark on the left side of board or paper for pupil to begin drawings.

3. Application and Generalization
   a. Pledge of allegiance: Stand on *right* side of the desk with *right* hand on the heart.
   b. Picture identification: Show photographs and magazine pictures of persons and directional objects and have pupil identify. Use colored slides and films for directional discussion.

Figure 9-6 (Copyright 1967, by Fearon Publishers.)

c. Chalkboard and paper orientation: Practice marking and doing exercises on right, left, top, bottom, middle, etc. Use marble boards.

d. Map projects: Locate directions, common buildings, and places on city and area maps. Draw map of school and neighborhood.

e. Writing: Trace patterns and words with crayon, beginning at left side marker and proceeding to the right. Have children sign their names on paper in upper *left* corner to avoid reversals.

f. Sequential activities: Arrange sequence puzzles or cartoons from left to right on desk, floor, chalkboard trays, etc. Arrange wooden number series and word forms from left to right.

SAMPLE PROGRAM

Activity A is an orientation game requiring the child to write "right" or "left" on the object or objects indicated.

Activity B continues the exercise to "up" and "down" objects.

Program C uses a marble board for the pupil to follow directions. "Place a marble second row, upper right side," etc.

Exercise D provides simple left to right tracing exercises.

All programs should be modified or extended to meet the needs of individual pupils.

REFERENCES

1. Related Programs
   a. *Developing Body-Space Perception Motor Skills,* Album 2 (Record), Educational Record Sales, 500 S. Douglas Street, El Segundo, Calif.
   b. *Which Way?* Rand McNally & Co., P. O. Box 7600, Chicago, Ill. 60680
   c. *Marching Along* (Record), Educational Record Sales
   d. "Differentiating Left from Right," *The Frostig Program for the Development of Visual Perception: Teacher's Guide,* 1964, pp. 54-68, Follett Publishing Co., Chicago, Ill. 60607
   e. Kephart, Newell C., *The Slow Learner in the Classroom* (Directionality programs), 1962, pp. 46-69, Charles E. Merrill Books, Inc., Columbus, Ohio 43216
   f. Zweig-Bruno Stereo-Tracing Exercise Pads (For proper directionality), Keystone View Company, Meadville, Pa. 16335

2. Instructional Materials
   a. Judy See-Quees, Series 12, The Judy Company, Minneapolis, Minn. 55401
   b. Mazes and directional puzzles
   c. Old jewelry bracelets for arms and legs
   d. Colored ribbons for activity programs
   e. Record player
   f. School-made map and layout, city, state, U.S., world maps
   g. Felt pens and drawing paper
   h. Stencils and forms for directional tracing
   i. Wood lower-case letters, #A561; Wood numerals, #A562, Creative Playthings, Princeton, N.J.

3. Further Evaluation
   a. Money Roadmap Test of Direction Sense, Johns Hopkins Press, Baltimore, Md. 21218
   b. Porteus Maze Tests
   c. Subjective appraisal of pupil response to directional commands, drawing, and writing activities

4. General Reference
   Benton, Arthur L., *Right-Left Discrimination and Finger Localization,* 1959, Paul B. Hoeber Co., New York, N.Y.

Figure 9-6—*Continued*

Directionality

A   NAME THE OBJECT "RIGHT" OR "LEFT"

B   NAME THE OBJECT "UP" OR "DOWN"

Figure 9-6—*Continued*

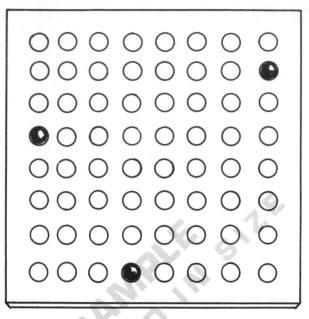

C   MARBLE BOARD

D   TRACING

Figure 9-6—*Continued*

LESSON PLAN FOR TEACHER USE

Learning Area: Perceptual-motor skills
Basic Learning Ability: Auditory decoding
Materials Required: Beginning activity—four rhythm sticks
Middle stage activity—none
Advanced activity—none

Learning Tasks

Beginning Activity

I'm going to tap a rhythm with these sticks. Listen very carefully. When I finish, I want you to tap the same rhythm. (Use rhythms below.)

1. __   _____ _____ _____
2. _____ _ _ _____ _____
3. _ _ _ _ _____ _____
4. _____ _____ _ _ _
5. _ _ _____ _ _ _____
6. _____ _ _ _____ _ _

Middle Stage Activity

Listen very carefully to this sentence. Then I want you to say exactly the same thing.
    1. The elephant is gray.
Good! Now I'm going to add another word to the sentence. Listen and say it after I finish.
    2. The big elephant is gray.
Fine! I'll add another word now.
    3. The big circus elephant is gray.
Let's continue now in the same way. Each sentence will be a little harder than the one before.
    4. The big circus elephant is gray and has large ears.
    5. The big circus elephant is gray and has large, droopy ears.
    6. The big circus elephant is gray and has large, droopy ears and a long trunk.
    7. The big circus elephant is gray and has large, droopy ears and a long trunk full of
       water.
(Use the sentences above until the child cannot remember and repeat them.)

Advanced Activity

I'm going to read a short poem. I want you to listen very carefully to hear what the ducks do in this poem.

Flip, flop,   Splish, splash,
Flip, flop,   Splish, splash,
Ducks marching in a row.   They dive and swim about.
Flip, flop,   Then phlot, phlot,
Flip, flop,   Phlot, phlot,
A-swimming they all go.   They shake the water out.

Now can you tell me the things that the ducks did? (Allow time for response.) What did they do first? Second? Next? Last? (Then proceed to teach the poem to the child in a rote manner, one line at a time, continually repeating.)

Figure 9-7

LESSON PLAN FOR PUPIL USE

Specific Learning Task: To develop reading comprehension.

Directions: Read the story. Write in the answers to the questions. Group the words in the lists by writing them in the boxes where they belong.

Billy lives in Sacramento, California. His father works in a department store as one of the managers. Billy often visits his father on Saturdays. This Saturday is very special, for Billy's father has promised him a big surprise.

What do you suppose Billy saw when he visited the store and rode up the escalator? Many balloons of all sizes and colors were drifting around everywhere! In some departments clowns were helping the shoppers! The circus had come to help the store celebrate its 120th birthday!

But where were the animals? Ah . . . that was the best surprise of all! The animals were in their cages on the circus wagons ready for the big parade down the main street. And that's not all! Billy will ride in a car in the parade with his father.

1. What was Billy's father's job?_____

2. Why was this Saturday a special day?_____

3. What did Billy see in the store?_____

4. Who had a birthday?_____

5. What was the best surprise?_____

now	shoes	lettuce	yo-yo
bread	milk	after	glove
drum	dress	ice cream	before
sweater	scooter	wagon	later

later	dress	ice cream	yo-yo

Figure 9-8

10

Program Organization

The actual programming of learning disabilities in the public schools occurs within a distinctive institutional system. The crucial aspects of this system are reflected in the organizational pattern of the local school and in the kinds of educational opportunities it offers its pupils. Financial resources of the school district obviously have much to do with the scope and variety of programs offered. Population characteristics and numbers also have significant impact on organizational possibilities since school size, number of classes, class size, and availability of consulting personnel are all important factors over which school principals and teachers have little or no control.

However, within the given school setting a number of alternate organizational possibilities exist. Once a commitment is made to the early identification and prevention of learning disabilities it can be achieved in part through the actual organizational and grouping pattern used in assigning pupils to teachers and classes. The individual class organization, room layout, and the special equipment and materials to be used all need to be considered as part of the problem of program organization.

School Organization

Only a few of the most important aspects of school organization affecting early identification, programming, and prevention of more serious learning disabilities will be considered here. The starting point should always be with the nature of the *preschool program* since it is here that much early identification and remediation can take place. Many schools already have provisions for cooperative nursery schools or compensatory Head Start-type programs. The crucial programming and organizational problem here is to provide adequate consulting help so that the psychoeducational needs of the prekindergarten child can be evaluated and the necessary educational interventions made. It is essential, for instance, that early childhood programs include consulting psychological and speech development services.

For the vast majority of children formal education will not begin until kindergarten or later. Thus the problems of evaluation and programming often need to be confronted initially at this level. The kindergarten years should be recognized as the most important in the learning sequence; classes should be kept small and adequate teacher time should be allowed to do the job that is required. It is advocated here that kindergarten teachers be assigned a reasonable number of pupils (no more than 20) on a three-hour daily basis. The remainder of their time during the school day would be devoted to working with individual children and families, and to lesson planning. During the first three months of school there can be general random grouping when free play, introduction to organized activities, and systematic observation by the teacher comprise the class program. In the afternoon individual evaluations can be made using such instruments as the Developmental Survey,[1] and counseling and planning with the family as to the child's specific educational needs can be accomplished. Following Christmas vacation, the initial evaluation period should be completed, and children should be reorganized into various kindergarten classes according to behavioral level and developmental needs. For example, by using the Developmental Survey and other data it is quite possible to arrive at the following behavioral groupings:

1. *Mature group:* Developmentally advanced, no significant learning problems apparent. Advanced in specific language and conceptual skills. Obviously ready for more formal learning programs as offered in traditional first-grade programs.
2. *Average group:* Normal preschool/kindergarten development. In need of continued maturation and developmental readiness experience.
3. *Immature group:* Developmentally speaking, four years of age or younger with obvious immaturity in basic motor, perceptual, language, and conceptual skills requiring special intervention. A two-year kindergarten and/or special experimental program may be required.

In addition to initial kindergarten evaluation and programming, school organization should provide some means of continued placement and grouping taking into consideration both developmental level and achievement. The new nongraded methods of elementary school organization offer the greatest flexibility to this end. Through placement of pupils in classes according to their actual performance level in the learning skill or tasks of concern, a high probability of successful accomplish-

---

[1] *Valett Developmental Survey of Basic Learning Abilities* (Palo Alto, Calif.: Consulting Psychologists Press, 1966).

ment can be assured. In addition to nongraded level groupings, provisions should be made for early and late classes for small-group language skill instruction. Instruction could be intensified by scheduling the most immature pupils in language skills in any class for separate early morning attendance. Then, after these children go home in the early afternoon, the more mature language arts pupils are afforded their special instructional time as well. In addition, some selected kindergarten or primary teachers should have an hour or so in the afternoon set aside for individual work with both primary and upper elementary pupils with specific learning disabilities. Such a tutorial system built into the regular organizational schedule can be of inestimable value as both a remedial and preventive provision.

School organization must also provide effective faculty orientation and involvement in the total programming of pupils with learning disabilities. Through faculty and in-service training meetings various ideas about scheduling, exchange programs, tutorial and evaluation approaches, and other relevant procedures can be investigated. If a special education program for remediating learning disabilities is to be established in the school, it is imperative that the faculty be given orientation and be involved in screening, referral, identification, and programming problems as early as possible. Once the special program has been established there should be continued faculty involvement through such means as regular case conferences on special pupils of concern. The special teacher should work cooperatively with regular teachers to further success experiences for the pupil integrated in some regular class activities. There might also be an arrangement whereby regular teachers could visit the special class in their school to observe the program in action and to consider some of the programming implications for their own classes.

Special Class Organization

A special class for the remediation of pupils with learning disabilities should be organized to permit as much integration with the regular program as possible. Although some children may require a complete self-contained classroom placement throughout their entire school career, most pupils can be integrated for part of the day. Integration normally begins with placement in those classes or school activities where the probability of success is high. With many youngsters this may result in gradual integration into nonacademic subjects such as art, music, and physical education. The degree of integration possible depends on the size of the school and the classes, and on the receptive nature of the regular teachers.

In order to accomplish the primary goal of remediation, such factors as the size of the special class, age range, and priority criteria for placement need to be considered. If remediation is to be successful, the special teacher should be limited to working with a relatively small number of pupils. Whenever there is an age span of more than three years it is usually necessary to limit the class to between nine and eleven children and to provide a full-time teacher's aide. On the other hand, if teachers work on a resource-centered class basis and provide intensive tutoring with one or two children at a time, it may be possible to work with a dozen or more pupils without a teacher's aide. Ideally, it is wise to restrict pupil age span in one class to three years or less. It is also recommended that new programs be started with at least two teachers working cooperatively in the same school so that they can offer support and encouragement to one another. When priority criteria have to be established, it is suggested that primary-aged and younger elementary pupils be given preference because of the preventive value of early remediation. Hence, a school district might begin a program with one class for children aged six to eight and a second class for pupils aged eight to ten. An alternate approach often used is to begin one primary self-contained class and to organize the second class as a resource-centered group with all elementary-aged pupils who come and go as needed for special tutorial remediation.

Once the age range and number of pupils has been decided some flexible daily programming schedule must be arranged. A model "Recommended Daily Schedule for Elementary Learning Disability Classes" is presented in Figure 10-1. This schedule divides the day into the major areas of remedial instruction for both early and late language skills groups. For example, the early group, consisting of five or six children, would arrive at 8:35 A.M. and immediately become involved in gross motor skill programs that would help both to remediate and to relax them for the more demanding programs to follow. A one-hour language skills session would then provide for varied language activities including silent and oral reading, writing, and vocabulary development. The late group then arrives, and the entire class continues as a whole until the early group leaves and the late group receives its intensified language instruction.

A very important aspect of this model schedule is the built-in provision for periodic evaluation approximately every 20 minutes; the actual evaluation procedure will be discussed in detail in Chapter 11.

RECOMMENDED DAILY SCHEDULE FOR ELEMENTARY LEARNING DISABILITY CLASSES

Gross Motor Skills

8:35	Early group arrives.
8:40-8:55	Individual and group calisthenics, muscular strength, health, and body schema activities (outside of classroom)
8:55-9:00	*Performance evaluation*

Language Skills

9:00-9:15	Language development
	Fluency and encoding—(oral speaking)
	Articulation—(show and tell, Peabody Kit and lessons)
9:15-9:20	*Performance evaluation*
9:20-9:35	Reading group A—(silent, taped, and programmed reading)
	Reading group B—(oral reading, writing, and vocabulary development)
9:35-9:40	*Performance evaluation*
9:40-9:55	Reading group B—(silent, taped, and programmed reading)
	Reading group A—(oral reading, writing, and vocabulary development)
9:55-10:00	*Performance evaluation*
10:00-10:15	Early group recess

Gross Motor Skills

9:55-10:10	Late group arrives and has gross motor skills training.
10:10-10:15	*Late group performance evaluation*

Figure 10-1

Conceptual Skills

10:15-10:35	Number and arithmetic concepts (both groups working together)
10:35-10:40	*Performance evaluation*
10:40-11:00	General concepts: classification/comprehension/thinking skills
11:00-11:05	*Performance evaluation*

Sensory-Motor Integration

11:05-11:25	Balance and rhythm, body-spatial organization, reaction speed-dexterity, tactile discrimination, directionality, laterality, time orientation activities
11:25-11:30	*Performance evaluation*

Break

11:30-11:50	Lunch
11:50-12:00	Recess

Perceptual-Motor Skills

12:00-12:25	Auditory, visual, visual-motor training
12:25-12:30	*Performance evaluation*

Social Skills

12:30-12:50	Social acceptance, anticipation, value judgments, responsibility training (social science units, audio-visual presentation and discussion)
12:50-12:55	*Performance evaluation*
12:55-1:15	Citizens' Council and peer group evaluation

Break

1:15	Early group leaves. (Selected children may be enrolled for both early and late language skills class.)
1:15-1:25	Late group recess

Language Skills

1:25-1:40	Reading group C (silent, taped, and programmed reading)
	Reading group D—(oral reading, writing, and vocabulary development)
1:40-1:45	*Performance evaluation*
1:45-2:00	Reading group D—(silent, taped, and programmed reading)
	Reading group C—(oral reading, writing, and vocabulary development)
2:00-2:05	*Performance evaluation*
2:05-2:20	Language development
	Fluency and encoding—(oral speaking)
	Articulation—(Peabody Kit and lessons)
2:20-2:25	*Performance evaluation*
2:30	Late group leaves.

Figure 10-1—*Continued*

Classroom Organization

The physical organization of the classroom also greatly affects the learning process. If adequate equipment and learning centers are available, pupil programming in accordance with the suggested model schedule becomes more feasible because both individual and small group specialized instruction is enhanced. The following is a recommended basic equipment and programmed materials list for an elementary class.

1. *General requirements*
   a. Full-sized room with built-in sink and storage units
   b. Teacher's desk, chair, and locked file
   c. Eleven single-unit pupil study desks and attached chairs
   d. Four private study offices (2½' square x 4' high)
   e. Three movable screens (5' x 6')
   f. Eleven movable pupil chairs
   g. Adequate chalkboard and bulletin board areas
   h. Folding cot
2. *Gross motor training center*
   a. Exercise mat (4' x 7')
   b. Walking board
   c. Balance beam
   d. Jumping board
   e. Jump ropes
   f. Selected weights, balls, and remedial physical education equipment
3. *Sensory-motor training center*
   a. Sand table
   b. Craft table and selected arts and crafts materials
   c. Double painting easel
   d. Piano
   e. TAC—Training of Attention and Concentration Program (Educational Research Associates)
   f. *The Letter Form Board* (Houghton Mifflin Company)
   g. Music center with listening posts and selected records
4. *Perceptual-motor training center*
   a. Tape recorder and listening post
   b. Kinesthetic alphabet
   c. Form and puzzle board and blocks
   d. Winter Haven templates and various geometric inserts and frames
   e. Etch-a-sketch and similar perceptual-motor toys
   f. ERIE Program 1 (Teaching Resources, Inc.)
   g. TRY—Experiences for Young Children (Noble & Noble Publishers, Inc.)
5. *Language training center*
   a. Primary typewriter
   b. Language Master or EFI Model 101 System
   c. Individual filmstrip projector and selected filmstrips
   d. Peabody Language Development Kit, Level 1
   e. *Handwriting with Write and See* (Lyons & Carnahan)
   f. Lift-off to Reading (SRA)
   g. Sullivan programmed reading series
   h. Library of assorted reading materials

6. *Conceptual-cognitive skills training center*
   a. Science table and experimental equipment
   b. Cuisenaire rods and programs
   c. Learning To Think series (SRA)
   d. Let's Look at Children Program (Educational Testing Services)
   e. Chess and other cognitive games
   f. Assorted science and math books, riddles, games, etc.
7. *Social skills training materials* (no special center)
   a. Filmstrips on manners and social skills
   b. Selected records and picture books
   c. Books on values and social skill themes (Human Values Series by Steck-Vaughn Company, etc.)

Figure 10-2 shows a model room layout with a central working area surrounded by the various learning centers. A rest area, which can also serve for isolation purposes, is screened off from the remainder of the room. Because of the heavy utilization of audiovisual materials, it is recommended that electrical outlets be available on all walls. In addition to other equipment listed, the room should contain a portable cartridge tape recorder with earphones that can be moved rapidly from center to center or desk to desk as the occasion demands. Adequate storage space should also be provided in each work center area.

MODEL ROOM LAYOUT FOR LEARNING DISABILITY CLASSES

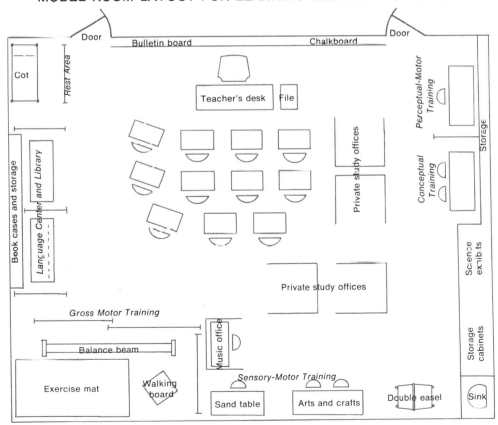

Figure 10-2

Program Materials and Equipment

The first part of this chapter has covered some of the basic aspects of program organization for schools and classes concerned with the remediation of learning disabilities. In larger school districts it may be desirable to organize classes for a very narrow age group. If this happens, organizing curricular materials and providing for scope and sequence throughout the entire program becomes a major problem.

The remainder of this chapter consists of recommended program materials covering kindergarten through senior high schools. A sample item listing of furniture and capital outlay equipment recommended for use in primary (P), intermediate (I), and upper elementary (U) is included. The chapter concludes with a brief listing of major professional teacher references of proven value in beginning learning disability programs. These lists should be considered as illustrations of the type of detailed information that must be made available to teachers and principals involved in program development and in the requisitioning of related materials. Each school district must, of course, develop its own specific list with code numbers and current prices. It is also strongly recommended that professional reference books and instructional program materials be obtained for use in preliminary in-service training programs for teachers well in advance of the actual opening of classes for pupils with learning disabilities.

PROGRAM MATERIALS

Kindergarten Learning Disabilities Class: Ages 5-7

Learning Area	Materials	Equipment
Social skills	*Your World,* Series I and II, 5 books each series (Taylor Publishing Co.) Social Skills section, *The Remediation of Learning Disabilities* (Fearon Publishers)	
Conceptual skills	*Kindergarten Evaluation of Learning Potential Program* (McGraw-Hill) *Concept Picture Puzzles and Charts* (set) (Harcourt, Brace & World) Conceptual Skills section, *The Remediation of Learning Disabilities* (Fearon Publishers) *Color Concepts,* Record CL18 (Bowmar Records)	Record player
Language skills	*Readiness in Language Arts* (Behavioral Research Laboratories) *Invitations to Story Time Series,* #2767-66 (Scott, Foresman) *Peabody Language Development Kit,* Kindergarten (American Guidance Service, Inc.) *Goldstein-Levitt Reading Readiness Program* (Follett Publishing Co.)	

Learning Area	Materials	Equipment
Language skills— Continued	Language Skills section, *The Remediation of Learning Disabilities* (Fearon Publishers) *An Experience-centered Language Program* (Franklin Publications, Inc.)	
Perceptual- motor skills	*My Weekly Reader Series*: Zips Book of Animals, Wheels, Puzzles (American Education Publications) *Perceptual Form Home Training Guide Kit* and teachers' templates (Winter Haven Lions' Research Foundation) Perceptual-Motor Skills section, *The Remediation of Learning Disabilities* (Fearon Publishers)	Tape recorder
Sensory- motor skills	*Let's Find Out Program* (Scholastic Magazines, Inc.) Touch ABC Boards (Warren's Educational Supplies) *Letters Are for Fun,* kinesthetic book (Touch Aids) Sensory-Motor Skills section, *The Remediation of Learning Disabilities* (Fearon Publishers)	Piano Sand table, #ID920 (Lakeshore Equipment Co.) Balance board, #WP52 (Creative Playthings)
Gross motor skills	*Basic Songs for Exceptional Children,* Records #1, 2, 3 (Children's Music Center) *Animals Rhythms,* Records (Educational Record Sales) Gross Motor Skills section, *The Remediation of Learning Disabilities* (Fearon Publishers)	School play mat, 4' x 6', #E8006 (Lakeshore Equipment Co.) Jumping board, BJ (California Correctional Industries) Tricycles, wagons, etc.

Primary Learning Disabilities Class: First year, Ages 7-8

Learning Area	Materials	Equipment
Social skills	Basic Social Studies Discussion Pictures (Harper & Row) *Useful Language 1* (Continental Press) Social Skills section, *The Remediation of Learning Disabilities* (Fearon Publishers) *Values* story record (Bowmar Records)	Filmstrip projector Record player
Conceptual skills	*Math Concepts,* Record CL21 (Bowmar Records) *Let's Look at Children,* Conceptual Training Materials (Educational Testing Service)	

Learning Area	Materials	Equipment
Conceptual skills— *Continued*	*Learning To Think Series*: Red Book (Science Research Associates) *Numbers in Color Cuisenaire Rods* (Cuisenaire Co.) *Number Concepts, Level 1; Measurement, Level 1* (Continental Press) *Greater Cleveland Mathematics Program,* Kndg.-Gr. 1 (Science Research Associates) Conceptual Skills section, *The Remediation of Learning Disabilities* (Fearon Publishers) *Concepts*, Record CL27 (Bowmar Records)	
Language skills	*Reading Readiness* (Behavioral Research Laboratories) *Lift-off to Reading*, Cycles I (Science Research Associates) *Sullivan Associates Programmed Reading*, Series I, Books 1-7 (Webster Division, McGraw-Hill Book Co.) *Reading-Thinking Skills* Pre-primer, Primer level 1 & 2 (Continental Press) *My Little Pictionary,* #2783 (Scott, Foresman) *Peabody Language Development Kit*, Level 1 (American Guidance Service) *Beginning Sounds 1* (Continental Press) *Reading Road to Spelling Series*, Book 1 (Harper & Row) *Language Experience in Reading*: LI-1, *I Learn To Read and Write*; LI-2, *Growing Up* (Encyclopaedia Britannica) Language Skills section, *The Remediation of Learning Disabilities* (Fearon Publishers) *Handwriting with Write and See*, Book 1 (Lyons & Carnahan) *Listen and Do*, Records and worksheets (Houghton Mifflin Co.)	Tape recorder Listening post Model 101 Self-learning System (Electronics Futures, Inc.)
Perceptual-motor skills	*Listen and Do*, 16 recordings and worksheets (Houghton Mifflin Co.) *Rhyming 1* (Continental Press) *The Developmental Program in Visual Perception*: *Beginning Pictures and Patterns* (Follett Publishing Co.) ERIE Program 1—Perceptual-Motor Teaching Materials (Teaching Resources) Geometric Inserts, #AP72 (Lakeshore Equipment Co.)	Kinesthetic alphabet, #KA84 (R. H. Stone Products)

Learning Area	Materials	Equipment
Perceptual motor skills— *Continued*	*Perceptual Form Home Training Guide Kit* and teachers' templates (Winter Haven Lions' Research Foundation) Perceptual-Motor Skills section, *The Remediation of Learning Disabilities* (Fearon Publishers) *Child's World of Sounds*, Record (Bowmar Records)	
Sensory-motor skills	*Time 1* (Continental Press) *The Letter Form Board* (Houghton Mifflin Co.) *Nursery Rhymes for Dramatic Play*, Record (Educational Record Sales) *The Five Senses*, Record (Bowmar Records) Sensory-Motor Skills section, *The Remediation of Learning Disabilities* (Fearon Publishers)	Primary typewriter Balance board, #WP52 (Creative Playthings) Rider roller, #111 (Creative Playthings)
Gross motor skills	*Self-image*, Record CL20 (Bowmar Records) *Basic Songs for Exceptional Children,* Records #1, 2, 3 (Children's Music Center) *Physical Fitness for the Younger Set*, K-2, Record (Educational Record Sales) Gross Motor Skills section, *The Remediation of Learning Disabilities* (Fearon Publishers) *Rope Jumping and Ball Handling*, Record (Bowmar Records)	School play mat, 4' x 6', #E8006 (Lakeshore Equipment Co.) Magna-sized Jigsaw Family #SL-110A Educational Record Associates) Jumping board, BJ (California Correctional Industries) Varied physical education equipment

Primary Learning Disabilities Class: Second year, Ages 8-9

Learning Area	Materials	Equipment
Social skills	*A Book About Me* (Science Research Associates) *Useful Language*, 2 & 3 (Continental Press) *Good Manners*, Filmstrip series (Educational Record Sales) Social Skills section, *The Remediation of Learning Disabilities* (Fearon Publishers)	Filmstrip projector
Conceptual skills	*Let's Look at Children*, Conceptual Training Materials (Educational Testing Service) *Learning To Think Series*: Blue Book (Science Research Associates)	Record player

Learning Area	Materials	Equipment
Conceptual skills— *Continued*	*Numbers in Color Cuisenaire Rods* (Cuisenaire Co.) *Number Concepts*, Level 2; *Measurement*, Level 2 (Continental Press) *Greater Cleveland Mathematics Program*, Kndg.-Gr. 2 (Science Research Associates) Conceptual Skills section, *The Remediation of Learning Disabilities* (Fearon Publishers) *Imagination and Insight*, Record (Bowmar Records)	
Language skills	*Sullivan Remedial Reading Program*, Programmed Structural Linguistics (Behavioral Research Laboratories) *Lift-off to Reading*, Cycles II and III (Science Research Associates) *Sullivan Associates Programmed Reading*, Series I, Books 1-7 (Webster Division, McGraw-Hill Book Co.) *Reading-Thinking Skills*, First reader, Level 1 & 2 (Continental Press) *My Little Pictionary*, #2783-64 (Scott, Foresman) *Peabody Language Development Kit*, Level 1 (American Guidance Service) *Beginning Sounds 2* (Continental Press) *Reading Road to Spelling Series*, Book 2 (Harper & Row) *Language Experience in Reading*: LT-3, *Magic Plastics;* LT-4, *Sounds Around Us* (Encyclopaedia Britannica) Language Skills section, *The Remediation of Learning Disabilities* (Fearon Publishers) *Handwriting with Write and See*, Book 2 (Lyons & Carnahan) *Famous Classics in Children's Literature*, Record CL17 (Bowmar Records)	Tape recorder Listening post Model 101 Self-learning System (Electronics Future, Inc.)
Perceptual-motor skills	*Listen and Do*, 16 recordings and worksheets (Houghton Mifflin) *Rhyming 2* (Continental Press) *The Developmental Program in Visual Perception: Intermediate Pictures and Patterns* (Follett Publishing Co.) *Listening Time*, Albums 1, 2, 3, Records (Children's Music Center) *Visual-Perceptual Skills,* Filmstrips (Educational Record Sales)	Kinesthetic Alphabet, #KA84 (R. H. Stone Products)

Learning Area	Materials	Equipment
Perceptual motor skills— *Continued*	Perceptual-Motor Skills section, *The Remediation of Learning Disabilities* (Fearon Publishers) *Sights and Sounds Feeling and Perceiving*, Record (Bowmar Records) TRY—Experiences for Young Children (Noble and Noble)	
Sensory-motor skills	*The Letter Form Board* (Houghton Mifflin Co.) *Listening and Moving*, Vols. 1-2, Records (Children's Music Center) *Developing Body-Space Perception Motor Skills*, Album 1, Record (Educational Record Sales) Sensory-Motor Skills section, *The Remediation of Learning Disabilities* (Fearon Publishers)	Primary typewriter Balance board, #WP52 (Creative Playthings) Rider roller, #R111 (Creative Playthings)
Gross motor skills	*Skip Rope Games*, Record (Educational Record Sales) Gross Motor Skills section, *The Remediation of Learning Disabilities* (Fearon Publishers) *Fun and Fitness*, Record (Bowmar Records)	School play mat, 4' x 6', #E8006 (Lakeshore Equipment Co.) Jumping Board, BJ (California Correctional Industries) Varied physical education equipment

Intermediate Learning Disabilities Class: Third year, Ages 9-10

Learning Area	Materials	Equipment
Social skills	*Fables*, Record CL22 (Bowmar Records) *Values To Learn* (Steck-Vaughn Co.) *Seven Stories for Growth* (Pitman Publishing Corp.) *Teaching Children Values*, Vol. 1, Record (Children's Music Center) Social Skills section, *The Remediation of Learning Disabilities* (Fearon Publishers)	Filmstrip projector Record player
Conceptual skills	*Learning To Think Series*: Green Book (Science Research Associates) *Thinking Skills, Level 1, Number Concepts*, Level 3 (Continental Press) *Greater Cleveland Mathematics Program*, Gr. 2-4 (Science Research Associates) *U.S. Money*, Level 1-3 (Continental Press)	

Learning Area	Materials	Equipment
Conceptual skills— *Continued*	*Numbers in Color Cuisenaire Rods* (Cuisenaire Co.) Conceptual Skills section, *The Remediation of Learning Disabilities* (Fearon Publishers)	
Language skills	*Sullivan Associates Programmed Reading*, Series II, Books 8-14 (Webster Division, McGraw-Hill Book Co.) *The Skyline Series*, Book A (Webster Division, McGraw-Hill Book Co.) *Reading-Thinking Skills*: Grade 2, Level 1-2; Grade 3, Level 1-2 (Continental Press) *Instant Words*, Filmstrip IW1-12 (McCurry's) *My Second Dictionary*, #2777-64 (Scott, Foresman) *Peabody Language Development Kit*, Level 2 (American Guidance Service) *Reading Road to Spelling*, Book 3 (Harper & Row) *Language Experience in Reading:* LI-5 *Animals Everywhere*; LI-6, *From Roller Skates to Rockets* (Encyclopaedia Britannica) *Phonics Practice,* Filmstrip, #PhP1-12 (McCurry's) Language Skills section, *The Remediation of Learning Disabilities* (Fearon Publishers) *Handwriting with Write and See*, Book 3 (Lyons & Carnahan) *Fun with Language*, Record (Bowmar Records)	Tape recorder Listening post Model 101 Self-learning System (Electronics Futures, Inc.)
Perceptual-motor skills	*The Developmental Program in Visual Perception: Advanced Pictures and Patterns* (Follett Publishing Co.) *Fairbanks-Robinson Program I in Perceptual-Motor Development* (Teaching Resources) *Visual-Perceptual Skills*, Filmstrips (Educational Record Sales) *Independent Activities*, Level 1 (Continental Press) Perceptual-Motor Skills section, *The Remediation of Learning Disabilities* (Fearon Publishers)	Stereo-reader Training Materials, AA + BB (Keystone View Co.) Tachist-o-Flasher (McCurry's)
Sensory-motor skills	*The Letter Form Board* (Houghton Mifflin Co.) *Listen—These Are Sounds About You*, Record and Filmstrip (Guidance Associates) *TAC—Training of Attention and Concentration Program* (Educational Research Associates) *Developing Body-Space Perception Motor Skills*, Album 2, Record (Educational Record Sales) Sensory-Motor Skills section, *The Remediation of Learning Disabilities* (Fearon Publishers)	Primary typewriter Balance board, #WP52 (Creative Playthings) Rider roller, #R111 (Creative Playthings)

Learning Area	Materials	Equipment
Gross motor skills	Gross Motor Skills section, *The Remediation of Learning Disabilities* (Fearon Publishers)	School play mat, 4' x 6', #E8006 (Lakeshore Equipment Co.) Jumping board, BJ (California Correctional Industries) Varied physical education equipment

Intermediate Learning Disabilities Class: Fourth year, Ages 10-11

Learning Area	Materials	Equipment
Social skills	*Values To Learn* (Steck-Vaughn Co.) *Seven Stories for Growth* (Pitman Publishing Corp.) *Teaching Children Values*, Vol. 2, Record (Children's Music Center) Social Skills section, *The Remediation of Learning Disabilities* (Fearon Publishers)	Filmstrip projector Record player
Conceptual skills	*Learning To Think Series*: Green Book (Science Research Associates) *Thinking Skills*, Level 1; *Measurement*, Level 3 (Continental Press) *Greater Cleveland Mathematics Program*, Gr. 2-4 (Science Research Associates) *U.S. Money*, Level 1-3 (Continental Press) *Numbers in Color Cuisenaire Rods* (Cuisenaire Co.) Conceptual Skills section, *The Remediation of Learning Disabilities* (Fearon Publishers)	
Language skills	*Conquests in Reading Workbook*, Kottimeyer and Ware (Webster Division, McGraw-Hill Book Co.) *Sullivan Associates Programmed Reading*, Series II, Books 8-14 (Webster Division, McGraw-Hill Book Co.) *The Skyline Series, Book A* (Webster Division, McGraw-Hill Book Co.) *Reading-Thinking Skills*: Grade 2, Level 1-2; Grade 3, Level 1-2 (Continental Press) *My Second Dictionary*, #2777-64 (Scott, Foresman)	Tape recorder Listening post Model 101 Self-learning System (Electronics Futures, Inc.)

Learning Area	Materials	Equipment
Language skills— Continued	*Peabody Language Development Kit*, Level 2 (American Guidance Service) *Reading Road to Spelling*, Book 4 (Harper & Row) *Language Experience in Reading:* LII-1 *About Me and My Friends*; LII-2 *What I Can Do* (Encyclopaedia Britannica) Language Skills section, *The Remediation of Learning Disabilities* (Fearon Publishers) *Handwriting with Write and See*, Book 4 (Lyons & Carnahan)	
Perceptual-motor skills	*Visual-Motor Skills 1, Visual-Discrimination 1* (Continental Press) *Visual Readiness Skills 1, Seeing Likeness and Differences 1* (Continental Press) *Seeing Skills*, Filmstrip SSB1-12 (McCurry's) *Independent Activities*, Level 2 (Continental Press) Perceptual-Motor Skills section, *The Remediation of Learning Disabilities* (Fearon Publishers)	Stereo-reader Training Materials, AA + BB (Keystone View Co.) Tachist-o-Flasher (McCurry's)
Sensory-motor skills	*Time 2* (Continental Press) *The Letter Form Board* (Houghton Mifflin Co.) *TAC—Training of Attention and Concentration Program* (Educational Research Associates) Sensory-Motor Skills section, *The Remediation of Learning Disabilities* (Fearon Publishers)	Primary typewriter Balance board, #WP52 (Creative Playthings) Rider roller, #R111 (Creative Playthings)
Gross motor skills	Gross Motor Skills section, *The Remediation of Learning Disabilities* (Fearon Publishers)	School play mat, 4' x 6', #E8006 (Lakeshore Equipment Co.) Jumping board, BJ (California Correctional Industries) Varied physical education equipment

Upper Elementary Learning Disabilities Class: Fifth year, Ages 11-12

Learning Area	Materials	Equipment
Social skills	*Values to Share* (Steck-Vaughn Co.) *Unfinished Stories for Use in the Classroom* (NEA)	Filmstrip projector

Learning Area	Materials	Equipment
Social skills— *Continued*	*Guidance Stories*, Filmstrip (Educational Record Sales) Social Skills section, *The Remediation of Learning Disabilities* (Fearon Publishers)	
Conceptual skills	*Learning To Think Series: Gold Book* (Science Research Associates) *Thinking Skills*, Level 2 (Continental Press) *Arithmetic Practice*, Filmstrip AP1-12 (McCurry's) *U.S. Money*, Level 3 (Continental Press) *Learning New Skills in Arithmetic*, Levels 1-6 (Continental Press) Conceptual Skills section, *The Remediation of Learning Disabilities* (Fearon Publishers)	
Language skills	*Conquests in Reading Workbook*, Kottimeyer and Ware (Webster Division, McGraw-Hill Book Co.) *Sullivan Associates Programmed Reading*, Series III, Books 15-21 (Webster Division, McGraw-Hill Book Co.) *The Skyline Series*, Books B and C (Webster Division, McGraw-Hill Book Co.) *Reading-Thinking Skills*: Grades 4 and 5, Level 1-2 (Continental Press) *Peabody Language Development Kit*, Level 3 (American Guidance Service) *Instant Word Phrases*, Filmstrip IWP1-12 (McCurry's) *Reading Road to Spelling*, Book 5 (Harper & Row) *Language Experience in Reading*, LII-3, *All Kinds of Weather*; LII-4, *Exploring Wildlife Around Us* (Encyclopaedia Britannica) Language Skills section, *The Remediation of Learning Disabilities* (Fearon Publishers) *Handwriting with Write and See*, Book 5 (Lyons & Carnahan)	Record player Tape recorder Listening post Model 101 Self-learning System (Electronics Futures, Inc.)
Perceptual-motor skills	*Visual-Motor Skills 2, Visual-Discrimination 2* (Continental Press) *Visual Readiness Skills 2, Seeing Likenesses and Differences 2* (Continental Press) *TAC—Training of Attention and Concentration Program* (Educational Research Associates) Perceptual-Motor Skills section, *The Remediation of Learning Disabilities* (Fearon Publishers)	Stereo-reader Training Materials, AA + BB (Keystone View Co.) Tachist-o-Flasher (McCurry's)

Learning Area	Materials	Equipment
Sensory-motor skills	*Time 3* (Continental Press) *The Letter Form Board* (Houghton Mifflin Co.) Sensory-Motor Skills section, *The Remediation of Learning Disabilities* (Fearon Publishers)	Primary typewriter Balance board, #WP52 (Creative Playthings) Rider roller, #R111 (Creative Playthings)
Gross motor skills	Gross Motor Skills section, *The Remediation of Learning Disabilities* (Fearon Publishers)	School play mat, 4' x 6', #E8006 (Lakeshore Equipment Co.) Varied physical education equipment

Upper Elementary Learning Disabilities Class: Sixth year, Ages 12-13

Learning Area	Materials	Equipment
Social skills	*Values to Share* (Steck-Vaughn Co.) *Unfinished Stories for Use in the Classroom* (NEA) *Developing Your Personality*, Filmstrip (Educational Record Sales) Social Skills section, *The Remediation of Learning Disabilities* (Fearon Publishers)	Filmstrip projector
Conceptual skills	*Conquests in Reading Workbook*, Kottimeyer and Ware (Webster Division, McGraw-Hill Book Co.) *Learning to Think Series*: Gold Book (Science Research Associates) *Thinking Skills,* Level 2 (Continental Press) *U.S. Money*, Level 3 (Continental Press) *Learning New Skills in Arithmetic*, Levels 1-6 (Continental Press) Conceptual Skills section, *The Remediation of Learning Disabilities* (Fearon Publishers)	
Language skills	*Sullivan Associates Programmed Reading*, Series III (Webster Division, McGraw-Hill Book Co.) *The Skyline Series*, Books B and C (Webster Division, McGraw-Hill Book Co.) *Reading-Thinking Skills*: Grades 4 and 5, Levels 1-2 (Continental Press)	Record player Tape recorder Listening post Model 101 Self-learning Systems (Electronics Futures, Inc.)

Learning Area	Materials	Equipment
Language skills— *Continued*	*Peabody Language Development Kit*, Level 3 (American Guidance Service) *Reading Laboratory*, 4, 5, 6 (Science Research Associates) *Pilot Library*, 4-5 (Science Research Associates) *Reading Road to Spelling*, Book 6 (Harper & Row) *Language Experience in Reading:* LII-5, *What's That?*; LII-6, *From Fact to Fancy* (Encyclopaedia Britannica) Language Skills section, *The Remediation of Learning Disabilities* (Fearon Publishers) *Handwriting with Write and See*, Book 6 (Lyons & Carnahan)	
Perceptual-motor skills	*Visual Readiness Skills 2, Seeing Likenesses and Differences 3* (Continental Press) Perceptual-Motor Skills section, *The Remediation of Learning Disabilities* (Fearon Publishers)	Tachist-o-Flasher (McCurry's)
Sensory-motor skills	Sensory-Motor Skills section, *The Remediation of Learning Disabilities* (Fearon Publishers)	Primary typewriter Rider roller, #R111 (Creative Playthings)
Gross motor skills	Gross Motor Skills section, *The Remediation of Learning Disabilities* (Fearon Publishers)	School play mat, 4′ x 6′, #E8006 (Lakeshore Equipment Co.) Varied physical education equipment

Junior High Learning Disabilities Class: Seventh year, Ages 13-15

Learning Area	Materials	Equipment
Social skills	*Values to Live by* (Steck-Vaughn Co.) Social Skills section, *The Remediation of Learning Disabilities* (Fearon Publishers)	Filmstrip projector
Conceptual skills	*Fitzhugh Plus Program: Language and Numbers Workbook* 4 (Allied Education Council) *How Far?* (Rand McNally & Co.) *Learning New Skills in Arithmetic*, Levels 3-8 (Continental Press) *Reading-Thinking Skills*, Grades 4-8, Levels 1-2 (Continental Press)	

Learning Area	Materials	Equipment
Conceptual skills— *Continued*	Conceptual Skills section, *The Remediation of Learning Disabilities* (Fearon Publishers)	
Language skills	*Conquests in Reading Workbook*, Kottimeyer and Ware (Webster Division, McGraw-Hill Book Co.) *Deep Sea Adventure Series* (Field Educational Publications) *Pacemaker Story Books*, 18 separate books (Fearon Publishers) *Reading Laboratory,* 4, 5, 6, and 7-8 (Science Research Associates) *Pilot Library*, 6-7 (Science Research Associates) Language Skills section, *The Remediation of Learning Disabilities* (Fearon Publishers)	Tape recorder Record player Listening post
Perceptual-motor skills	*Michigan Tracking Program*: Symbol Tracking, Visual Tracking, Word Tracking (Ann Arbor Publishers) Perceptual-Motor Skills section, *The Remediation of Learning Disabilities* (Fearon Publishers)	Tachist-o-Flasher (McCurry's)
Sensory-motor skills	*Time and Telling Time*, B. Wiley (Fearon Publishers) Sensory-Motor Skills section, *The Remediation of Learning Disabilities* (Fearon Publishers)	Pica typewriter
Gross motor skills	Adaptive and special physical education classes Gross Motor Skills section, *The Remediation of Learning Disabilities* (Fearon Publishers)	

Senior High Learning Disabilities Class: Ages 15-19

Learning Area	Materials	Equipment
Social skills	*Values and Goals*, Home Economics Packet #22 (Minnesota Mining & Manufacturing Co.) *Getting a Job*, F. Randall (Fearon Publishers) *Eddie in School*, B. Piltch (Fearon Publishers) *Turner-Livingston Reading Series* (Follett Publishing Co.)	Filmstrip projector
Conceptual skills	*Learning New Skills in Arithmetic*, Levels 4-8 (Continental Press) *Mathematics in Living Series*, Workbooks 1-4 (Pruett Press, Inc.)	

Learning Area	Materials	Equipment
Conceptual skills— *Continued*	*Reading-Thinking Skills*, Grades 5-8, Levels 1-2 (Continental Press)	
Language skills	*Turner-Livingston Reading Series* (Follett Publishing Co.) *Pacemaker Classics*, series (Fearon Publishers) *Reading Laboratory*, 7-8 and 8-9 (Science Research Associates) *Reading in High Gear*, Grades 7-12 and Adults (Science Research Associates) *Pilot Library*, 6-7 and 8-9 (Science Research Associates)	Record player Tape recorder Listening post
Perceptual-motor skills	*Fitzhugh Plus Program*: Spatial Organization Workbooks 1-3, Language and Numbers Workbooks 1-5 (Allied Educational Council)	Tachist-o-Flasher (McCurry's)
Sensory-motor skills		Pica typewriter
Gross motor skills	Adaptive and special physical education classes	

Program Materials References

Allied Education Council, Distribution Center, Galien, Mich. 49113

American Education Publications, Columbus, Ohio 43216

American Guidance Service, Inc., Publishers Bldg., Circle Pines, Minn. 55014

Ann Arbor Publishers, 610 S. Forest, Ann Arbor, Mich. 48104

Behavioral Research Laboratories, Box 577, Palo Alto, Calif. 94302

Bowman Records, Curtis Audiovisual Materials, Curtis Publishing Co., Independence Square, Philadelphia, Pa. 19105

California Correctional Industries, 1400 S Street, Sacramento, Calif.

Children's Music Center, Inc., 5373 West Pico Blvd., Los Angeles, Calif. 90019

The Continental Press, Inc., 367 S. Pasadena Ave., Pasadena, Calif.

Creative Playthings, Princeton, N.J.

Cuisenaire Company of America, Inc., 9 Elm Ave., Mt. Vernon, N.Y.

Educational Record Associates, P.O. Box 305, Fort Washington, Pa.

Educational Record Sales, 500 S. Douglas St., El Segundo, Calif.

Educational Research Associates, Inc., P.O. Box 6604, Philadelphia, Pa. 19149

Educational Testing Service, Princeton, N.J.

Electronics Futures, Inc., 57 Dodge Ave., North Haven, Conn. 06473

Encyclopaedia Britannica, Inc., 425 N. Michigan Ave., Chicago, Ill. 60611

Fearon Publishers, 2165 Park Blvd., Palo Alto, Calif. 94306

Field Educational Publications, Inc., 609 Mission St., San Francisco, Calif. 94105

Program Materials References—*Continued*

Follett Publishing Co., 1010 W. Washington Blvd., Chicago, Ill. 60607
Franklin Publications, Inc., 367 S. Pasadena Ave., Pasadena, Calif. 91105
Ginn & Co., Statler Bldg., Back Bay P.O. 191, Boston, Mass. 02117
Guidance Associates, Pleasantville, N.Y.
Harcourt, Brace & World, 757 Third Ave., New York, N.Y. 10017
Harper & Row, Publishers, 2500 Crawford Ave., Evanston, Ill. 60201
Houghton Mifflin Co., 2 Park St., Boston, Mass. 02107
Keystone View Co., Meadville, Pa. 16335
Lakeshore Equipment Co., 6036 Claremont Ave., Oakland, Calif. 94618
Lyons & Carnahan, 407 E. 25th St., Chicago, Ill. 60616
McCurry's, Eighth and Eye Streets, Sacramento, Calif.
McGraw-Hill Book Co., 330 W. 42nd St., New York, N.Y. 10036
Minnesota Mining & Manufacturing Co., St. Paul, Minn.
National Education Association, 1201 16th St. N.W., Washington, D.C.
Noble & Noble, Publishers, Inc., 750 Third Ave., New York, N.Y. 10017
Pitman Publishing Corp., 20 E. 46th St., New York, N.Y. 10017
Pruett Press, Inc., 2930 Pearl St., Box 80301, Boulder, Colo. 80302
R. H. Stone Products, Box 414, Detroit, Mich. 48231
Rand McNally and Co., Box 7600, Chicago, Ill. 60680
Scholastic Magazines, Inc., 902 Sylvan Ave., Englewood Cliffs, N.J. 07632
Science Research Associates, Inc., 259 E. Erie St., Chicago, Ill. 60611
Scott, Foresman & Co., 1900 E. Lake Ave., Glenview, Ill. 60025
Steck-Vaughn Company, P.O. Box 2028, Austin, Tex. 78767
Taylor Publishing Co., P.O. Box 597, Dallas, Tex. 75221
Teaching Resources, 334 Boylston St., Boston, Mass. 02116
Touch Aids, C. & E. Krueger, 1790 S. Juniper St., Escondido, Calif.
Warren's Educational Supplies, 1252 Sylvan Ave., West Covina, Calif.
Webster Division, McGraw-Hill Book Co., Manchester, Mo. 63011
Winter Haven Lions' Research Foundation, Inc., Box 1045, Winter Haven, Fla. 33881

PROGRAM EQUIPMENT

Stock Number	Qty.*	Item Description	Unit of Issue	Unit Price	Recommended for P	I	U
		Furniture and Capital Outlay Equipment					
		Chair, teacher		$ 7.00	x	x	x
		Desk, teacher		80.00	x	x	x
	12	Chairs, pupil (11″, 12″, 13″)		72.00	x	x	x
	12	Desks, pupil (open front)		288.00	x	x	x
	2	Tables, reading-utility (36″ x 72″, adjustable)		72.00	x	x	x
		File, two-drawer, locked, letter-sized, green		75.00	x	x	x
		Screen, projection		50.00	x	x	x
		Record player and listening posts with cart		175.00	x	x	x

*All equipment and supplies are recommended for purchase in single units unless indicated otherwise.

Stock Number	Qty.	Item Description	Unit of Issue	Unit Price	Recommended for		
					P	I	U
		Typewriter, primary, with table*		$230.00			
		Typewriter, 11″ pica, with table*		230.00			
		23″ TV set*		165.00			
		Tape recorder and listening post with cart		275.00	x	x	x
		Filmstrip projector with table, screen, and cart		120.00	x	x	x
		Overhead projector with cart		165.00	x	x	x
		TV cart*		35.00			
		Blackout curtains		200.00	x	x	x
		16 mm. movie projector with cart*		450.00			

Instructional Supplies

Stock Number	Qty.	Item Description	Unit of Issue	Unit Price	Recommended for		
					P	I	U
04-01990		Brushes, bristle, ½″	box	1.82	x	x	x
04-02090		Brushes for pasting	pkg.	.43	x	x	x
04-03500		Chalk, assorted colors	box	1.32	x	x	x
04-04060	6	Clay boards, 12″ x 12″	each	.44	x	x	x
04-04080		Clay jar	each	3.68	x	x	x
04-04100		Clay, mixed	25 lbs.	1.79	x	x	x
30-04075		Clay crock, dolly, circular—DCC mounted on casters	1	5.55	x	x	x
04-04930	12	Crayons	box	.23	x	x	x
04-14130	3	Oil cloth	yard	.55	x	x	x
04-14600		Paints, cold water, black	each	.35	x	x	x
04-14610		Paints, cold water, blue	each	.35	x	x	x
04-14620		Paints, cold water, brown	each	.35	x	x	x
04-14630		Paints, cold water, flesh	each	.40	x	x	x
04-14650		Paints, cold water, green	each	.40	x	x	x
04-14670		Paints, cold water, orange	each	.36	x	x	x
04-14680		Paints, cold water, red	each	.41	x	x	x
04-14730		Paints, cold water, white	each	.55	x	x	x
04-14740		Paints, cold water, yellow	each	.35	x	x	x
04-14760		Paints, finger, black	each	.79	x	x	x
04-14770		Paints, finger, blue	each	.59	x	x	x
04-14780		Paints, finger, green	each	.67	x	x	x
04-14790		Paints, finger, orange	each	.71	x	x	x
04-14800		Paints, finger, red	each	.61	x	x	x
04-14810		Paints, finger, yellow	each	.72	x	x	x
04-15600		Paper, construction, black	pkg.	.58	x	x	
04-15610		Paper, construction, blue	pkg.	.56	x	x	
04-15650		Paper, construction, tan	pkg.	.66	x	x	
04-15670		Paper, construction, dark brown	pkg.	.56	x	x	
04-15680		Paper, construction, green	pkg.	.56	x	x	
04-15720		Paper, construction, red	pkg.	.57	x	x	
04-15760		Paper, construction, white	pkg.	.57	x	x	
04-15770		Paper, construction, yellow	pkg.	.64	x	x	
04-15920		Paper, drawing, manila	case	8.04	x	x	x
04-15960		Paper, fibre tint, green	ream	.78	x	x	

*This equipment is recommended for a three-room center.

Stock Number	Qty.	Item Description	Unit of Issue	Unit Price	Recommended for		
					P	I	U
04-16010		Paper, fibre tint, yellow	ream	$ .81	x	x	
04-15990		Paper, fibre tint, red	ream	.80	x	x	
04-16000		Paper, fibre tint, tan	ream	.79	x	x	
04-16370	10	Paper, tissue, dark blue	pkg.	.06	x	x	
04-16380	10	Paper, tissue, green	pkg.	.06	x	x	
04-16390	10	Paper, tissue, red	pkg.	.07	x	x	
04-16400	10	Paper, tissue, white	pkg.	.06	x	x	
04-15810		Paper, crepe, black	pkg.	.29	x	x	
04-15820		Paper, crepe, blue	pkg.	.28	x	x	
04-15830		Paper, crepe, green	pkg.	.26	x	x	
04-15840		Paper, crepe, orange	pkg.	.26	x	x	
04-15850		Paper, crepe, pink	pkg.	.25	x	x	
04-15600		Paper, crepe, purple	pkg.	.26	x	x	
04-15700		Paper, crepe, red	pkg.	.26	x	x	
04-15880		Paper, crepe, white	pkg.	.25	x	x	
04-15890		Paper, crepe, yellow	pkg.	.27	x	x	
04-17260		Paste, school	carton	3.15	x	x	x

General Supplies

Stock Number	Qty.	Item Description	Unit of Issue	Unit Price	P	I	U
16-00430		Alphabet chart	each	1.76	x	x	x
16-01620	2	Books, teacher plan	each	.83	x	x	x
16-02910		Cards, Ginn: Pre-primer and Primer	set	1.09	x		
16-02920		Cards, Ginn: Pre-primer, Unit I	set	11.22	x		
16-02939		Cards, Ginn: Primer, Unit II	set	5.22	x		
16-02990		Cards, filing index, 3 x 5	pkg.	.21	x		
16-02900		Cards, filing index, 5 x 8	pkg.	.51	x		
16-03880		Chart rack	each	14.47	x	x	
16-03900		Charts, word study	set	15.51	x		
16-05690		Dispenser, scotch tape	each	1.56	x	x	x
16-07070		Erasers, classroom	box	1.79	x	x	x
16-07350		File box	each	1.05	x	x	x
16-07790		Flag, classroom, 2' x 3'	each	2.09	x	x	x
16-08970		Glue, Elmer's	pkg.	3.04	x		
16-13190		Money kits	each	2.18	x	x	x
16-13970	11	Number Aid—student	each	1.76	x	x	
16-14500		Paint easels	each	20.35	x	x	x
16-17080		Paper, penmanship, 1" lines	case	5.89	x		
16-17090		Paper, penmanship, ¾" lines	case	7.62		x	
16-17110		Paper, penmanship, ½" lines	case	7.36			x
16-17510		Pencils, classroom	box	1.07	x	x	x
16-19830		Records, Ginn & Co., *Let's Listen*	set	8.95	x		
16-21100		Scissors, 4½"	box	2.72	x		
16-21110		Scissors, 5"	box	2.91		x	
16-21120		Scissors, 6"	box	3.47			x
16-21130		Scissors, 8"	pair	1.67	x	x	x
16-24660		Tape, scotch	pkg.	4.40	x	x	x
16-22950		Stapler	each	4.25	x	x	x
16-22960		Staples	box	.30	x	x	x
16-24940		Thermometer, classroom	each	1.08	x	x	x

Stock Number	Qty.	Item Description	Unit of Issue	Unit Price	Recommended for		
					P	I	U
30-26550		Scale, school balance	each	$ 16.25	x	x	x
30-10160		Airplane, jet cargo—wooden 14″ wing spread	each	9.00	x		
30-09520		Screen, movable, wooden	each	12.56	x	x	
16-18400		Chart, pocket	each	5.59	x	x	x
16-19830		Records, Ginn: *Let's Listen*, Gr. 1 & 2	set	9.31	x	x	
16-20800		Rulers, 12″ (not metal edge)	box	1.20		x	x

Physical Education

Stock Number	Qty.	Item Description	Unit of Issue	Unit Price	P	I	U
36-01010		Baseball, rubber, 9″	each	.87	x	x	x
36-07920		Fleece ball	each	.77	x	x	x
36-09420		Horseshoes, rubber indoor	set	4.15	x	x	x
36-12595		Marla-bar, 7′ rope	each	2.20	x	x	
36-12596		Marla-bar, 8′ rope	each	2.75			x
36-22200		Soccer ball	each	4.21	x	x	x
36-22360		Softball, 12″ rubber	each	1.07	x	x	x
36-24220		Table game—checkers	each	.38	x	x	x
36-24210		Table game—checkers, board	each	.39	x	x	x
36-24230		Table game—chessmen	each	2.51			x
36-24250		Table game—dominoes	each	1.37	x	x	x
36-24360		Table game—Monopoly	each	3.62			x
36-24280		Table game—tiddlywinks	each	1.03	x	x	x
36-24290	2	Table game—jacks & ball	set	.28	x	x	
36-24300		Table game—anagrams	set	3.74		x	x
36-24310	2	Table game—bean bags	set	.41	x	x	x
36-25910		Utility ball	each	1.56	x	x	x
36-22230		Bat, softball, elementary school	each	1.50	x	x	x
36-24240		Table game—checkers, Chinese	set	1.17	x	x	x
36-26320		Whistle, small	each	.31	x	x	x

Music

Stock Number	Qty.	Item Description	Unit of Issue	Unit Price	P	I	U
34-01240		Bells, melody chromatic	each	4.95	x	x	x
34-01250		Bells, melody colored	each	4.95	x	x	x
34-03220	3	Castanets, handle	each	1.65	x	x	
34-05450		Cymbals	pair	2.34	x	x	
34-10920		Jingle bells	pair	.51	x	x	
34-20400	2	Rhythm sticks, hollow	pair	.22	x	x	
34-24470	2	Tambourine	each	2.82	x	x	
34-25600	2	Triangle and striker	each	.65	x	x	
34-25650		Tub drum	each	7.92	x	x	
34-25660		Tub drum mallet	each	1.34	x	x	

Instructional Aids

Stock Number	Qty.	Item Description	Unit of Issue	Unit Price	P	I	U
30-01120		Bead laces, black, 36″	dozen	.43	x	x	x
30-01130		Beads, ½″, colored wood spheres, cubes	box	6.01	x	x	x
30-01140		Beads, 1″, colored wood spheres, cubes	box	3.88	x	x	x
30-02610		Building blocks, solid floor	box	20.68	x	x	

Stock Number	Qty.	Item Description	Unit of Issue	Unit Price	Recommended for P	I	U
30-10200		Instruc. toy—farm animals, rubber, set of 15	box	$ 14.25	x		
30-10220		Instruc. toy—baby doll, Negro, with sunsuit and nursing bottle	each	1.69	x	x	
30-10230		Instruc. toy—baby doll, white, with sunsuit and nursing bottle	each	1.82	x	x	
30-10360		Instruc. toy—cash register, Tom Thumb	each	3.85	x	x	x
30-10361		Instruc. toy—construction blocks to make cars	set	6.71	x	x	
30-10430		Instruc. toy—domino blocks, wooden, 2¾″ x ¾″ with dots	box	7.39	x	x	x
30-10460		Instruc. toy—wooden family, set of 6: mother, father, 6″; brother, sister, 5″	box	5.96	x	x	
30-10550		Instruc. toy—parquetry block container, wooden, shop-made	each	.99	x	x	x
30-10560		Instruc. toy—parquetry design blocks	box	2.09	x	x	x
30-10570		Instruc. toy—people, wooden, doctor, 6″	each	.95	x		
30-10580		Instruc. toy—people, wooden, farm worker, 6″	each	.96	x		
30-10590		Instruc. toy—people, wooden, fireman, 6″	each	.95	x		
30-10610		Instruc. toy—people, wooden, milkman, 6″	each	.96	x		
30-10620		Instruc. toy—people, wooden, nurse, 6″	each	.96	x		
30-10640		Instruc. toy—people, wooden, postman, 6″	each	.93	x		
30-10650		Instruc. toy—people, wooden, truck driver, 4″	each	.95	x		
30-10710	2	Instruc. toy—telephone, plastic	each	1.09	x	x	
30-10720		Instruc. toy—tinker toy	box	3.35	x	x	x
30-17860		Pictures—basic social studies discussion pictures, 24 colored, 22½″ x 30″	box	24.06	x	x	
30-18830		Puzzles, animals—cat, 11 pcs.	each	1.87	x		
30-18850		Puzzles, animals—dog, 13 pcs.	each	1.87	x		
30-18860		Puzzles, animals—duck, 8 pcs.	each	1.85	x		
30-18870		Puzzles, animals—elephant, 15 pcs.	each	1.87		x	
30-18900		Puzzles, animals—little brown bear, 9 pcs.	each	1.54	x		
30-18910		Puzzles, animals—monkey, 15 pcs.	each	1.49	x	x	
30-18920		Puzzles, animals—rabbit, 19 pcs.	each	1.87	x	x	
30-18950		Puzzles, animals—turtle, 10 pcs.	each	1.87	x		
30-18960		Puzzle case, wooden, holds 12 puzzles	each	8.36	x	x	x
30-18970		Puzzles, community helpers—doctor, 12 pcs.	each	1.92	x		
30-18980		Puzzles, community helpers—farmer, 10 pcs.	each	1.87	x		

Stock Number	Qty.	Item Description	Unit of Issue	Unit Price	Recommended for		
					P	I	U
30-18990		Puzzles, community helpers—fireman, 15 pcs.	each	$ 1.87		x	
30-19000		Puzzles, community helpers—milkman, 8 pcs.	each	1.89	x		
30-19010		Puzzles, community helpers—policeman, 10 pcs.	each	1.85	x		
30-19040		Puzzles, folk tales—Gingerbread Boy, 5 pcs.	each	1.85	x		
30-19050		Puzzles, folk tales—Goat's Gruff, 19 pcs.	each	1.87		x	
30-19060		Puzzles, folk tales—Jack and Beanstalk, 21 pcs.	each	1.87		x	
30-19070		Puzzles, folk tales—mama bear, 22 pcs.	each	1.87		x	
30-19110		Puzzles, holidays and seasons—clown, 13 pcs.	each	1.95	x		
30-19140		Puzzles, holidays and seasons—Santa Claus, 24 pcs.	each	1.83		x	x
30-19170		Puzzles, misc.—Billy, 9 pcs.	each	1.83	x	x	
30-19180		Puzzles, misc.—house, 19 pcs.	each	1.96	x	x	
30-19210		Puzzles, misc.—merry-go-round, 20 pcs.	each	1.87		x	x
30-19220		Puzzles, misc.—Susie, 12 pcs.	each	1.68	x	x	
30-19290		Puzzles, Mother Goose—Miss Muffet, 15 pcs.	each	1.49	x		
30-19320		Puzzles, Mother Goose—Old King Cole, 22 pcs.	each	1.49		x	
30-19330		Puzzles, Mother Goose—Old Woman in Shoe, 18 pcs.	each	1.68		x	
30-19360		Puzzles, transportation—airplane, 14 pcs.	each	1.49		x	x
30-19370		Puzzles, transportation—bus, 18 pcs.	each	1.85		x	x
30-19400		Puzzles, transportation—fire engine, 12 pcs.	each	1.74	x		
30-19430		Puzzles, transportation—train, 20 pcs.	each	1.85		x	
30-19440		Puzzles, transportation—tugboat, 16 pcs.	each	1.49		x	
30-10480		Toy—flat bed, wooden, 7″ x 28″	each	10.45	x		
30-10520		Ironing board	each	7.27	x		
30-10500		Toy iron, metal, hp 117	each	1.17	x		
30-10660		Pots and pans	set	6.51	x		
30-10440		Toy dust brush, hp 113	each	.72	x		
30-10450		Dustpan, hp 113	each	.61	x		
30-10530		Mop, hp 124	each	.95	x		

Science

Stock Number	Qty.	Item Description	Unit of Issue	Unit Price	P	I	U
44-12610		Magnets, horseshoe	each	1.15	x	x	x
44-12630		Glass, magnifying	each	5.36	x	x	x
44-00660		Aquarium, 11¾″ x 8¼″ x 7¾″	each	5.93	x	x	x

Stock Number	Qty.	Item Description	Unit of Issue	Unit Price	Recommended for		
					P	I	U
44-00670		Aquarium top, 12″ x 8½″	each	$ .56	x	x	x
44-09010		Aquarium gravel, 10 lb.	pkg.	.68	x	x	x
44-02680		Cages, insect cylindrical screen wire	each	.72	x	x	x

Creative Playthings, Inc., Princeton, N.J.

Stock Number	Qty.	Item Description	Unit of Issue	Unit Price	P	I	U
AA-441		Workbench with vise (27″)	each	52.50		x	x
AA-445		Tools: Auger bit, ¼″	each	1.40		x	x
AA-446		Auger bit, ½″	each	1.50		x	x
AA-447		Auger bit, ¾″	each	1.75		x	x
AA-448		Auger bit, 1″	each	1.95		x	x
AA-449		Bit brace	each	4.95		x	x
AA-450		Block plane	each	4.50		x	x
AA-451		Chisel, ¾″	each	2.25		x	x
AA-453		Clamp, 3″	each	.95		x	x
AA-454		Claw hammer, 13 oz.	each	4.50		x	x
AA-455		Claw hammer, 16 oz.	each	4.50		x	x
AA-456		Coping saw, 10 oz.	each	1.00		x	x
AA-457		Coping blades	24	.05		x	x
AA-458		Hand drill	each	3.95		x	x
AA-459		Drill bits (set of four)	set	2.55		x	x
AA-460		Hand saw, 16″	each	1.95		x	x
AA-462		Screwdriver	each	.65		x	x
AA-465		Wood rasp	each	1.95		x	x
AM-364		Autoharp, 12 chord	each	32.95	x	x	x
AH-335		Chair, rocking	each	13.95	x	x	
AB-88		House, doll	each	14.95	x		
AD-265		Doll house family	each	4.50	x		
AG-450		Puppets, hand, rubber, white family	set	6.95	x	x	x
AG-550		Puppets, hand, rubber, Negro family	set	6.95	x	x	x
AT-660		Magnasticks	box	4.50	x	x	
AT-334		Lacing boot	each	3.00	x		
AN-113		Pegboard, rubber	6	.50	x	x	x
AN-117		Pegs, straight	box	.50	x	x	x
AT-671		Pattern play abstracts	set	2.75	x	x	
AT-330		Lincoln logs	each	4.00	x	x	x
AA-352		Puzzle, U.S. map	each	4.00		x	x
AS-394		Cage, hamster	each	7.75	x	x	x
AA-280		Easel, economy	each	12.95	x	x	
AA-375		Thermometer, education	each	.85		x	x
AF-605		Rest cot, aluminum	each	11.95	x		
AP-157		Blocks and boards, balance	set	16.95	x	x	x

Learning Through Seeing, Inc.,
c/o McCurry's Camera Store, 8th and Eye Sts., Sacramento, Calif.

Stock Number	Qty.	Item Description	Unit of Issue	Unit Price	P	I	U
SSB 1-12		Tachist-o-Flasher sets:					
		Seeing Skills	set	35.50		x	x
NRA 1-12		Number recognition	set	35.50		x	x
IW 1-12		Instant words	set	35.50		x	x

Stock Number	Qty.	Item Description	Unit of Issue	Unit Price	Recommended for		
					P	I	U
PhP 1-12		Phonics practice	set	$ 35.50		x	x
IWP 1-12		Instant word phrases	set	35.50		x	x
AP 1-12		Arithmetic practice	set	35.50		x	x

Continental Press, Inc., 367 So. Pasadena Ave., Pasadena, Calif.

		Number Concepts, Level 1, Book, 16 lessons		3.20	x	x	
		Number Concepts, Level 2, Book, 16 lessons		3.20	x	x	
		Number Concepts, Level 3, Book, 16 lessons		3.20		x	x
		Measurement, Level 1, Book, 16 lessons		3.20	x	x	
		Measurement, Level 2, Book, 16 lessons		3.20	x	x	
		Measurement, Level 3, Book, 16 lessons		3.20			x
		U. S. Money, Level 1, Book, 16 lessons		3.20	x	x	
		U. S. Money, Level 2, Book, 16 lessons		3.20	x	x	
		U. S. Money, Level 3, Book, 16 lessons		3.20			x
		Time, Level 1, Book, 16 lessons		3.20	x	x	
		Time, Level 2, Book, 16 lessons		3.20		x	x
		Time, Level 3, Book, 16 lessons		3.20			x
		Useful Language, Level 1, Book, 16 lessons		3.20	x	x	
		Useful Language, Level 2, Book, 16 lessons		3.20	x	x	
		Useful Language, Level 3, Book, 16 lessons		3.20	x	x	
		Rhyming, Level 1, Book, 24 lessons		3.20	x	x	
		Rhyming, Level 2, Book, 24 lessons		3.20	x	x	
		Visual-Motor Skills, Level 1, Book, 24 lessons		3.20	x	x	x
		Visual-Motor Skills, Level 2, Book, 24 lessons		3.20	x	x	x
		Visual Discrimination, Level 1, Book, 24 lessons		3.20	x	x	
		Visual Discrimination, Level 2, Book, 24 lessons		3.20		x	x
		Beginning Sounds, Level 1, Book, 24 lessons		3.20	x	x	
		Beginning Sounds, Level 2, Book, 24 lessons		3.20		x	x
		Independent Activities, Level 1, Book, 24 lessons		3.20	x	x	x

Stock Number	Qty.	Item Description	Unit of Issue	Unit Price	Recommended for		
					P	I	U
		Independent Activities, Level 2, Book, 24 lessons		$ 3.20	x	x	x
		Thinking Skills, Level 1, Book, 24 lessons		3.20	x	x	x
		Thinking Skills, Level 2, Book, 24 lessons		3.20	x	x	x

Warren's Educational Supplies, 1252 Sylvan Ave., West Covina, Calif.

Stock Number	Qty.	Item Description	Unit of Issue	Unit Price	P	I	U
		Touch ABC boards	set	39.95	x		
		Touch ABC lowercase letters	set	2.95	x	x	x
		Judy clock	each	3.50	x		
		Judy 100 pegboard	each	5.75	x	x	x
1010W		Pegboards, wood, 10″ x 10″	each	1.10	x	x	x
		Calculating blocks	set	2.75	x	x	
		Fraction inlay board—circles	each	1.75		x	x
		Dolch material					
2203		Group word teaching game	set	1.59		x	x
2204		Basic sight cards	set	1.10	x	x	x
2205		Sight phrase cards	set	1.00		x	x
2200		Picture word cards	set	1.00	x	x	x
2300		What the letters say	each	1.98		x	x
2304		Consonant lotto	each	1.98		x	x
2305		Vowel lotto	each	1.98		x	x
2303		Take	each	1.50		x	x
2302		The syllable game	each	2.10		x	x
2301		Group sounding game	each	2.10		x	x
2201		Popper words, Set I	set	1.00		x	x
2202		Popper words, Set II	set	1.00		x	x
		Popper Numbers Flashcards					
2408		Addition	set	1.00	x	x	x
2409		Subtraction	set	1.00	x	x	x
2410		Multiplication	set	1.00		x	x
2411		Division	set	1.00		x	x
2403		Say-it arithmetic game	each	7.92	x	x	x
2405		Pay the cashier	each	3.95		x	x
60		Number matchettes	set	2.00	x		
3002		Counting frame	6	2.60	x	x	
C-12		Clock dials (class)	2	.50	x	x	x
C-4		Clock dials (pupil)	set	2.50	x	x	x
9309		Quizmo (add-subtract)	each	2.00		x	x
100-C		Cubes, colored	box	3.30	x	x	x
9375		Tell Time Quizmo	each	2.50		x	x
AJ-112		Fractional squares board	each	6.95		x	x
AJ-101		Jumbo sconed rods	each	4.95	x	x	
AA-295		Go-together lotto	each	1.00	x		
AA-330		Dominoes, picture	each	1.00	x		
AA-806		Letters, individual kinesthetic	set	5.95	x	x	
AA-729		Ben-G reading readiness puzzles	set	3.50	x		

Stock Number	Qty.	Item Description	Unit of Issue	Unit Price	Recommended for P	I	U
	Follett Publishing Co., 1010 W. Washington Blvd., Chicago, Ill. 60607
		The Frostig Program for the Development of Visual Perception	set	$105.00	One set per school		
	Cuisenaire Company of America, Inc., 9 Elm Ave., Mt. Vernon, N.Y.
		Sample teacher's kit	kit	10.00	x	x	x
	R. H. Stone Products, Box 414, Detroit, Mich. 48231
31		Solid wood color cubes	set	2.00	x	x	x
KA84		Kinesthetic alphabet	set	35.00	x	x	
26		Plastic play tiles	set	4.00	x	x	x
	Lakeshore Equipment Co., 6036 Claremont Ave., Oakland, Calif. 94618
J710		Judy numberite	each	2.95	x		
P5C		Fort Lincoln logs	set	4.50	x		
P770		U.S. map inlay puzzle	each	3.50		x	x
CA402		Magnetic form board	each	2.50	x	x	x
M31		Color cubes	set	1.75	x	x	x
SM58		Design tiles	set	1.85	x	x	x
M26		Senior pegboard play tiles	set	3.40	x	x	x
WP52		Balance board	each	13.00	x		
M1		Pillow rest mat	each	3.40	x	x	x
CA400		Magnetic alphabet board	each	2.55	x	x	x
CA407		Extra lowercase letters		.85	x	x	x
BG14		Ben G ready-to-read puzzles	each	3.50	x		
TK1A		Beaded alphabet lowercase	set	3.95	x	x	x
E111		Picture dominoes	set	.85	x	x	
E100		ABC lotto	each	.85	x		
E101		Zoo lotto	each	.85	x		
E115		World about us lotto	each	.85	x	x	
E120		What's missing lotto	each	.85	x	x	
E127		Object lotto	each	.85	x	x	
W4201		Life on the farm lotto	each	.85	x		
W4202		How we live lotto	each	.85		x	x
W4203		What's in a store lotto	each	.85		x	x
W4204		How we travel lotto	each	.85		x	x
3001		Counting frame	each	2.60	x	x	
2106		Match sets I	set	1.00	x	x	
2107		Match sets II	set	1.00	x	x	
9502		Alphabet picture flash cards	each	2.00	x	x	
272-2		Magic cards—consonants	each	1.90		x	x
273-2		Magic cards—blends and digraphs	each	.70		x	x
274-2		Magic cards—vowels	each	1.40		x	x
262		Phonic talking letters	each	1.25		x	x
L705		Basic lego	each	4.50	x	x	
9503		Link letters	each	1.00	x	x	x
8134		Economo sentence builder	each	.50		x	x
7503		Educational password	each	2.00		x	x

Stock Number	Qty.	Item Description	Unit of Issue	Unit Price	Recommended for		
					P	I	U
8252		Phonetic drill cards	each	$ 2.00		x	x
270		Reading readiness charts	each	4.25	x		
271		Classification—opposites, sequence charts	each	5.00	x	x	
KR2		Prefixes, suffixes, and blends	each	3.00			x
5		Flannel board	each	4.50	x	x	x
7802		Flannel board numbers	each	2.00	x		
7807		Flannel board fractional parts	each	3.00	x		
SN436		Pick-up sticks	each	.25	x	x	x
2210		My puzzle books I	each	.56	x		
2211		My puzzle books II	each	.56	x		

Palfrey's School Supply Co., 7715 E. Garvey Blvd., So. San Gabriel, Calif.

Stock Number	Qty.	Item Description	Unit of Issue	Unit Price	P	I	U
2156-A		Phonic rummy	each	1.50		x	
2156-B		Phonic rummy	each	1.50		x	
2156-C		Phonic rummy	each	1.50		x	x
2156-D		Phonic rummy	each	1.50		x	x
		Go fish sound game	each	1.50		x	x
		Go fish blend game	each	1.50		x	x
		Learner's ruler	each	.25	x	x	
		New felt-riter, blue	each	.49	x	x	x
		New felt-riter, black	each	.49	x	x	x
		New felt-riter, red	each	.49	x	x	x
		New felt-riter, green	each	.49	x	x	x
		My first crossword puzzle book	each	1.25		x	x
		My first dictionary	each	1.50		x	x
		My picture dictionary	each	.69	x	x	x
		The picture dictionary for children	each	2.95		x	x
		The golden picture dictionary	each	2.00		x	x

Webster Division, McGraw-Hill Book Co., Inc., Manchester, Mo. 63011

Stock Number	Qty.	Item Description	Unit of Issue	Unit Price	P	I	U
		M. Sullivan and C. Buchanan *Programmed Reading Series* *Pre-reading Series*					
62351		Programmed pre-reading (teacher's guide)	each	1.11	x	x	
62352		Programmed primer	each	.93	x	x	
62356		Pupil alphabet cards	each	1.38	x	x	
62354		Teacher alphabet cards	set	2.70	x	x	
62353		Reading readiness tests	set	1.80	x	x	
62319		Alphabet strips	each	1.11	x	x	
62363		Eight sound-symbol cards	each	1.35	x	x	
		Series I (Grade level 1.7-3.5) Teacher's guide to series I	each	.99		x	x
62291		Programmed reading, book I	each	.99		x	x
62525		Storybook 1, *Pins and Pans*	each	.99		x	x
62292		Programmed reading, book 2	each	.99		x	x
62526		Storybook 2, *The Bag in Sand*	each	.99		x	x
62296		Programmed reading, book 3	each	.99		x	x
62527		Storybook 3, *The Red Mitten*	each	.99		x	x

Stock Number	Qty.	Item Description	Unit of Issue	Unit Price	Recommended for		
					P	I	U
62298		Programmed reading, book 4	each	$ .99		x	x
62528		Storybook 4, *Witch and Bat*	each	1.11		x	x
62304		Programmed reading, book 5	each	.99		x	x
62529		Storybook 5, *Pick a Pet*	each	1.11		x	x
62306		Programmed reading, book 6	each	.99		x	x
62530		Storybook 6, *Jars and Jars of Jam*	each	1.11		x	x
62308		Programmed reading, book 7	each	.99		x	x
62531		Storybook 7, *The Starship*	each	1.11		x	x
62357		29 symbol cards (sound)	set	3.15		x	x
62532		Test booklet for series I	each	.69		x	x
62533		Teacher's guide to test booklet for series I	each	.36		x	x
		Series II (Grade level 3.6-4.5)					
62318		Teacher's guide to series II	each	.99			x
62311		Programmed reading, book 8	each	.99			x
62312		Programmed reading, book 9	each	.99			x
62313		Programmed reading, book 10	each	.99			x
62314		Programmed reading, book 11	each	.99			x
62315		Programmed reading, book 12	each	.99			x
62316		Programmed reading, book 13	each	.99			x
62317		Programmed reading, book 14	each	.99			x
62320		Test booklet for series II	each	.69			x
62321		Teacher's guide to test booklet for series II	each	.36			x
		Vanishing marking pencils					
62410		Holders	pkg.	5.40	x	x	x
62411		Fillers	pkg.	4.50	x	x	x

American Guidance Service, Inc., Publishers Bldg., Circle Pines, Minn. 55014

Stock Number	Qty.	Item Description	Unit of Issue	Unit Price	P	I	U
		The Peabody Language Development Kit					
		Kindergarten	each	125.00	x		
		Level 1	each	52.00		x	
		Level 2	each	58.00			x

Distribution Services, Cooperative Test Division, Educational Testing Service, Princeton, N.J.

Stock Number	Qty.	Item Description	Unit of Issue	Unit Price	P	I	U
		New York City Project Materials:					
		From theory to the classroom	each	.30	x		
		Let's look at first graders	each	2.00	x		
		Instructional and assessment materials for first graders	each	1.00	x		
		Written exercises	each	1.00	x		
		Written exercises: manual of directions	each	1.00	x		
		Sequence card game:					
		Teacher's set	each	1.50	x		
		Student's set	each	6.00	x		
		Directions card game:	set	5.00	x		
		Answer sheets	each	1.00	x		

Teacher References

GENERAL REFERENCES

ARENE, JOHN (ed.). *Teaching Educationally Handicapped Children.* San Rafael, Calif.: Academic Therapy Publications, 1967.

CRUICKSHANK, WILLIAM. *The Brain-injured Child in Home, School and Community.* Syracuse, N.Y.: Syracuse University Press, 1967.

FERNALD, GRACE. *Remedial Techniques in Basic School Subjects.* N.Y.: McGraw-Hill Book Company, 1943.

FRIERSON, EDWARD C., and BARBE, WALTER B. (eds.). *Educating Children with Learning Disabilities.* N.Y.: Appleton-Century-Crofts, 1967.

JOHNSON, DAVIS, and MYKLEBUST, HELMER. *Learning Disabilities.* N.Y.: Grune & Stratton, Inc., 1967.

KEPHART, NEWELL. *The Slow Learner in the Classroom.* Columbus, O.: Charles E. Merrill Books, Inc., 1960.

SUTPHIN, FLORENCE. *A Perceptual Testing-training Handbook for First-grade Teachers.* Winter Haven, Fla.: Winter Haven Lions' Research Foundation, Inc., 1964.

VALETT, ROBERT E. *The Remediation of Learning Disabilities.* Palo Alto, Calif.: Fearon Publishers, 1967.

SPECIAL SKILLS

ENGEL, ROSS; REED, WILLIAM; and RUCKER, DONALD. *Language Development Experiences for Young Children.* Los Angeles, Calif.: Department of Exceptional Children, School of Education, University of Southern California, 1966.

GARDNER, WARREN. *Test Manual for Remedial Handwriting.* Danville, Ill.: The Interstate Printers and Publishers, Inc.

HADSOTT, L. C., and JENSEN, R. G. *A Guide to Movement Exploration.* Palo Alto, Calif.: Peek Publications.

MOORE, JANE; PALMER, MARGARET; and PATE, JOHN. *Handbook of Kindergarten Activities for Every Day of the Year.* Darien, Conn.: Teachers Publishing Corp. 1965.

SCOTT, L. B., and THOMPSON, J. J. *Talking Time.* Manchester, Mo.: Webster Publishing Co.

TUDYMAN, AL, and GROLLE, MARVIN. *A Functional Basic Word List for Special Pupils.* Pittsburgh, Pa.: Stanwix House, Inc.

VAN ALLEN, ROACH, and VAN ALLEN, CLARYCE. *Language Experience in Reading Teachers' Resource Book* (Level I and II). Chicago: Encyclopaedia Britannica, Inc., 1966.

WAGNER, GUY, *et al. Arithmetic Games and Activities.* Darien, Conn.: Teachers Publishing Corp., 1966.

————. *Games and Activities for Early Childhood Education.* Darien, Conn.: Teachers Publishing Corp., 1967.

————. *Science Games and Activities.* Darien, Conn.: Teachers Publishing Corp., 1967.

11

Behavior Modification Through
Psychoeducational Programming

A few years ago B. F. Skinner predicted that ". . . total control of the environment from birth is within range" of becoming a reality.[1] Although such a possibility undoubtedly has its positive and negative aspects, there is little question but that the educator of children with learning disabilities can learn much of value from the new behavior technology. Through a systematic application of the principles of learning in programming the pupil and designing his total learning environment, we can now insure that the nonlearner will begin to achieve. In cooperation with parents and community agencies, the special educator and the psychologist can now begin to shape a preventive environment. Through means such as early intervention programs on the preschool level, educational teams working with parents and children as young as 18 months of age are already having dramatic results in effecting

[1]B. F. Skinner, "Operant Behavior," *American Psychologist*, Vol. XVIII, No. 8 (1963), pp. 503-515.

changes in human behavior, as demonstrated by Rhodes.[2] Although it may be questionable whether or not it will be possible to program the entire educational environment within the near future, the teacher of children with learning disabilities will undoubtedly have to become a more effective human engineer than at the present time. Some of the beginning behavior modification systems presented here should be of some value to the professional educator interested in moving in this direction.

Rationale for Behavior Modification

Children with neurological perceptual problems, mental retardation, emotional disturbances, and specific learning dysfunctions often have behavior disorders that are characterized by inattentiveness, distractibility, hyperactivity, and lack of self-control. Most experienced teachers have occasionally seen these same disorders manifested in regular classrooms. When such behavior is allowed to continue, the child experiences increasing failure in learning, together with growing frustration and social maladjustment, and may seriously interfere with the educational program of the entire class. In such situations it is obvious that there must be some positive intervention if the entire learning situation is not to be jeopardized.

Every teacher has some system of classroom and pupil control that supposedly enhances effective learning. In most cases, an interested teacher with a flexible curriculum, well-organized lesson plans, and a realistic marking system is sufficient to provide the structure, motivation, and reward essential to learning. However, children with chronic behavior disorders need more than these basic essentials. First, they require a teacher capable of love and understanding, who is concerned about doing more to help the child learn. Of equal importance is the teacher's ability to define the pupil's educational needs, develop specific learning programs with realistic goals, set consistent limits, provide direction, training, and guidance, and encourage gradual and continued success through reinforcement systems of praise and rewards.

For learning to occur, the pupil must be motivated to attend, concentrate, and respond to appropriate stimuli. To maintain motivation, there must be some measure of success and reward for effort expended by the child. Many children with behavior problems lose their motivation as a result of repeated failure and uninteresting lessons. The pupil who is continually given work beyond his basic skills or ability seldom experiences sufficient success to motivate him to keep working. Obviously, a strong and well-organized system of rewards is essential if we wish to keep children interested in learning.

Most children who have been reared in a home and community environment where their primary needs of physical care, love, and attention have been adequately provided for have been taught to respond to such secondary reinforcers as encouragement and recognition. These children are more capable of self-control and of deferring immediate gratification of their inclinations. Other pupils whose primary needs have not been met must be taught to attend, respond, and cooperate; only then can they gradually acquire self-control and responsible behavior.

It is well accepted that children can be taught appropriate responses through conditioning procedures that reinforce or reward the specific desired behavior.

[2]W. C. Rhodes, "The Disturbing Child: A Problem of Ecological Management," *Exceptional Children*, Vol. XXXIII, No. 7 (1967), pp. 449-455.

Now it is necessary to develop a reinforcement system around the appropriate responses that have been clearly identified. Furthermore, to be educationally effective, the system must provide for immediate and primary rewards to the single pupil when necessary and must also encourage total classroom or peer group support of the individual and the group learning situation.

Applying Behavior Modification Techniques

Through the years considerable data has accumulated regarding the efficacy of applying the principles of learning in behavior modification situations. With the current widespread use of candy reinforcers, it is difficult to realize that this is not a new technique, but was used in the early experiments of Ivanov-Smolensky. (Candy was delivered into a child's mouth when he squeezed a rubber bulb.[3]) Since that time, both theory and technique have advanced rapidly and have been applied in the school system. A number of recent studies have attempted to relate behavior modification to educational programming and classroom structure and organization.

Steven Doubros recently demonstrated that verbal behavior can be successfully conditioned in high-level retarded adolescents.[4] A dramatic presentation of the effectiveness of using primary food reinforcers in a language development program for compensatory preschool children has been reported by Risley.[5] The importance of relating reinforcement to appropriate intervention techniques in a structured classroom has been stressed by Hewett.[6] Manipulation of teacher behaviors to "correct" pupil responses, including the importance of using the pupil's name, touching him, turning away from him (negative reinforcement), and programming him with suitable materials, has been discussed by Allen, et al.[7] Public awareness of the effectiveness of using behavior modification techniques has been growing, as evidenced by a *Newsweek* magazine report on the value of keeping dropouts in school and transforming low achieving pupils into honor students.[8]

An increasing sophistication in the application of these principles has been demonstrated in many programs. In a recent paper Llorens emphasized the importance of reinforcement in specific remediation procedures. He stressed that the pupil should be programmed with realistic expectations of success and should have ample opportunity for independent practice and support.[9] The author has developed a series of social reinforcement techniques for teacher use in which reinforcement contingencies are integrated in the daily program and systematically reported.[10] It has also been encouraging to find that adolescents have responded favorably to

[3]A. G. Ivanov-Smolensky, "On Methods of Examining Conditioned Food Reflexes in Children and in Mental Disorders," *Brain*, Vol. 50 (1927), pp. 138-141.

[4]S. G. Doubros, "Behavior Therapy with High-level, Institutionalized, Retarded Adolescents," *Exceptional Children*, Vol. XXXIII, No. 4 (1966), pp. 229-232.

[5]T. Risley, "Learning and Lollipops," *Psychology Today*, Vol. I, No. 8 (1968), pp. 28-31 and pp. 62-65.

[6]F. M. Hewett, "Educational Engineering with Emotionally Disturbed Children," *Exceptional Children*, Vol. XXXIII, No. 7 (1967), pp. 459-467.

[7]K. E. Allen, et al., "Control of Hyperactivity by Social Reinforcement of Attending Behavior," *Journal of Educational Psychology*, Vol. LVIII, No. 4 (1967), pp. 231-237.

[8]"Golden Grades," *Newsweek*, Vol. LXVII, No. 14 (1966), p. 62.

[9]L. A. Llorens, "Remediation Procedures" (Paper presented at Symposium on Utilizing Cognitive-Motor Approaches with Learning and Adjustment Problems, 45th Annual International CEC Convention, March 30, 1967, St. Louis, Missouri).

[10]R. Valett, "A Social Reinforcement Technique for the Classroom Management of Behavior Disorders," *Exceptional Children*, Vol. XXXIII, No. 3 (1966), pp. 185-189.

conditioned learning situations, including the use of small gifts, food, cash bonuses, and verbal praise.[11] For secondary school students the use of controlled access to learning centers, together with a point system that converts points to free time for handicrafts, typing, woodworking, games, and science units, has been found by Nolen, *et al.* to be a powerful motivator for this age group.[12] A report by O'Leary and Becker demonstrates that a structured token system with the systematic use of varied rewards, such as candy, peanuts, comics, perfume, and popsicles, for the entire class can be very effective in shaping desirable classroom behavior (such as remaining in one's seat, facing the front, raising hand, etc.).[13]

School psychologists are rapidly applying behavior modification techniques to both individual pupils and group situations; for example, Dickinson has developed a highly effective contract system for use with individual pupils. His system also provides a prescriptive approach for teacher involvement.[14] An excellent review of behavior modification rationale and technique for use by school psychologists has been presented by Franks and Susskind and includes several references to studies involving parents in behavior modification programs.[15] Similarly an article by David Ryback,[16] although oversimplified and somewhat misleading, did focus attention on the involvement of parents in behavior modification programs similar to the work being done by Dr. Gerald Patterson's research group at the University of Oregon, where parents are systematically trained to observe and modify the behavior of their children.[17]

It is quite apparent from these and other studies that the principles of learning are being applied systematically to the classroom in a wide variety of situations, including both regular and exceptional pupils. For clarification purposes these basic principles are summarized here with an illustration of the application of each in the programming of learning disabilities.

Principles of Learning

1. **Readiness:** A child will learn when he has the interest and the desire to learn and when he recognizes purpose and meaning in the task at hand. The programming of learning disabilities should begin by determining strengths and interests, and by utilizing both intrinsic and extrinsic motivation.

   Example: Bill's readiness to learn was stimulated by teacher exploration of his interest in and curiosity about horses. He was motivated to complete his assigned learning tasks through an extrinsic reward system culminating in weekly horseback riding privileges.

[11]R. Schwitzgebel, "Short-term Operant Conditioning of Adolescent Offenders on Socially Relevant Variables," *Dissertation Abstracts,* Vol. XXV, No. 8 (1963), pp. 503-515.

[12]P. A. Nolen, H. P. Kunzelmann, and N..C. Haring, "Behavioral Modification in a Junior High Learning Disabilities Classroom," *Exceptional Children,* Vol. XXXIV, No. 3 (1967), pp. 163-167.

[13]K. D. O'Leary and W. C. Becker, "Behavior Modification of an Adjustment Class: A Token Reinforcement Program," *Exceptional Children,* Vol. XXXIII, No. 9 (1967), pp. 637-642.

[14]D. J. Dickinson, "Changing Behavior with Behavioral Techniques," *Journal of School Psychology* (Winter, 1968-69).

[15]C. M. Franks and D. J. Susskind, "Behavior Modification with Children: Rationale and Technique," *Journal of School Psychology,* Vol. VI, No. 2 (1968), pp. 75-88.

[16]D. Ryback, "A Parent's Guide for Use of Operant Conditioning with Disturbed Children," *California State Federation, Council for Exceptional Children Journal,* Vol. XVII, No. 1 (1967), pp. 16-19.

[17]G. Patterson, "Mother and Father Behavior Modifiers" (Invited address at the California Association of School Psychologists' and Psychometrists' Annual Conference, March, 1968).

2. **Effect:** Pupils should be programmed with educational tasks that are appropriate for their developmental and achievement levels and that have a high probability of success.
   Example: In order to obtain Ralph's cooperation in learning to read, he was programmed with material on an achievement level that both challenged him and assured him a good chance of accomplishment.

3. **Cue discrimination:** Learning tasks should be programmed in small structured units, systematically proceeding from material that has been successfully accomplished to the next level of difficulty. Be sure the child has recognized the new material to be learned.
   Example: Betty's body coordination and balance gradually improved through the use of sequential exercises with the balance beam and jump rope.

4. **Immediate reinforcement:** Upon successful accomplishment of new learning tasks children should be rewarded with praise and extrinsic symbols. If necessary, primary rewards, such as food and tokens, should be used.
   Example: Barbara was taught to talk by immediately placing M & M candy in her mouth every time she correctly repeated the names of simple objects presented to her.

5. **Intermittent reinforcement:** Once the child has learned the task he should continue to be rewarded, but evaluation and reward can now be given upon completion of several tasks or at the end of an assignment period.
   Example: Tom's arithmetic work was evaluated and rewards were given every 20 minutes. However, Tom's teacher would also occasionally give him M & M candy when he was working extra hard or attending unusually well.

6. **Social reinforcement:** The school peer group must be recognized as a powerful source of reinforcement for behavior modification. When primary rewards are used with the individual pupil, a related bonus reward should be given to the class as a whole. The class peer group should also be involved in giving special rewards and recognition to individual pupils.
   Example: On Friday afternoon Mrs. Thompson's class enjoyed sharing the candy that had been earned as a bonus reward for the group by individual pupils who had completed varied assignments during the week.

7. **Negative reinforcement:** Occasionally, the child should be deprived of privileges or carefully punished for *not* doing the assigned task. (Negative reinforcement must be used with caution since emotional behavior is easily conditioned in an undesirable way by traumatic association.)
   Example: Steve was restricted at home for the weekend because he failed to do his assigned chores during the week.

8. **Drill and feedback:** Repeated success and varied reinforcement experiences should be provided before moving pupils to significantly more difficult material. Children should be involved in evaluating their own performance and in the correction of their mistakes.
   Example: Mr. Brown rewarded Alan with 20 bonus points for correcting his arithmetic mistakes.

9. **Transfer and generalization:** The teacher should provide opportunities for skills already learned to be used in varied and related situations. The child should be helped to analyze the new situation and to apply relevant skills.
   Example: John transferred his new word attack skills learned from practice on simple materials to direct use with the regular classroom readers under the tutoring of his special teacher.

10. **Extinction:** Do not reward or pay attention to behavior that you do *not* want
    to be learned; remember that inappropriate behavior is inhibited ("un-
    learned") through fatigue and nonreinforcement.
    Example: Joan's mother paid no attention to her when she acted out her
    frustration in temper tantrums. After a while, the tantrums lessened and then
    disappeared altogether.

11. **Insight and understanding:** The pupil must be led to understand what is
    desired or expected in the learning situation and how this new knowledge
    may be used in problem solving. Hopefully, the child will become aware of
    the change in his "system of knowledge" and will know how to apply this
    new insight.
    Example: Joe was taught to role-play the logical consequences of various
    forms of social behavior. As a result, his personal behavior toward others
    improved considerably.

In devising educational programs for the remediation of learning disabilities, an
effort should be made to apply these principles of learning. The educational environment should be organized in such a way that the entire system, including the
daily schedule, learning task assignments, and the rewards and punishments to be
used, is fully understood by the pupils involved. (The reader is referred to Hunter's
excellent book entitled *Reinforcement Theory for Teachers,* which gives a practical
programmed introduction to the application of learning theory in the classroom.[18])
Teachers in special learning disability programs should have in-service training
meetings, and deliberate consideration should be given to the development of practical behavior modification systems in their own classrooms.

The Reinforcement Hierarchy

Any behavior modification system devised for classroom operation must recognize the need to provide a hierarchy of reinforcements for the pupils involved. In
accordance with the preceding principles, the system must provide for social reinforcement (such as peer group recognition), immediate primary reinforcement
(such as candy), if necessary, and eventually, intrinsic rewards through a developing sense of personal satisfaction resulting from achievement and recognition.

SOCIAL REINFORCEMENT

Classroom organization and the structure of the learning environment are crucial
in the development of an effective social reinforcement system. The structure
should provide for the following forms of social reinforcement:

1. *School acceptance:* The pupil must be capable of entering into an educational
   setting; moreover, he must want to attend school. The school, in turn, must
   accept the child if he meets the minimum criteria for placement. It should be
   recognized, however, that all programs have their limitations, and that it may
   not be possible for some children to meet the minimum demands of the
   situation. For example, lack of toilet training, bizarre or highly disrupting
   behavior, etc., may make it essential to limit the child's attendance to a
   shorter day, to place him on home teaching, or in extreme cases to exempt him

[18]M. Hunter, *Reinforcement Theory for Teachers* (El Segundo, Calif.: TIP Publications,
1967).

from school attendance. Most children with learning problems and behavior disorders can learn to control themselves for given periods of time, and reduction of attendance to a half-day, a period or two, or even for only the amount of time that self-control can be maintained permits these children to attend school. Sometimes, such pupils are further aided by a mild tranquilizing medication that, together with a limited day, may make some school attendance possible. Over a period of time most children come to prefer the stimulation of their peer group; therefore, school attendance in itself is accepted and becomes a strong social reinforcer.

2. *Class privileges:* Membership within the class should denote several privileges that acknowledge the awareness and involvement of the individual pupil and that can be manipulated for reinforcement purposes. Such activities as participation in class discussions, projects, leadership roles, in-school work placement, field trip attendance, etc., can be built into the system.

3. *Direct physical contact:* The teacher can and should use direct physical contact with pupils as a social reinforcer. Of course, these contacts must be adapted to the level of the pupils and will cover the entire gamut from the kissing, hugging, and actual stroking of young children to clapping with touching and an occasional pat on the back or hand for older pupils.

4. *Verbal reinforcement:* Verbal reward can be a powerful social reinforcer. It includes direct praise and recognition, the indirect involvement of listening and attending to pupils, and an occasional personal acknowledgment through the use of positive exclamations and grunts.

5. *Group dynamics and shaping:* One of the most successful social reinforcers that should be built into the system is the conscious use of peer group pressure to motivate learning and to shape and control behavior. Through the development of classroom codes of behavior and the use of a special "Citizens' Council" such as outlined by Stiavelli and Shirley,[19] specific pupil behaviors can be subjected to continual evaluation by the group and shaped or modified in accordance with deliberate rewards or punishment as decided by the group itself.

PRIMARY REWARDS

Once the over-all system of social reinforcement has been established, provision should be made for the utilization of primary rewards as necessary. In this context primary rewards are defined as any material object that can provide immediate gratification to the pupil concerned. With young children food may be used to reward every initial correct response; with older pupils more complex but tangible rewards may prove to be more effective. The possible range of reinforcers is vast and includes sunflower seeds, peanuts, raisins, fruit loops, M & M's, chocolate drops, single pieces of varied candies, candy bars, lollipops, cookies, cakes, soft drinks, ice cream, milk, sandwiches and lunches, toy rings and other jewelry, treasure box toys of assorted values, grab bags, comics, magazines (*Hot Rod, Teen Age, Mad*, etc.), movie tickets, athletic admission tickets, direct use of swimming pools, direct access to use of body weights, educational toys, and puzzles, and controlled access to special exploratory and learning centers in the room.

[19] R. S. Stiavelli and D. T. Shirley, "The Citizens' Council: A Technique for Managing Behavior Disorders in the Educationally Handicapped Class," *Journal for School Psychology*, Vol. VI, No. 2 (1968), pp. 147-153.

When primary rewards are administered, they should always be accompanied with secondary reinforcement, such as verbal praise and acknowledgment. Provision should also be made within the system to move from immediate reinforcement to more intermittent reinforcement where gratification is put off for longer periods of time.

In the establishment and administration of a reinforcement hierarchy consideration must also be given to the use of tokens as substitutes for immediate primary reinforcements. Every educational system uses some token rewards, such as letter and numerical grades. These have seldom proved effective with pupils with specific learning disabilities and behavioral disorders as they are too general, too abstract, relatively infrequent, and are more often perceived as punishments than as rewards. A good token system must be discriminatory in that the pupils can recognize the basis for the rating. It must also be quantitative, cumulative, and have an exchange value if the learner desires to use it. Tokens should be directly related to the hierarchy of primary and social reinforcement so that they have functional value in the total learning program. In order to accomplish its purpose, the token system should be written out and displayed in a way similar to that presented in the following sections.

A variety of tokens are available for classroom use—colored stars, rubber stamps (animal pictures), C marks for correct responses, "hash marks" for correct responses (/), paper tickets, score cards for accumulating marks, marbles, poker chips, pennies, cash slips or checks, and privilege passes—to name just a few of those most commonly used. Whatever the token, it is essential that it be negotiable for something of value to the pupil.

INVOLVEMENT

Another aspect of the reinforcement hierarchy to be considered here is the system of involvement. All of the important people involved with the learner are meaningfully integrated into the dispensation of rewards. In effect, this means that the pupils' peer group, his special teacher, other teachers, and his parents must all cooperate in a consistent approach to the reinforcement of desired behaviors. Therefore, some means of systematic communication must be developed for use by the special teacher and others involved with the child, including the parents. Where this cooperation is developed and where the behavior modification system relates to specific psychoeducational tasks to be programmed within the school situation, we can assume that learning will occur.

Developing Behavior Modification Systems

THE PUPIL PERFORMANCE RECORD

The first example is concerned with the recording, rating, and rewarding of pupil performance behaviors in the special classroom setting. Since the pupil with significant learning disabilities must be programmed accordingly, some provision must be made for evaluating and rewarding those specific psychoeducational tasks that have been programmed. One method is to build-in the evaluation and reward system as part of the daily prescription for learning. On the sample "Daily Lesson Assignment" sheet (*Fig. 11-1*) a task has been prescribed in each of the six major learning areas. For each task performed, the pupil is rated according to how well he pays attention, how hard he works, if he completes the work, and his general

DAILY LESSON ASSIGNMENTS

Name __Billy__   Date __1/17/68__

	Pays Attention (starts work)	Works Hard (good posture and attitude)	Completes Work (neatly done)	Accuracy Fair some correct	Good most correct	Exc. all correct	Special Behavior Award (1 to 3 bonus points)
Points Earned	/	/	/	/	/		

Gross Motor Development

Rolling
Sitting
Crawling
Walking
Running
Throwing
Jumping
Skipping
Dancing
Self-identification
Body localization
Body abstraction
/ Muscular strength
General physical health

Beginning time: 8:40
1. Do three push-ups and ten jumping jacks.

Points Earned							
1.	/	/	0	/	/		/
2.	/	/	/	/			

Sensory-Motor Integration

Balance and rhythm
Body-spatial organization
Reaction speed-dexterity
1,2 Tactile discrimination
Directionality
Laterality
Time orientation

Beginning time: 11:00
1. Play the Feeley Meeley Game.
2. Discriminate all wooden letters of the alphabet in the Feeley Meeley box.

Figure 11-1

	Pays Attention (starts work)	Works Hard (good posture and attitude)	Completes Work (neatly done)	Accuracy Fair some correct	Good most correct	Exc. all correct	Special Behavior Award (1 to 3 bonus points)
Points Earned	1. /	/	/	/			
	2. /	/	0	0			

Perceptual-Motor Skills

Auditory: Acuity
A-Vocal association
A-Decoding
A-Memory
/ A-Sequencing
Visual: Acuity
V-Coordination and pursuit
V-Form discrimination
V-Figure/ground
2 V-Memory
Visual-Motor: Memory
VM-Fine muscle coordination
VM-Spatial-form manipulation
VM-Speed of learning
VM-Integration

Beginning time: 12:30
1. Carry out a series of sequential directions to be given by the teacher.
2. Play the Concentration card game with George.

Points Earned	1. /	/	/	/	/	/	
	2. /	0	0	0	Quit	work	

Language Development

Vocabulary
Fluency and encoding
Articulation
/ Word attack skills
2 Reading comprehension
Writing
Spelling

Beginning time: 8:50
1. Complete the Fun with Phonics Exercise sheet (from Highlights for Children).
2. Read assigned story and answer questions.

Figure 11-1—_Continued_

	Pays Attention (starts work)	Works Hard (good posture and attitude)	Completes Work (neatly done)	Fair some correct	Accuracy Good most correct	Exc. all correct	Special Behavior Award (1 to 3 bonus points)
Points Earned	/	/	/	/	/		

Conceptual Skills

Number concepts
Arithmetic processes
Arithmetic reasoning
General information
/ Classification
Comprehension

Beginning time: 10:00
1. Complete the Classification Game.

Points Earned	/	/	/	/			3

Social Skills

Social acceptance
/ Anticipatory response
Value judgments
Social maturity

Beginning time: 10:30
1. Play checkers and discuss alternate moves. (Special behavior award points for helping Tommy at recess.)

Got in a fight.

Citizens' Council Code Awards

Respects Other's Rights (lines up, takes turns, (does not hit))   0

Respects Other's Property (helps keep school clean, does not destroy or take things)   /

Attempts To Understand Others' Feelings (does not call names, is courteous and kind)   /

Tries To Be a Good Neighbor (cooperates, raises hand, helps others)   /

Total Points Earned Today *42*

Figure 11-1—Continued

accuracy; in each of these areas he can earn one point for each task. In addition, it is possible to earn up to three points at any time for completion of special assignments or as a reward for exceptional behavior that the teacher may wish to shape; for example, one or more points might be awarded for correcting prior errors, extra good work or effort, manners, correctly reading new words, improving reading speed in a three-minute period, unusual self-control, etc. Figure 11-1 shows that Billy earned a total of 42 points on that day for his performance in the areas indicated. This included three points awarded through the "Citizens' Council" by a decision of his peer group.

The major value of such a system is that it provides a specific record for use by the pupil as well as by the teacher. If the assignment sheets are maintained in an individual three-ring binder for each child, the reports provide a continual record of pupil performance that will be of use in future programming. The use of these assignment sheets also contributes to the development of a meaningful sense of involvement, progress, and direction for the pupil concerned.

THE DAILY BEHAVIOR RECORD

The second example illustrates one method of recording daily behavior ratings from regular teachers and parents as well as from the special teacher (*Fig. 11-2*). Through the use of such a record, the pupil becomes aware that his total behavior is of concern and that he is being cooperatively evaluated and rewarded by many different persons. This form of record is usually most helpful in shaping the behavior of difficult pupils. It must, of course, be worked out and developed in full cooperation with the parents and the other teachers involved. In the illustration presented, Billy was able to earn 6 points in the regular program, 42 points from his special teacher, and 5 points from his behavior at home. It should be noted that in this system the pupil carries his record sheet with him when he goes out to attend a regular class; the regular teacher awards points and immediately signs her name or initials. The record is then carried home from school each night and presented to the parents for their use and completion at the end of the day. Family rewards are usually given on a weekly basis, although they can be awarded daily if the situation demands it. Generally, however, family rewards for the preceding week are given on Friday night.

A CONTINGENCY SYSTEM

The third and last example concerns the nature of the contingency system employed and the means by which the pupil may cash in his points for whatever he values. The basic unit in the system recommended here is the single white poker chip. The poker chip is an attractive and tangible token and is quickly recognized by most pupils as having significant exchange value. The recommended procedure is to begin immediate primary reinforcement by giving single M & M's (or similar food items), and then quickly substitute poker chips for the candy with the explanation that one chip can be exchanged at any time for a single candy. Upon receipt of his poker chip, the child should place it in a distinctive plastic container on his desk so that he can frequently see the chips and use them as counters or manipulating devices. Following initial orientation to the system, the child should be switched to intermittent reinforcement upon completion of assignments—evaluation and poker chips can be awarded approximately every 20 minutes. Although the teacher awards the chips, it is important that the child record on his "Daily Lesson Assignment" record sheet *why he is being rewarded*.

DAILY BEHAVIOR RECORD

Pupil's name _Billy_   Date _1/17/68_

Regular Class Behavior

Class _Physical Education_ Teacher's initials _A. E._

	Poor (0)	Fair (1)	Good (2)	Exc. (3)
Pays attention		✓		
Works hard and has good attitude	✓			
Completes work		✓		
Accuracy	✓			

Class _Music_ Teacher's initials _F. Q._

	Poor (0)	Fair (1)	Good (2)	Exc. (3)
Pays attention		✓		
Works hard and has good attitude		✓		
Completes work		✓		
Accuracy		✓		

Class _____ Teacher's initials _____

Pays attention				
Works hard and has good attitude				
Completes work				
Accuracy				

Special Class Behavior

	Total Special Class Points Earned
Pays attention	9
Works hard and has good attitude	8
Completes work	6
Accuracy	12
Special behavior awards	4
Citizens' Council awards	3

Home Behavior

	Poor (0)	Fair (1)	Good (2)	Exc. (3)
General attitude and actions			✓	
Home chores and responsibilities		✓		
Other _Helped little brother._			✓	

Total points earned for the day _53_

(Parents are to total all points earned during the day and retain the record; family rewards should be given on Friday night for the preceding week.)

Figure 11-2

The following is a recommended exchange or contingency system; an explanation of the system should be placed on the bulletin board with samples of poker chips and other objects involved in order to motivate the pupils to understand the rationale and to regulate their behavior accordingly.

One white poker chip	= Praise + one single candy	(1 point)
Ten white poker chips	= Praise + one red poker chip *or* special penny candy	(10 points)
Five red poker chips	= Praise + one blue poker chip *or* candy bar	(50 points)
Two blue poker chips	= Praise + one green ticket *or* ice cream, fruit, etc., *or* admission to field trip *or* admission to selected learning center for 20 minutes	(100 points)
Three green tickets	= Praise + surprise grab bag *or* special magazine *or* admission to learning center *or* free time for a one-hour period *or* one gold privilege pass	(300 points)
Two gold privilege passes	= Movie, sports admissions, special work privileges in the school, etc. Special rewards upon arrangement with parents	(600 points)
Citizenship Pin	= The Citizenship Pin is awarded to those pupils who have been elected to the "Citizens' Council" and who have remained there for two weeks. Wearers of the pin auto- matically derive privileges of being first in line, class monitors, office messengers, game leaders, etc.	

Some form of day-to-day tabulation of total points earned needs to be kept (*Fig. 11-3*). This record should be placed on the bulletin board or wall and constantly kept up-to-date. Most pupils can be taught to maintain their record, which also is a valuable aid in developing interest, attention, and numerical skill. It must be emphasized that the child is recording his own behavior and is not in competition with others since his learning program is a highly individualized one.

INDIVIDUAL PUPIL TOTAL AWARD RECORD

Name _Billy_   School _Washington_

Date	Points previously earned and saved	+ Points earned today	− Points used today	= Total cumulative points	Gold privilege passes	Member of Citizens' Council	
						Yes	No
1/17	226	53	0	279	0	✓	
1/18	279	41	10	310	1	✓	
1/19	310	67	58	319	1	✓	
1/20	319	12	300	31	0		✓
1/21	31	72	0	103	0	✓	

Figure 11-3

The "class party" system is a related technique to further social reinforcement by involving class members in helping one another and by encouraging individual pupil performance. Every other Friday afternoon the entire class is given a free period with candy or other refreshments. The refreshments for the class are based on the work of the individual pupil—for every 50 points earned by the individual pupil, 5 additional points are awarded to the class party fund. Thus, if Billy earned 490 points in a two-week period, an additional 45 points would be placed in the party fund. The total party fund could then be used to purchase refreshments that all class members would share equally.

In such a contingency system it is obvious that some special financial allocations must be made in order to purchase rewards and refreshments. Each district operating such a program should allocate the amount necessary to fund each pupil involved in the program. For special education pupils these funds can justifiably be charged to special instructional allowances. If work-experience programs are involved, with cash payments for older pupils, other financial sources may be available. In many districts PTA's may be willing to donate to such programs; in others the parents of the children involved may be able to donate. The parents of pupils with learning and behavior disorders should always be intimately involved in the behavior modification program, including the reinforcement system itself. One common means of direct involvement is for the parents to reward the child over and above the school and in addition to any family allowance system. As mentioned earlier, one child who was highly interested in horses was rewarded with horseback riding on Saturdays on the basis of ten minutes of riding for every 50 points earned during the previous week. Needless to say, such a cooperative system can be highly effective for all concerned.

12

Supporting Programs and Services

Introductory Concepts

When planning and organizing learning disability programs, adequate provision must be made for supporting services. Supporting services are those direct auxiliary services for the special classroom teacher that are essential for a successful program. Without these essential programs and services, it is almost impossible for the best-intentioned and trained teacher to maintain a learning disabilities program. Too often school districts begin special programs for children with learning disabilities, but fail to plan for the necessary supporting services from the very beginning. In most cases it is best not to begin any new program unless a carefully developed plan and rationale that includes necessary supporting services has been decided upon.

Before considering some of the specific supporting programs and services for learning disability programs, it must be recognized that all pupils, handicapped and regular, could profit from a number of additional services that most school districts now provide only in very limited ways. A notable example is the need for widespread and well-developed preschool screening, early problem identification, and cooperative preschool programs; the value of such programs in preventing the development of more serious learning problems in later school years is almost self-evident. A second example is the nongraded school program, which is receiving more acceptance with the growing awareness of the importance of providing for individual differences throughout the school system. General prevocational work exploration and later actual work-experience programs that are coordinated through the schools are also becoming of increasing importance to the handicapped and nonhandicapped student alike. For years the need for more personal counseling and guidance programs, smaller class sizes, and increased instructional material and library resources—to name just a few things—has been recognized, but these programs and services, although regarded as an integral part of any sound educational system, are still utilized only on a limited basis.

Ideally, these supporting services should be provided for *all* children. Even though it is quite evident that the above services are important for both regular and handicapped children, the fact remains that they are generally not available on any widespread scale. The district that has all of these programs for its students is indeed fortunate, but it is also very rare. If these supporting services exist in school at all, because of financial limitations they are too often limited to special education classes instead of being applied to all students, both regular and handicapped.

In addition to the above general supporting services, the following specific programs and services must be considered as essential elements for success when organizing a learning disabilities program.

1. *Psychological services:* The school psychologist is involved in the initial screening, evaluation, and placement of the special pupil and in the follow-up consultation and programming. If there is to be adequate psychoeducational consultation for teacher, pupil, and parents, it is recommended that there be one psychologist for a maximum of every 125 pupils *enrolled* in the program.

2. *Health services:* Medical screening, liaison, and nursing services must be provided in a higher ratio than for regular pupils because of the greater incident of health and related physical problems experienced by pupils with learning disabilities.

3. *Innovative programs and applied research:* Since educational programs for children with learning disabilities are relatively new in most school districts, those concerned with the development and administration of these programs must recognize the necessity for a conscious awareness of the limited knowledge available in the field and must be dedicated to seeking out available research data that may have applied implications. Then they must be willing to proceed in the development of innovative and evolving programs.

4. *Parent involvement programs:* With regular pupils parent involvement is rather incidental, but with children with learning disabilities parent involvement is basic to the success of the entire program. Formal parent education, participation programs, conferences, discussion groups, and counseling should be included in the total program.

5. *In-service training:* Experience has demonstrated that good regular teachers can be retrained to work with pupils with learning disabilities. It is impractical, however, to count on formal training institutions to provide all of the required training, and it is imperative that a well-developed, supporting in-service training program be maintained by the school district itself.

6. *Instructional and resource services:* Because of the nature of specific learning abilities and the demands of the prescriptive teaching approach, special provision must be made for unique equipment, books, materials, and supplies that are quite different from those used or required in the regular program.

7. *Coordination and supervision:* The organization, development, and direction of a learning disabilities program needs to be carefully integrated and coordinated. In most districts of any size a full-time coordinator-supervisor should be provided to handle screening procedures, placement, admission, in-service training, supervision and teacher program consultation, and curriculum development.

The preceding list of supporting programs is not all-inclusive and can probably be supplemented by the reader. Psychological and health services will not be discussed here since they both have been fully covered in previous chapters. The remainder of this chapter will consider some of these supporting services in depth and will present some tried and proven approaches to their implementation.

Innovative Programs and Applied Research

Since innovation and the application of existing knowledge are much needed in the planning of learning disability programs, these will be considered first. Specifically, the teaching of social skills is presently recognized as an area of great importance and one in need of innovation. It is readily apparent that the child or adult who lacks proper social skills, such as manners, techniques of gaining social acceptance, or the ability to accept social and personal responsibility, is bound to have considerable difficulty both in and out of school. Although the importance of these skills is recognized on the elementary and secondary level alike, relatively little has been done to develop a meaningful curriculum to teach these skills.

SECONDARY SCHOOL

Most people are fully aware that during the adolescent years in senior high school many young people lack value orientation, goals, or direction, and feel lonely, isolated, and alienated from peer group and society. These feelings often result in many problems, and the student may drop out of school or exhibit other maladaptive behavior. The problem, of course, has been how to meet the needs of students and how to involve them meaningfully in the entire educational process so that a commitment to both personal and social betterment results. Although the basic key to such involvement is the attitude and behavior of the teacher, who must be willing to work closely and directly with the student concerned, the need also exists for alternatives to the programs and teaching approaches currently being used in most school systems. A number of innovative approaches have been tried and appear to have some value for further investigation.

For some time now, extensive audiovisual materials have been used in group guidance and social skills courses. Over the past few years a number of individual guidance filmstrips and recordings covering everything from family problems to sexual reproduction and personal value orientation have been produced. Through the use of individual listening posts, filmstrip centers, taped class discussions of social skill problems, and other related materials and techniques, many new possibilities for programming exist in this field.

Community action programs also offer new innovative approaches worthy of exploration. Field trips to Head Start programs, maternity wards, jails, courts, city councils, community center projects, model legislature programs, etc., are being organized according to the developmental levels of pupils involved and are structured to introduce the pupil to meaningful social situations and to involve him in the processes of both thinking through the problems of concern and possibly doing something about them through such means as student tutoring and community work projects.

As mentioned previously, the working world also offers almost unlimited opportunity for involvement of pupils, especially those of secondary school age. Experience has shown that where pupils have been involved in sound and worthwhile work programs, many behavior problems are eliminated, and social skills are improved. The opportunity for exploration of fields of employment, followed by actual part-time work experience while in school and later placement in a job under school supervision, should be included in all secondary programs for handicapped pupils.

FUTURE PROGRAMS

A number of promising and innovative programs seem possible in the near future. Already some attempts have been made to introduce *transactional analysis*[1] into adolescent counseling and parent education groups, and some of Berne's concepts will undoubtedly find their way into the classroom as well. Problem simulation techniques, including the use of extended role playing and games are being incorporated into curricular programs; new family games and games of strategy such as Career, Life, and others offer many opportunities for classroom adaptation. A direct attempt at teaching value orientation is also being made using the classroom presentation of selected jokes, humorous situations and stories, parables, proverbs, and folklore, followed by analytical discussion and search for alternate interpretations and solutions to the problems presented. All of these approaches have promising features and offer much in the way of possible creative innovation in the organization of new learning disability programs.

Parent Involvement Programs

Meaningful parent involvement in learning disability programs should begin as soon as it is realized that there is a possibility that the child is in need of special help. A system of early parent contact and responsible reporting of learning strengths and weaknesses by the professionals concerned, together with teacher observation of total behavior, must be planned from the beginning. Ideally, the system should encourage frequent direct contact on the part of all teachers with parents. In this way a cooperative teamwork approach is engendered in the education of the child, and both parents and teachers are alerted by early learning difficulties. If continued review of the child's problem by those concerned results in the need for formal referral to special education or other treatment programs, the family should take an active role in the entire process.

Too often, however, it is found that children are placed in special programs and their parents have never been involved in any meaningful way. As discussed earlier,

[1]E. Berne, *Transactional Analysis in Psychotherapy* (New York: Grove Press, Inc., 1961).

it is recommended that at the point of actual referral for possible special program placement or treatment the referring teacher and principal again meet with both parents to discuss the entire learning problem and its implications. After the specialized evaluation by the school psychologist and the physician, there should be a follow-up conference to interpret the results of the examinations and to relate them to the future learning program in terms that the parents can understand.

TEACHER-PARENT CONTACT

Once the child has been placed in a special program, the special education teacher assumes the responsibility of working with him and with the parents in every possible way. Often, the first contact with parents is through arrangements for a home visitation prior to placement of the child in the program. This visit is highly recommended because it allows the teacher to meet the parents on their own ground, to make social contact with them, to observe the child in his natural environment, and to discuss some of his needs and interests with the parents. All of the information gained during the visitation should be helpful in programming him in the school situation. Many teachers of self-contained classes prefer to visit all of their assigned pupils in advance and then to arrange for them to come into the class one-by-one, according to a schedule allowing for the best possible orientation and integration of all pupils. The home visitation program has much to offer and should be an integral part of the professional responsibility of all teachers since it permits the teacher to be viewed in a different light by both parents and pupils. Although it is best that such visitations be made as often as is felt to be necessary and profitable, they should always be made at least twice a year, during the beginning and end of the school term.

EVALUATION AND RATING

Parents also need to be directly involved in the evaluation and rating of their children's behavior. Of course, this is already done to some extent, since during home visitations, initial interviews, etc., parents report specifics of their children's behavior that may have relevance to the educational situation. However, the parents should be brought into a more systematic evaluation of the educational progress of their children. For instance, psychologists have long relied on parent reporting to estimate the child's level of social competency, as measured by the Vineland Social Maturity Scale.[2]

Now many preschool programs are requesting parents to assess their children's specific readiness behaviors directly on such instruments as the School Readiness Survey.[3] The use of behavior checklists, systematic observations of specific behaviors of concern to both parents and educators, and other procedures hold promise for bridging the communication gap that exists between so many parents and the school.

CONFERENCES

Much also needs to be done to further the participation of parents in regular school-parent conferences within the school setting itself. Many schools are estab-

[2]E. Doll, *Vineland Social Maturity Scale* (Minneapolis, Minn.: Educational Test Bureau-Educational Publishers, Inc., 1947).

[3]F. L. Jordan and J. Massey, *School Readiness Survey* (Palo Alto, Calif.: Consulting Psychologists Press, Inc., 1967).

lishing parent conference weeks in the fall and spring of the school year. During these weeks teachers are placed on a limited teaching day and given time to schedule conferences with all parents at the school. Although this is a valuable adjunct to the regular reporting system, which too often consists only of traditional grade markings, the conference is usually so limited in time that it does not permit a meaningful parent-teacher relationship, where the parent feels free to discuss his concerns and feelings regarding the entire educational program to be developed. Some special means need to be provided for the parent of the child with a learning disability to confer with the teacher and/or the school administrator on a much more frequent and involved basis than is true with the regular pupil. It must be recognized and accepted by the principal concerned that he will be involved with a good many families in this type of joint conference.

REPORTING PROGRESS

Consideration must also be given to the problem of formal reporting of pupil progress. Although there is no simple solution to this perplexing problem, it must be recognized that the usual letter or number marks have little meaning for the child with specific learning problems. If letter or number grades are to be given, it is recommended that they be awarded for progress relative to the child's own ability and handicap rather than to some arbitrary class standard. In most cases report cards should carry written descriptions of the progress made in the pupil's individual learning program and should contain recommendations for helping the child to progress in the school term to come. Because of the problem of misunderstanding, it has been found helpful to convey grades in a personal letter of interpretation to the parents; this may then be followed up by a parent-teacher conference at a later date to discuss the ensuing educational plan.

PARENT PARTICIPATION

Throughout the school year, many opportunities present themselves for parents of children with learning disabilities to become involved in the educational process. A planned approach to direct parent involvement is necessary, however, since even the most interested parents need to be invited to participate and to be shown how their time and effort can be used. Although parents have long been involved in cooperative programs such as preschool teacher's aide assignments, it has only been in recent times that serious consideration has been given to having parents serve as aides in the elementary classroom. Admittedly, there are many difficulties inherent in such an arrangement, but it does appear as though parents could begin work in learning disability classes as participant-observers and then gradually move into specific teacher's aide assignments. For example, parents could assist in the construction of learning materials, preparation of art media, supervision of learning centers and special activities, and also in the direct tutoring of children under the assignment and supervision of the special teacher. If it is felt to be unwise for the parent to work with her own child, assignments could be undertaken with other children in either the same or different classrooms.

Another means of gradual parental involvement is to hold class orientation meetings for parents a few weeks after school has started. At this time the teacher and psychologist could review the educational program, answer questions, and encourage participation. Throughout the course of the year, follow-up meetings can be held when special demonstrations of instructional materials, lesson assignments, etc., can be presented and meaningfully discussed. After these introductory meetings parents might themselves be involved in giving occasional classroom demonstrations, assisting in field trips, arranging for special visits to businesses of some relevance or interest to a pupil, and helping in many other ways. It must be recognized that most parents are vitally interested in the education of their children and many are eager and willing to help. Unfortunately, reluctance on the part of professional educators has retarded parental involvement more than can be logically justified; thus, it is a promising area for constructive change.

PARENT EDUCATION

Much has been written about the value of formal parent education programs, although most districts have done relatively little in working with parents of exceptional children. A great need exists to make such programs available to all interested parents on a regular basis. Courses might deal with broad program concerns and be entitled, "The Educationally Handicapped Child," "The Exceptional Child in School," etc.; they could include both formal and informal presentations, films, classroom visitations, speakers, parent panels, role playing, and problem case discussions. Other parent education programs may focus on the book and program, *Parent Effectiveness Training*,[4] transactional analysis in family situations, or how to deal with problems of communication, discipline, and related concerns as advocated by various experts such as Gesell,[5] Ilg and Ames,[6] Ginott,[7] and others. Whatever the formal content of such programs, adequate provision must be made for parents to meet in small informal discussion groups and to talk with the teacher and psychologist working directly with their child.

If the program is organized to permit ready access of parents to educators, it must be expected that, sooner or later, the following questions will be raised:

1. What is my child's major learning problem at this time?
2. How does his present educational program relate to the remediation of his learning problems?
3. Should he have special homework, or should we tutor him at home in special areas? (How can we help him at home with his work?)
4. How long will he require special education?
5. Just how does the psychologist work with my child, and what does he do with him?
6. How can we help with improving his behavior at home?
7. Will he be able to finish school? Will he be able to go to college or receive special training?
8. How can we help him in school?
9. Does he need any additional special help? If so, where can we obtain this for him?

It can also be expected that professional educators will eventually be requested to give personal evaluations of the value of private school placement, special therapy programs, intensive tutoring such as remedial reading, speech therapy,

[4]T. Gordon, *Parent Effectiveness Training*, 110 South Euclid Avenue, Pasadena, Calif., 1964.
[5]A. Gesell and F. Ilg, *The Child from Five to Ten* (New York: Harper & Row, Publishers, 1946).
[6]F. Ilg and L. Ames, *Child Behavior* (New York: Harper & Row, Publishers, 1955).
[7]H. Ginott, *Between Parent and Child* (New York: The Macmillan Company, 1965).

"patterning programs," and family counseling, and many other related concerns. It is obvious that the teacher and/or psychologist will not be in a position to respond adequately to many of these requests for help, and parents will have to be referred to other sources. It is apparent, however, that the special educator must become involved with the parents both as a teacher and educational counselor and that this role must be accepted as part of the over-all professional responsibility in working with children with learning disabilities.

In-service Training

Every special program for the education of children with learning disabilities must provide supporting in-service training for teachers, administrators, nurses, physicians, aides, and other personnel involved. With the rapid development of program innovations, new materials, and the accumulating data from research in this field, an integrated in-service training program has become a necessity.

NEW TEACHERS

In-service training begins with the careful orientation of new teachers and personnel at the time of employment. This should take the form of a thorough explanation of the program philosophy and the professional demands on the teacher, together with an explanation of the necessity of her commitment to participation in regular in-service training. Initial orientation is best followed up with preassignment workshops and informal classes where the entire program is discussed in detail. Ample opportunity should be provided to visit classes, evaluate instructional materials, become acquainted with evaluation and curricular structure, and to become fully cognizant of the operating policy and rationale. In many systems, it is possible to offer such courses during the school year itself. These may be supplemented with all-day special workshops and extended summer workshops preceding the opening of school. Summer workshops should be organized to give the teachers the opportunity to be stimulated by outside consultants and to become involved in some detailed study or the development of relevant ideas that may be of significant value to the total program.

REGULAR PERSONNEL

Provision should also be made for the ongoing in-service training of regular staff members. In most districts regular in-service teacher meetings should be established on a frequent basis, perhaps weekly, to allow for meaningful teacher involvement. If there are four meetings per month, the content should be varied each week. At one all-teacher meeting new materials, films, or ideas of general concern could be presented. A second meeting could well be devoted to small group discussions with the consulting psychologist, with emphasis upon the open consideration of general psychological matters, such as the development of behavior modification systems, the possibility of applying the results of recent research in learning disability programs, understanding and applying the principles of learning, discipline problems, diagnostic evaluation of pupils and follow-up programming, etc. Another meeting could well be spent on group discussions when primary, elementary, junior high, and senior high school teachers could meet by themselves for selected case presentations; in this program, teachers should take turns selecting a pupil of concern for their case presentation to fellow teachers. The presentation should include specification of the educational problems and open consideration of alternate possible solutions. At least one meeting should be given over entirely to curriculum, instructional, and organizational problems.

GENERAL SUGGESTIONS

It is also important for districts to arrange for teachers and others involved to attend conferences and institutes, and to participate in various professional organizations. New teachers should be especially encouraged to attend formal training programs in colleges and universities and should be provided with financial aid through the district, PTA, or other concerned organizations. Visiting programs out of the local district is usually a most effective training procedure for new personnel, and the resulting infusion of new ideas and enthusiasm is well worth the limited cost involved. Cooperative projects with colleges or other institutions, and government research and demonstration projects also present many opportunities for in-service training resulting in professional growth.

Whatever the means of training may be, it is essential that the personnel involved look upon the program as an opportunity for personal professional growth and that they have some part in both the development and evaluation of the program. If teachers are provided with the means by which to communicate openly and freely with their colleagues and administrators through in-service training, the total program will flourish. Where the training program is conventional, formal, stilted, and planned without teacher and administrator involvement, little of any real value will be accomplished. Since the programming of learning disabilities is a relatively new and challenging field, professional people are usually eager for training. If in-service training is organized as a vital supporting service to the total program, the opportunity for meaningful contact with colleagues and administrators should stimulate all teachers.

The Learning Resource Center Approach

A need exists for supporting programs and services to be systematically integrated in order to meet the demands of an extensive program for exceptional children most adequately. One of the more successful recent approaches to this problem is through the development of learning resource centers for exceptional children. The primary purpose of the center is to make available necessary consultative, diagnostic, evaluative, training, parent education, educational therapy, and research services, together with a resource-material center, for all persons concerned with the remediation of learning disabilities and the education of exceptional children. Such a center is organized and operated through the special education office and the special funds available to the district.

STAFFING

Although the learning resource center can house as large a staff as desired, there are at least four crucial positions. The *director* of the center is usually a psychoeducational specialist whose major function is to serve as a professional consultant to special education personnel in the development of innovative and applied research projects and in the special evaluation and psychoeducational programming of specially referred children. An *educational psychologist* is a key staff member, with the primary responsibility of research design and evaluation, pupil evaluation, and experimental programming with pupils and parents. An *educational therapist* is assigned to the center with primary responsibility for doing direct educational therapy with selected pupils and parents and for serving as the liaison with the regular classroom teacher. If a *demonstration teacher* is provided, the center then has the flexibility to experiment with the introduction of new programs and instructional ideas into the classrooms.

SPACE REQUIREMENTS

Ideally, such a center should also provide space for a psychoeducational clinic and examining rooms, speech therapy, library materials, and administrative offices. The resource center should be large enough to provide adequate conference and in-service training space for regular teacher meetings, staff functions, and parent education programs. Cooperative training projects with students from local colleges or universities could also be coordinated here, and the center would become the focal point for badly needed applied research projects in all special education programs. The learning resource center must be recognized as being just a supplementary resource center of personnel and material and not a physical entity for centralizing all special education programs in one building or location. The center concept merely provides for the coordination and easier implementation of the vital auxiliary programs and supporting services of concern in any effective approach to the remediation of learning disabilities.

Coordination and Supervision

A successful learning disabilities program requires good coordination and careful supervision. The coordinator of such a program should have a teaching background and some further training in special education and educational psychology. Direct experience with children with learning disabilities is almost a prerequisite to supervision of others. Several facets of the coordinator's role are somewhat unique and warrant consideration here.

COORDINATOR'S ROLE

If the program is to have a fairly uniform rationale, the coordinator has the responsibility to insure that the basic district policy and program philosophy are being put into effect. The processing of referrals, admission and placement of pupils, classroom organization, allocation of equipment and instructional materials, and in-service training are usually the major coordinating functions. A few of the more important specific responsibilities include:

1. Interpreting the program to teachers, administrators, parents, and others concerned. Aiding teachers and administrators to understand the behavioral characteristics of pupils with learning disorders and assisting them in the screening, identification, and referral of such pupils.
2. Consulting with and training special diagnostic teachers in the use of individual psychoeducational evaluation instruments, such as the Developmental Survey, Psychoeducational Inventory, Frostig Test of Visual Perception, Spache Reading Scales, Wide Range Achievement Tests, and others.

3. Assisting teachers in the development and use of weekly lesson plans and daily pupil learning prescriptions based on profiles of strengths and weaknesses resulting from teacher evaluation of her children.
4. Assisting teachers in the organization of their initial parent conferences, pupil evaluation sessions, and in the subsequent profiling of learning strengths and weaknesses; aiding the teacher in group consultation meetings with parents.
5. Working with the teacher in the development of behavior modification systems and in the development and application of applied research projects within the classroom setting.
6. Consulting with principals, directors, and other administrators regarding the organization, development, evaluation, and improvement of preventive and remedial programs.

In order to perform these functions adequately, time must be provided for the coordinator to visit classrooms, observe teachers in action, and to work on special problem areas. Consequently, the coordinator should also serve as program supervisor, since he will undoubtedly be the most intimately acquainted with the entire program operation.

AIDING THE NEW TEACHER

Special supervisory aid needs to be made available to the new or relatively inexperienced teacher. Such aid should consist of in-service orientation and training followed by personal consultation with the coordinator. In most cases the building principal will be the direct administrator of the program and will be responsible for the evaluation and rating of teachers within his school building; seldom, however, will the principal have the background or skills to evaluate the new teacher meaningfully and to provide the specific help that will undoubtedly be required. One solution to this apparent dilemma is to have the coordinator consult with the principal regarding the evaluation ratings in advance and to sit in on the evaluation of new teachers. As part of this process the coordinator should discuss the teacher's strengths and weaknesses as they relate to the program policy and philosophy of the district and should propose concrete means of improving the program relative to recognized standards. Following the personal conference, it is recommended that a written summary of the session be prepared and presented to the teacher. Subsequently, a plan should be developed to give the teacher the aid that may be required. It is seldom that such constructive supervision is rejected or misunderstood by the teacher since it is supportive and positive in form. Often, almost no meaningful coordination and supervisory services are available, and teachers feel they are isolated, lack support, and are without direction in obtaining the vital help they need in coping with the many problems inherent in learning disability programs.

PROGRAM EVALUATION

Administrators may find the following "Basic Checklist for the Organization of Learning Disability Programs" of some help to them as an organizational aid (*Fig. 12-1*). This list should be used both as a guide and as a program evaluation instrument at the end of the year when it should be completed by teachers and other professionals involved in order to determine their various perceptions of the program for use as a basis for subsequent planning and program improvement.

BASIC CHECKLIST FOR THE ORGANIZATION OF LEARNING DISABILITY PROGRAMS

	Rating Scale		
	No (0)	Somewhat (1)	Yes (2)
1. The entire school faculty was involved in preparing for the new learning disability program through initial orientation meetings.			
2. The most experienced teachers are assigned to learning disability programs and provided with equivalent status and remuneration.			
3. Learning disability teachers and principals are provided adequate in-service training both before and after assignment to the program.			
4. Provision is made for the development of special learning disability programs for slow learners and culturally deprived pupils.			
5. Pupils are systematically introduced to the learning disability program beginning with home visitations and psychoeducational evaluation by the teachers.			
6. Teachers prescribe individual learning programs for their pupils on a daily basis.			
7. Pupils with learning disabilities are programmed into selected regular classes on an audit basis.			
8. Teachers utilize a systematic behavior modification system in the classroom.			
9. Classrooms for pupils with learning disabilities are provided with varied learning centers and appropriate equipment and materials.			
10. A teacher aide is provided for each learning disability classroom with a maximum enrollment of 11 pupils.			
11. In lieu of traditional grading procedures teacher-parent conferences are held and followed up with individual pupil evaluation letters written by the teacher.			
12. The special teacher requests and chairs periodic case conferences on selected pupils of concern.			

Figure 12-1

BASIC CHECKLIST—*Continued*

	No (0)	Somewhat (1)	Yes (2)
	Rating Scale		
13. Parents are provided with parent education and parent counseling programs.			
14. All learning disability pupils are involved in frequent group counseling and guidance programs with their teacher.			
15. In senior high school programs learning disability pupils are involved in meaningful vocational exploration and work experience programs.			
16. In secondary programs teachers are assigned to work with core groups of special pupils and do not have full-time, departmentalized subject-matter assignments.			
17. The teacher visits and observes the pupil in his home and family situation.			
18. Pupils are involved in systematically evaluating themselves, their programs, and their teachers.			
19. Psychological consultation and related services are available to the teacher on a regular weekly basis.			
20. Teachers are provided with professional direction and supervision, including joint evaluation by their principal and supervisor. Follow-up written recommendations and consultation help are provided as necessary.			

Figure 12-1—*Continued*

Following use of the checklist, administrators might give themselves an over-all rating, although it must be recognized that this is just a rough guide for discussion purposes and for aiding in quantitatively comparing the differing perceptions of various staff members.

Total points	Rating	Comment
36–40	Excellent	Your program is a leader in the field!
31–35	Good	Keep up the good work!
21–30	Par	You're off to a good start!
10–20	Fair	You need help!
0–10	Poor	Are you sure you have a program?

Since most learning disability programs take about three years to become estab-lished, it must be expected by teachers, parents, and administrators alike that effective organization will result only from systematic attempts at improvement. Some direct effort should be made to evaluate the program yearly and to incorporate any necessary changes the following year. Little concern should be shown over a "fair" rating for the first year of the program operation. However, programs receiving a "fair" rating for more than one year or those receiving a "poor" rating had better look very closely at the entire operation to determine whether it is a worthwhile endeavor. Those programs with continued poor ratings may actually prove detrimental to the total educational system because they are obviously not designed as true learning disability programs. Such low scores almost certainly will be accompanied by teacher morale problems, pupil unrest and behavioral difficulties, high dropout rates, and other evidence of educational malfunctioning. It is then the responsibility of the school administration either to take drastic steps to provide the essential supporting services and the proper coordination or to discontinue the entire program.

Programs for the Future

Both present research and innovative school organization patterns indicate that many new auxiliary programs are in the process of development. Many of these educational innovations will have an effect on the organization and programming of learning disabilities. Four areas of promising development involve parent groups, district programs, community ventures, and state and federal projects.

PARENT ORGANIZATIONS

In many communities parents of handicapped children are organizing for the purpose of self-education and to offer direct help and encouragement to the school district in initiating new special education programs. Associations for retarded children have long been concerned with passing better legislation permitting districts to improve their programs and to start classes and workshops for the trainable mentally retarded; with the development of occupational training as a joint responsibility between school and sheltered workshops, a new cooperative pattern is emerging. The California Association for Neurologically Handicapped Children is another example of a parent group that has actively involved professional educators in a joint venture that includes the sponsoring of educational workshops in which parents are working with teachers in curriculum building and program innovation. Parents of aurally handicapped children have also been active in holding workshops concerning program standards and new approaches to teaching deaf and hard of hearing children.

The trend is definitely toward increased involvement of parent organizations and the individual family in the total educational process. One of the promising extensions of this trend in the future is the further involvement of parents in the actual tutoring and programming of their child outside of school hours but under the supervision of the educator. Parents will become more of a total part of the learning disability program in that they will aid in the evaluation process itself and will then supplement classroom lessons with prescriptive programs and approaches to specific disabilities at the request of the teacher. For example, the teacher of a child with specific language disabilities may have the parents working with selected kinesthetic sand vocabulary cards as a reinforcement to vocabulary development and auditory discrimination. Such programs will be carefully designed by individual teachers, but they will also be initiated by joint parent-educator committees and by parent associations themselves.

DISTRICT PROGRAMS

As new methods of school organization appear, they will have a marked effect on special education programs. Perhaps the most significant example on the scene today is the proposal for developing *educational parks* to serve all students from preschool through adult education in one huge center. One of the major advantages of this system for learning disability programs may be the additional services, such as psychological consultation and applied research programs, that would be more readily available under such an arrangement. Since the educational park system will include resource material centers, clinics, and provisions for counseling and parent education, the coordination and supervision of programs will be simplified.

Several school districts are conducting cooperative work experience programs with private enterprise for pupils with specific disabilities. A number of extended outdoor education programs, including school day camps, arboretums, nature trails, conservation camps, and resident camping, all offer new opportunities for reaching pupils with learning problems who may not respond adequately in the traditional school organizational system. Many other changes in the system, such as educational television, automated learning, adaptive and individual remedial physical education programs, will undoubtedly be integrated into special education offerings.

COMMUNITY PROGRAMS

Within the community itself a number of social changes will also affect learning disability programs. Certainly the organization of community-wide social action committees charged with implementing racial integration, providing increased job opportunities, and promoting new preschool programs such as Head Start will make a notable impact. From such ventures will come school involvement in expanded labor union training program agreements, community mental health centers, early medical evaluation of preschool-kindergarten children, and many other programs including joint research projects concerned with the efficacy of these approaches. Bardon has already prophesied that the school system of the future will be intimately involved with "community psychologists" whose function will be to apply social psychology to community and school related problems.[9]

STATE AND FEDERAL PROGRAMS

It can also be expected that federal aid to the schools will be continued and extended. Under the Elementary and Secondary Education Act provision has been made for handicapped children including those with learning disabilities. Much of the needed research in this field will result from local school projects financed under this act. In the future it can be anticipated that Title VI of Public Law 89-10 under the ESEA will be appropriately funded and will stimulate continued development of state and local projects. Regional materials centers for the handicapped, research laboratories, and central data processing will all offer

[9] J. Bardon, "School Psychology and School Psychologists," *American Psychologist*, Vol. XXXIII, No. 3 (1968), pp. 187-194.

services of value to local districts and will, in some cases, be cooperatively operated among local, state, and federal governments. The major contribution of government aid will undoubtedly be in the emphasis on applied research and the accompanying requirements for built-in evaluation procedures in learning disability programs. Through such cooperative endeavors it will be possible for learning disability programs to evaluate their ongoing program carefully and to develop systematically a meaningful and valid curricular and remedial approach to specific disabilities.

SELECTED REFERENCES

Selected References

This section consists of selected reading lists for teachers, parents, and psychologists. No attempt has been made to make these all-inclusive on the subject of learning disabilities. Instead, the intent has been to list a few of the major references proven of value as an introduction to several aspects of the programming of learning disabilities. The teacher's list emphasizes references containing teaching methodology and structure. The parent's list is a general reading list that will be of special use in parent counseling and parent education programs. The third list is for psychologists and stresses psychological theory and practice. The lists should not be perceived as being exclusive of one another, and the reader should be encouraged to explore all references of interest to him.

A Selected Reading List for Teachers

ARENE, J. *Teaching Educationally Handicapped Children.* San Rafael, Calif.: Academic Therapy Publications, 1967.

BARRY, H. *The Young Aphasic Child: Evaluation and Training.* Washington, D. C.: Alexander Graham Bell Association for the Deaf, Inc., The Volta Bureau, 1961.

BARSCH, R. H. *Achieving Perceptual-Motor Efficiency: A Space-oriented Approach to Learning.* Seattle, Wash.: Special Child Publications, 1967.

CHALL, J. *Learning To Read,* New York: McGraw-Hill Book Company, 1967.

CRATTY, B. *Developmental Sequences of Perceptual-Motor Tasks.* Freeport, L.I., New York: Educational Activities, Inc., 1967.

CRUICKSHANK, W. *The Brain-injured Child in Home, School, and Community.* Syracuse, N.Y.: Syracuse University Press, 1967.

ENGEL, R.; REED, W.; and RUCKER, D. *Language Development Experiences for Young Children.* Los Angeles, Calif.: Department of Exceptional Children, School of Education, University of Southern California, 1966.

FAIT, H. *Special Physical Education: Adaptive, Corrective, Developmental.* Philadelphia: W. B. Saunders Co., 1966.

FERNALD, G. *Remedial Techniques in Basic School Subjects.* New York: McGraw-Hill Book Company, 1943.

HACKETT, L. C., and JENSEN, R. G. *A Guide to Movement Exploration.* Palo Alto, Calif.: Peek Publications, 1966.

HELLMUTH, J. (ed.). *Educational Therapy,* Vol. I. Seattle, Wash.: Special Child Publications, 1966.

————. *Learning Disorders,* Vol. I, 1965; Vol. II, 1966. Seattle, Wash.: Special
Child Publications.

JOHNSON, D., and MYKLEBUST, H. *Learning Disabilities.* New York: Grune & Stratton, Inc., 1967.

KEPHART, N. *The Slow Learner in the Classroom.* Columbus, Ohio: Charles E. Merrill Books, Inc., 1960.

MONTESSORI, M. *Dr. Montessori's Own Handbook.* New York: Schocken Books,
Inc., 1964.

————. *The Montessori Method.* New York: Schocken Books, Inc., 1964.

MOSSTON, M. *Developmental Movement.* Columbus, Ohio: Charles E. Merrill
Books, Inc., 1965.

PETER, L. *Prescriptive Teaching.* New York: McGraw-Hill Book Company, 1965.

SCOTT, L. B., and THOMPSON, J. J. *Talking Time,* 2nd ed. Manchester, Mo.: Webster
Publishing, 1966.

SUTPIN, F. *A Perceptual, Testing-training Handbook for First-grade Teachers.* Winter Haven, Fla.: Winter Haven Lions' Research Foundation, Inc., 1964.

VALETT, R. *The Remediation of Learning Disabilities.* Palo Alto, Calif.: Fearon
Publishers, 1967.

WAGNER, G., *et al. Games and Activities for Early Childhood Education.* Darien,
Conn.: Teachers' Publishing Corp., 1967.

WITSON, B. *Perceptual Training Activities Handbook.* New York: Teachers' College
Press, 1967.

A Selected Reading List for Parents

ANDERSON, C. *Jan, My Brain-damaged Daughter.* Portland, Ore.: The Durham
Press, 1963.

AVERY, M., and HIGGINS, A. *Help Your Child To Learn How To Learn.* Englewood
Cliffs, N. J.: Prentice-Hall, Inc., 1962.

AXLINE, V. *Dibs in Search of Self.* Boston, Mass.: Houghton Mifflin Company, 1964.

CHALL, J. *Learning To Read.* New York: McGraw-Hill Book Company, 1967.

ENGLEMANN, S., and ENGLEMANN, T. *Give Your Child a Superior Mind.* New York:
Simon and Schuster, Inc., 1966.

GINOTT, H. *Between Parent and Child.* New York: The Macmillan Company, 1965.

HOLT, J. *How Children Fail.* New York: Pitman Publishing Corp., 1965.

ILG, F., and AMES, L. *Child Behavior.* New York: Dell Publishing Co., Inc., 1955.

LEWIS, R.; STRAUSS, A.; and LEHTINEN, L. *The Other Child,* 2nd ed. New York:
Grune & Stratton, Inc., 1960.

LOWELL, E., and STONER, M. *Play It by Ear: Auditory Training Games.* Los Angeles: John Tracy Clinic, 1963.

RADLER, D. H., and KEPHART, NEWELL C. *Success Through Play.* New York: Harper
& Row, Publishers, 1960.

SCHWARTZ, A. *A Parent's Guide to Children's Play and Recreation.* New York:
Crowell, Collier and Macmillan, Inc., 1963.

SPOCK, B., and LERRIGO, M. *Caring for Your Disabled Child.* New York: Fawcett
World Library, Crest Books, 1965.

WAGNER, G., *et al. Arithmetic Games and Activities.* Darien, Conn.: Teachers' Publishing Corp., 1966.

————. *Listening Games.* Darien, Conn.: Teachers' Publishing Corp., 1962.

————. *Reading Games.* Darien, Conn.: Teachers' Publishing Corp., 1967.

A Selected Reading List for Psychologists

BENTON, A. *Right-Left Discrimination and Finger Localization.* New York: Paul B. Hoeber, 1959.

BLOOM, B. *Stability and Change in Human Characteristics.* New York: John Wiley & Sons, Inc., 1964.

BRUECKNER, L., and BOND, G. *The Diagnosis and Treatment of Learning Difficulties.* New York: Appleton-Century-Crofts, 1955.

CRUICKSHANK, W.; BENTZEN, F.; RATZEBURG, F.; and TANNHAUSER, M. *A Teaching Method for Brain-injured and Hyperactive Children.* Syracuse, N.Y.: Syracuse University Press, 1961.

DELACATO, C. *Neurological Organization and Reading.* Springfield, Ill.: Charles C. Thomas, Publisher, 1966.

FLAVELL, J. H. *The Developmental Psychology of Jean Piaget.* New York: D. Van Nostrand Co., Inc., 1966.

FRIERSON, E., and BARBE, W. *Educating Children with Learning Disabilities.* New York: Appleton-Century-Crofts, 1967.

GARRETT, J., and LEVINE, E. (eds.). *Psychological Practices with the Physically Disabled.* New York: Columbia University Press, 1962.

GESELL, A., and ILG, F. *The Child from Five to Ten.* New York: Harper & Row, Publishers, 1946.

GESELL, A., *et al. The First Five Years of Life.* New York: Harper & Row, Publishers, 1940.

HAEUSSERMAN, E. *Developmental Potential of Preschool Children.* New York: Grune & Stratton, Inc., 1958.

HARING, N., and PHILLIPS, E. *Educating Emotionally Disturbed Children.* New York: McGraw-Hill Book Company, 1962.

HOFFMAN, M., and HOFFMAN, L. (eds.). *Review of Child Development Research,* Vol. I. New York: Russell Sage Foundation, 1964.

HUNT, J. M. *Intelligence and Experience.* New York: The Ronald Press Company, 1961.

ILG, F., and AMES, L. *School Readiness.* New York: Harper & Row, Publishers, 1965.

ITARD, J. *The Wild Boy of Averon.* New York: Appleton-Century-Crofts, 1962.

KRAUS, H. *Therapeutic Exercises,* 2nd ed. Springfield, Ill.: Charles C. Thomas, Publisher, 1963.

LOUTTIT, C. *Clinical Psychology of Exceptional Children,* 3rd ed. New York: Harper & Row, Publishers, 1957.

MONEY, J. (ed.). *Reading Disability: Progress and Research Needs in Dyslexia.* Baltimore, Md.: The Johns Hopkins Press, 1962.

RIESSMAN, F. *The Culturally Deprived Child.* New York: Harper & Row, Publishers, 1962.

STRAUSS, A., and KEPHART, N. *Psychopathology and Education of the Brain-injured Child,* Vols. I and II. New York: Grune & Stratton, Inc., 1955.

TAYLOR, E. *Psychological Appraisal of Children with Cerebral Defects.* Cambridge, Mass.: Harvard University Press, 1961.

VALETT, R. *The Practice of School Psychology: Professional Problems.* New York: John Wiley & Sons, Inc., 1963.

INDEX

Index